Algrove Publishing Limited
36 Mill Street, P.O. Box 1238
Almonte, Ontario, Canada K0A 1A0

Telephone: (613) 256-0350
Fax: (613) 256-0360
Email: sales@algrove.com

Library and Archives Canada Cataloguing in Publication

Williams, Morris
    Stair builders' guide / Morris Williams.

(Classic reprint series)
Reprint. First published: New York : D. Williams Co., 1914.
ISBN 1-897030-47-9

    1. Stair building. I. Title. II. Series: Classic reprint series
(Almonte, Ont.)
TH5667.W5 2006   690'.1832   C2005-907717-4

Printed in Canada
#1-4-06

Publisher's Note

When reprinting old books, it is critical to get the best possible original to work from. In some cases, and this book is a prime example, the originals were all a bit short on basic layout. They would have benefited from a larger page format and larger type size.

This book is not as easy to read as it should be but enlarging old text in the scanning process (during production of a reprint) has its pitfalls as well. All we can say is that this book is faithful to the original.

Leonard G. Lee
Publisher
Almonte, Ontario
April 2006

How We Make Our Books - You may not have noticed, but this book is quite different from other softcover books you might own. The vast majority of paperbacks, whether mass-market or the more expensive trade paperbacks, have the pages sheared and notched at the spine so that they may be glued together. The paper itself is often of newsprint quality. Over time, the paper will brown and the spine will crack if flexed. Eventually the pages fall out.

All of our softcover books, like our hardcover books, have sewn bindings. The pages are sewn in signatures of sixteen or thirty-two pages and these signatures are then sewn to each other. They are also glued at the back but the glue is used primarily to hold the cover on, not to hold the pages together.

We also use only acid-free paper in our books. This paper does not yellow over time. A century from now, this book will have paper of its original color and an intact binding, unless it has been exposed to fire, water, or other catastrophe.

There is one more thing you will note about this book as you read it; it opens easily and does not require constant hand pressure to keep it open. In all but the smallest sizes, our books will also lie open on a table, something that a book bound only with glue will never do unless you have broken its spine.

The cost of these extras is well below their value and while we do not expect a medal for incorporating them, we did want you to notice them.

Stair Builders' Guide

A Treatise on the Construction of
Straight Flight, Platform, Cylin-
drical and Eliptical Stairs, Explain-
ing the Theory and Practice so the
Average Building Mechanic May
Understand It, With Examples of
Work Ranging from the Simplest
to the Most Complex Forms

By Morris Williams

New York

1914

Algrove Publishing
Classic Reprint Series

PREFACE

THE fact cannot have failed to impress itself upon all students of stairbuilding that something of essential import is lacking in the literature of the art and science, for on no other ground can one account for the very small percentage of proficiency among carpenters and even stairbuilders in laying out and constructing stairways.

Stairbuilding differs materially from all other branches of carpentry; it is a science having its fundamentals in the solution of some of the most intricate problems in plane and solid geometry. The solutions of these problems have within the last century been the study of a number of scholarly mathematicians resulting in a variety of solutions known as "systems" of cylindrical handrailing. The one man who towers above all others in this connection is Peter Nicholson, to whom we are indebted for the discovery of the primary lines deduced from the developments of sections of solids (cylinder and prism) which are the bases of all the succeeding systems up to the present time. These are variously known as "Tangent Systems" due to the use made of the developed tangents in the construction of the Face Mold, Bevels and Joints of the wreath rails.

All attempts after Mr. Nicholson's great achievement were merely to simplify his solutions and so great has been the success in this connection that the most advanced handrailers claim the science to be so nearly perfection that further improvement is not to be expected.

The effort in this book is to explain the simplest method of the science in its present advanced stage. The arrangement of its plan in short chapters cannot fail to be of the greatest advantage to the reader. The first chapter treats upon the constructive details of the stairway, while the second, third, fourth and fifth chapters are devoted exclusively to the fundamental elements of wreath rail construction.

Special care has been taken in the preparation of these chapters to make them as clear as their importance demands because their subject matter constitutes the sub-strata upon which is founded every system of handrailing hitherto published.

What appears in the sixth chapter on the arrangement of risers will prove of paramount value. The remaining chapters

3

contain examples of stairways of all descriptions from the small straight flight to the most complex examples of cylindrical structures.   Each chapter represents a complete example of a special stairway including plan, elevation and rails.   The laying out of each working detail is carefully considered and explained accompanied by such illustrations as will render the explanation easily understood.   Many of the examples will be found to have been planned contrary to all prescribed standard rules of correct construction.   In the explanation furnished upon such examples their defects are noted and the correct plan considered.   What accounts for the presence of these examples is the fact that they were sent as queries by readers of Carpentry and Building— now known as The Building Age.   This also is the cause of the apparently needless representations which occur in the explanation supplied for the laying-out methods of many of the working details.

In presenting this work to the attention of carpenters, stair-builders and other building mechanics clever in the use of their tools, the author confidently asserts that they will find it to embrace the requisite information to enable them to thoroughly master the science of handrailing.   It should be studied intelligently in the order of its arrangement.   By following this plan, the knowledge obtained of the elementary principles supplied in the first six chapters will be found of inestimable value in making intelligible the methods explained for laying out the details attending the construction of the examples of stairways presented in the twenty-three remaining examples.

MORRIS WILLIAMS

May 10, 1914

CONTENTS

CHAPTER I

STRAIGHT FLIGHT AND PLATFORM STAIRWAYS 7

CHAPTER II

SECTIONS OF PRISMS 20

CHAPTER III

TANGENTS 30

CHAPTER IV

FACE MOLDS 38

CHAPTER V

WREATH RAIL BEVELS 55

CHAPTER VI

ARRANGEMENT OF RISERS IN AND AROUND CYLINDER 70

CHAPTER VII

STRAIGHT FLIGHT OF STAIRS 81

CHAPTER VIII

FLIGHT WITH WINDERS AT THE BOTTOM 84

CHAPTER IX

PLATFORM AND NEWEL STAIRWAY 86

CHAPTER X

CONSTRUCTION OF A PLATFORM STAIRWAY WITH STRETCHOUT CURVE
AT THE BOTTOM 93

CHAPTER XI

A STAIRWAY CONTAINING STRETCHOUT CURVE AT THE BOTTOM AND A
QUARTER TURN CURVE AT TOP LANDING 103

CHAPTER XII

METHOD OF CONSTRUCTING A SCROLL WREATH 116

CHAPTER XIII

SECOND METHOD OF CONSTRUCTING A SCROLL WREATH 121

CHAPTER XIV

THIRD METHOD OF CONSTRUCTING A SCROLL WREATH 127

CHAPTER XV

A WREATH RAIL OVER A 12-INCH CYLINDER CONTAINING EIGHT
WINDERS 134

CHAPTER XVI

A Wreath over a Cylinder Adjoining a Level Landing 140

CHAPTER XVII

Wreath for Stairway Containing a Curve more than a Quadrant at the Starting and a Quadrant Curve at the Intersection of Two Flights 145

CHAPTER XVIII

A Wreath in Sections over a 13½ inch Quadrant 151

CHAPTER XIX

A Wreath over a Cylinder at the Top of a Stairway 157

CHAPTER XX

A Wreath over a 4-inch Cylinder Adjoining a Top Landing . . 162

CHAPTER XXI

The Right and the Wrong Way of Treating a Quadrant between Two Flights 165

CHAPTER XXII

Examples of Curves Intersecting Flights and Landings . . . 168

CHAPTER XXIII

Wreaths for "Thumb-Ellipse" Plan Curves 178

CHAPTER XXIV

Wreaths over an Elliptical Plan Stairway 183

CHAPTER XXV

Rails for a Stairway containing Complicated Plan Curves . . 190

CHAPTER XXVI

Wreath Rail over a Thumb Ellipse Curve; and a Quadrant Intersecting Two Flights 198

CHAPTER XXVII

A Panel Soffit for a Circular Stairway 207

CHAPTER XXVIII

A Rail over a 24-inch Quarter Turn, at the Bottom of a Stairway 215

CHAPTER XXIX

Rail around a Cylinder containing 4 Risers at the Junction of a Flight and Top Landing 221

CHAPTER XXX

Photos showing Wood, Stone and Iron Stairs erected in Residences, Schools, Theatres and Public Buildings 228

CHAPTER I

STRAIGHT FLIGHT AND PLATFORM STAIRWAYS

The construction of stairways is considered the highest branch of joinery; far more care and knowledge are required in their planning; more ingenuity in setting them out; and more skillful workmanship in their execution, than in any other work about a building.

The prime object in designing stairways should be to obtain the utmost facility of access to the various stories with which they communicate. Care should be taken to secure proper head room while ascending and descending and the treads and risers should be arranged so as to secure easy travel.

The width of a stairway in a private house should never be less than *2* ft. *8* in.; and in a public building never less than *4* ft. *6* in.

An important item also that should never be neglected is the securing of harmony in the assembled members to produce appearance in the finished structure that will be beautiful and pleasing. This is evident when it is considered that stairways are among the most prominent features in a building. They are seen by every one; their convenience and beauty are readily appreciated; and their faults and defects instantly detected.

There are a few terms used in stairbuilding that should be known in order to intelligently understand the detailed explanations that follow.

The term *flight* designates a succession of steps between one starting place and the one next above it.

A *step* is what is made up of a tread and riser combined.

A *tread* is the horizontal part of a step, and a *riser* the upright or vertical part.

7

The *nosing* is the projection of a tread beyond the face of a riser.

What is termed *flier* is a straight step, and a *winder* a step consisting of a triangular tread.

Platforms are the spaces which constitute resting places between flights; known also by the term *landings*.

If a landing takes in the full width of a stairway it is called *half-space landing*; but when it takes only half the width of a stairway it is termed *quarter-space landing*.

The space required for landings is sometimes filled in by winders. This is especially the case in geometrical stairways, and those in which the run space is limited.

In every case it is the quantity of space in the run that decides the nature of the landing; whether it is to be half or quarter space or filled in with winders.

The term *bull-nose* step is applied to a step ending in a semicircle curve; and the term *curtail* step is applied to a step ending in the form of a horizontal spiral. This step is used under a *scroll* rail at the bottom of a stairway.

Stringers is the term for the side boards to support the steps. The one next to the wall is called *wall stringer* and the outside one the *front stringer*.

When a stringer is grooved to receive the treads and risers it is called a *housed stringer* and when cut horizontal for the tread and mitered for the riser it is known as a *cut and mitered stringer*.

The terms *carriages, horses* and *springing trees* are applied to the supporting timbers and are synonymous terms.

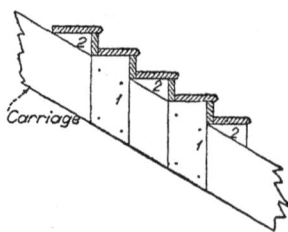

Sometimes the carriages are cut to the angle of treads and risers, so as to fit tight under the treads, and against the risers, but most often they assume the simple form of a straight scantling, placed tight against the soffit of the stairway.

FIG. 1—Showing scantling.

When used in the form of scantling, *1*-inch or sometimes *2*-inch cleats are nailed as shown at *1* in Fig. 1 to the side, and as at *2* upon the upper edge, the purpose being to support the treads. Care should be taken that the carriage timbers be of sufficient strength to support the stairway and the load it may have to support.

These timbers are utilized only when a heavy load is to be sustained by the stairway, such as in public buildings. In private houses and especially with platform stairways where the flights are of short length the custom is for the stairway to sustain itself, the soffit to be prepared for plastering by having few strips nailed to the angular intersection of the steps.

How Stairways Are Constructed

The simplest form of a stairway is the flight consisting of straight steps only.

The second simplest form is the stairway known by the term *platform and newel* stairway, which consists of two or more flights intervened by a platform or winders.

The third and considerably the most complex in its construction is the geometrical stairway, its peculiarity consisting in its plan being fully or partly curved, and necessitating the twisting of both stringers and handrails.

It is shown in Fig. 2 how to construct a simple straight flight.

The first operation will be to ascertain the *run* and the height, because it is the *run* that determines the number of treads and the height the number of risers.

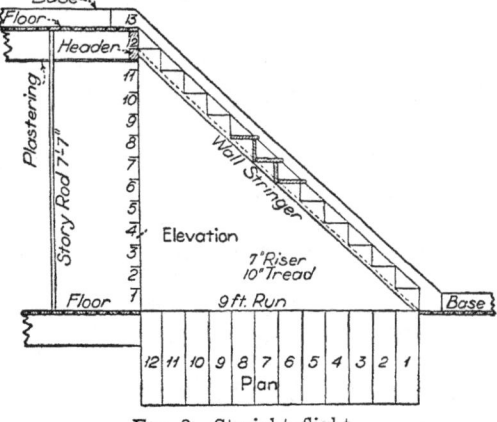

FIG. 2—Straight flight.

The plan Fig. 2 indicates a run of 9 ft. and upon the story-rod the height between the first and second floors is found to be 7 ft. 7 in. With these dimensions known the next operation will be to find the number of treads and risers required, and also the best proportional combination of the two to produce the best facility to ascend and descend.

A rule for efficient results is to guard against a tread too narrow and a riser too high.

In a private house stairway a tread of *10* inches and a riser *6½* inches is considered a good combination in a step.

If conditions allow, a tread *12* inches wide will be better providing the riser is proportionately adapted to the width of the tread.

In laying out the steps it is immaterial whether the size of the riser or the tread is first determined.   However, the custom in practice is to first find the size and number of the risers and then to find the best proportional width for the tread.

To find the riser for the stairway conditioned as represented in Fig. 2 when the total height between the floors is shown to be *7* ft. *7* in., the arithmetical method is to reduce the feet to inches and divide the total number of inches in the height tentatively with the number *7*, which represent approximately the standard size for a suitable riser.

Another method and the one oftener used in practice is to step along the story-rod with the compass opened out to measure *7* inches.

By either method will be found approximately the number and size of the risers.

An example of the first method is as follows: *7* ft. *7* in. reduced to inches equal *91* inches.

$$91 \div 7 = 13$$

which denotes the number of risers (*7* inches wide) the flight will contain to reach from one floor to the other.   To find a proportional tread for a riser *7* inches wide there are rules approved by long experience as standards.

The first is to double the width of the riser and to deduct the product from the number *24*.   For example, with a *7*-inch riser doubled, we obtain *14*, deducting *14* from *24* we obtain *10*, which will be the best possible width of a tread to combine with a *7*-inch riser to form a step to guarantee easy stepping in ascending and descending.

The second method is to consider the product of the tread and riser to equal the number *66* and whatever width we have for the riser to divide it into this number.   For example, let the riser be 7 inches then the width of the tread will be

$$66 \div 7 = 9\tfrac{3}{7} \text{ inches.}$$

A third method is of a different kind. As shown in Fig. 3 it graphically illustrates the principle of operation. The right-angle triangle shown in this figure has a base *a-b* of *24* inches and an altitude *b-c* of *11* inches.

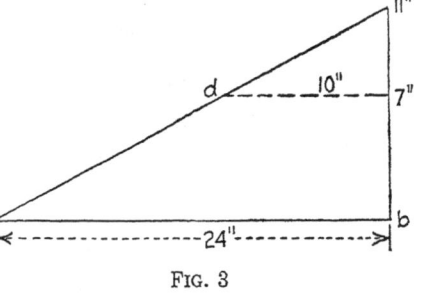

FIG. 3

To find the tread measure *7* inches from *b* to represent the riser, and draw a line as shown from *7* to cut the long edge of the triangle in *d*. The length of this line will indicate the width of a tread for a *7*-inch riser

These three rules may be used reversely by first determining the size of the tread and then proceed to find the best proportional riser.

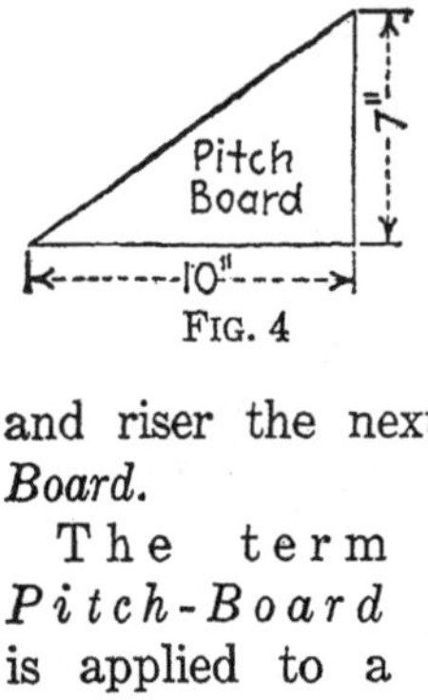

It will be observed that they do not produce identical results, yet the result of either one is considered sufficiently accurate for the purpose.

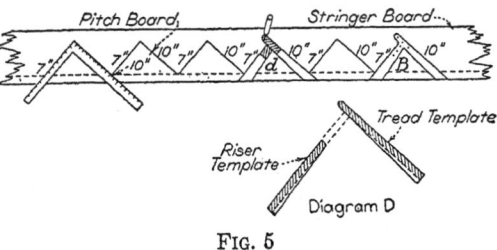

Pitch Board

FIG. 4

After determining the width of the tread and riser the next operation will be to lay out the *Pitch-Board.*

The term *Pitch-Board* is applied to a template in the form of a right-angle triangle, consisting of a base representing the width of a

Pitch Board   Stringer Board

Tread Template

Riser Template

Diagram D

FIG. 5

tread and an altitude the width of a riser. It is shown in Fig. 4 and is used as shown in Fig. 5 to mark the form of the steps upon a stringer board.

The steel square is also shown in Fig. 5 being used for the same purpose, and for a "common job" it may be considered preferable.

It is used in the same manner as when laying out a roof rafter, the tongue and blade respectively representing the dimensions of the tread and riser.

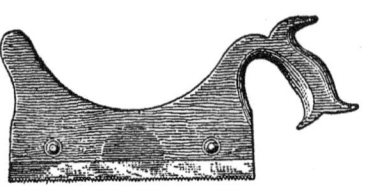

FIG. 6

After the steps are marked upon the face of the stringer the next operation will be the marking of the grooves or "housing" for the risers, treads and wedges.

For this purpose two thin templates are prepared and applied as shown at d in Fig. 5. How they are prepared is shown in diagram "D", where the shaded portions represent the thickness of the treads and risers while the parts not shaded indicate the shape of the wedges.

A brad-awl hole is made in the center of the nosing of the one for the treads so that when applied to the stringer as shown at d in Fig. 5 a brad-awl may be inserted to hold the template in place.

The one for the riser is pushed against the one for tread and close to the riser line already marked upon the stringer board. The brad-awl mark left upon the stringer after marking the grooves for

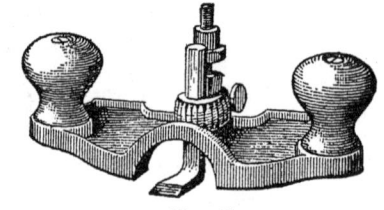

FIG. 7

all the steps required, will be the center for the brace bit that will be used to bore the hole for the nosing of the tread.

The method in use to work the grooves is as follows:

With the same size bit as the one used to bore for the nosing few other bores are made as shown at B in Fig. 5 for both the treads and risers.

This portion then is chipped off clean to the depth of the groove as shown by the shaded portion upon the step d in Fig. 5.

Then with a tenon saw or better still a regular Stairbuilder Saw shown in Fig. 6 the remainder of the groove for both treads and risers is sawed along the lines that have been marked upon the stringer for the grooves and roughly chipped off to the depth of the groove. Then by the use of a router plane shown in Fig. 7 all the grooves are cleaned to the depth required.

A part of a stringer is shown finished in Fig. 8 and one step placed in the groove ready for the wedging.

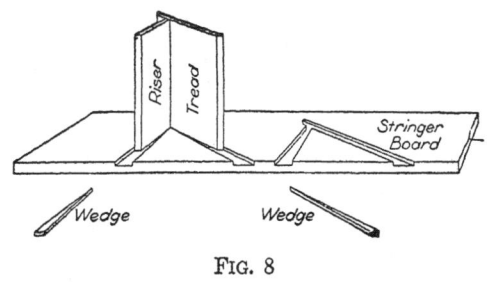

FIG. 8

This figure illustrates the "shop" method usually in practice of putting the stairs together. When the work is done on the "job" the method is to fix the stringers in place, and then the risers and treads; wedging each pair as the work proceeds.

Cut and Miter Stringer

When laying out a "cut and miter" stringer the pitch board

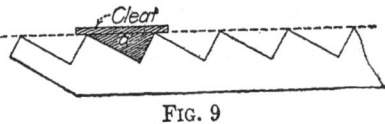

FIG. 9

is applied as at a in Fig. 9, having a narrow cleat nailed to its long edge projecting about ½ an inch beyond the face to form a guide.

When all the steps are marked, the tread lines are cut out square to the face of the stringer, and the riser marks to a miter as shown in Fig. 9a, where also is shown the treads cut square to the face of the stringer, the nosing only being cut to an angle to miter with the return nosing.

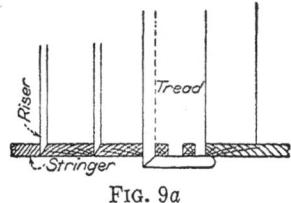

FIG. 9a

Bending Stringers and Risers

A platform stairway similar to the plan shown in Fig. 10 is often seen in reception halls in first-class private houses all over the country, the first and second risers being bent to improve the appearance.

There are different methods to bend these risers. One is shown in Fig. 11, where a solid block is shown to have been

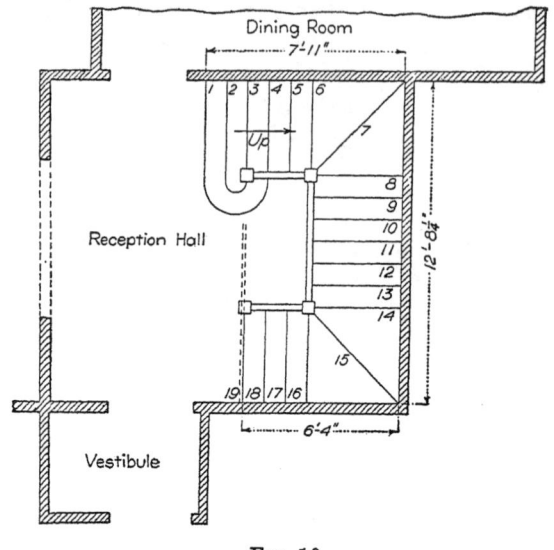

prepared to support the veneered part of the riser, which is screwed as shown at *b* to the block and bent around to *a*, where two wedges shown at *d* are driven tight to clamp it firmly against the block. Before it is clamped the back of the veneer is covered with glue.

FIG. 10

Another method in use is the one shown in Fig. 12. The veneer according to this method is ripped from the riser as from *a* right through to *b*, leaving no solid wood at *b* as in Fig. 11, and instead of a solid block the support for the veneer is made up in sections nailed together to the form required.

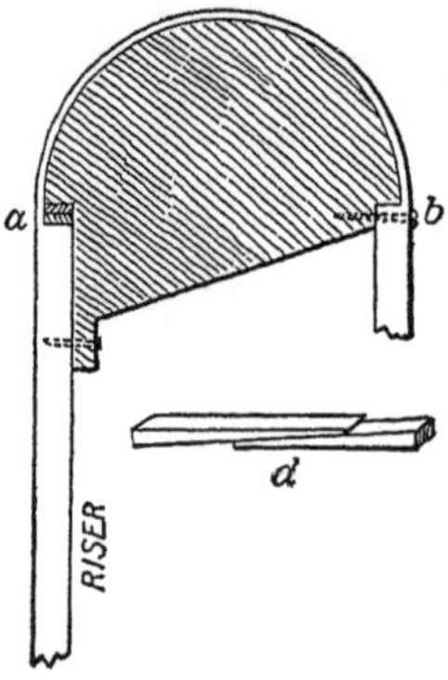

The veneer is glued to the form by means of hand-screws, and where hand-screws are not available, as the case often happens when a stairway is being con-

FIG. 11

FIG. 12

structed on the job, it is fastened to the form by means of cleats nailed to the form; pressing the veneer tight all around from *a* to *b*.

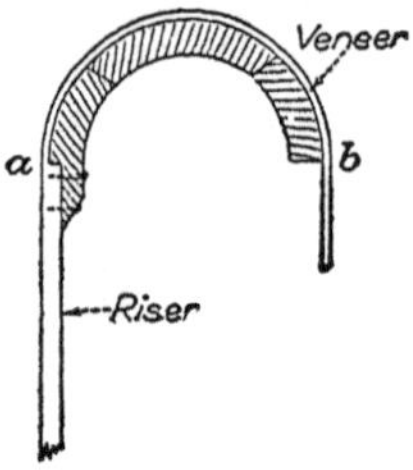

The riser after it is finished by this method is shown

in Fig. 13; and in Fig. 14 an edge view of it prepared for bending is shown. A third method is known by the term "kerfing".

In Fig. 15 is shown an edge view of the riser prepared for bending according to this method. It consists merely in making saw cuts at equal distances on the inside of the riser to weaken the stiffness of the material.

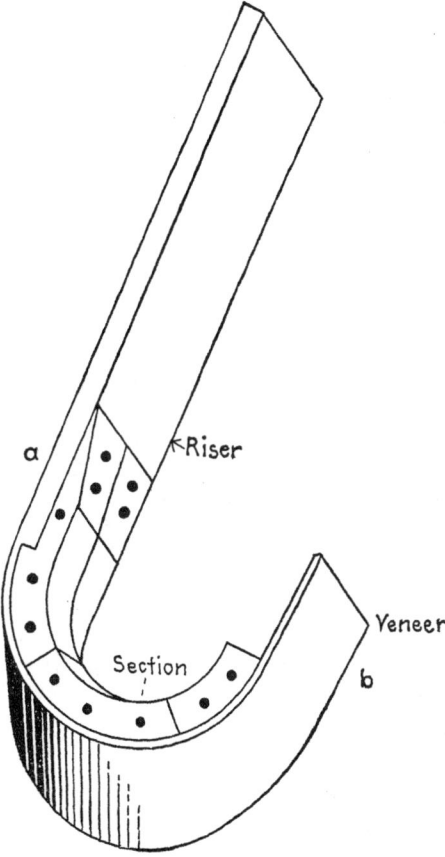

It is shown in Fig. 16 how to find the distances between the saw cuts to guarantee the best bending results.

The quadrant curve in this figure represents the sweep of the curve to be covered At a a saw cut is made on the inside to within 3-16 of an inch to the outside of the material to be bent. The distance from a to b is to be equal to the radius of the curve. Now press down the piece to be bent until the saw cut at a is closed. The piece after being pressed is shown

FIG. 13

in its second position at c: and the space between c and b will be the space between the kerfs shown in Fig. 15.

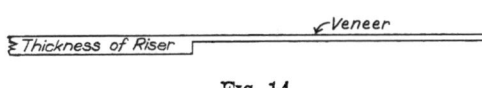

FIG. 14

In Fig. 17 is shown the kerfed piece bent around the drum.

The three foregoing methods are in use to bend risers and

stringers, but a better method especially for stringers is the one known by the term *laminated method.*

By this method the piece required is built up of thin layers of about ⅛

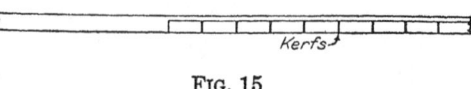

FIG. 15

inch thickness bent around a drum in the manner shown for

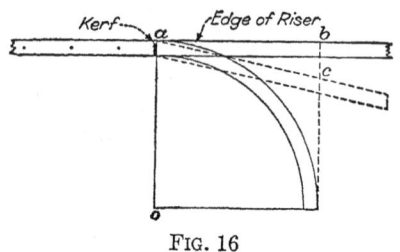

FIG. 16

the veneer and the kerfing methods. Each layer is thoroughly soaked with glue and pressed against one another by means of hand-screws or cleats and left upon the drum to set. When taken from the drum they will retain their bending form.

How to Lay Out Easements and Goose Necks

In the class of stairways that are known by the term "Platform and Newel stairways" the handrails often strike the intersecting newels at a different height.

To have uniform height for the handrail at the newel post is the object in the use of *goose-necks* and *easements.*

In Fig. 18 the handrail is shown in position above the steps of the three flights indicated in plan, Fig. 10. The flights are shown unfolded so as to show the rails to the best advantage in relation to the steps.

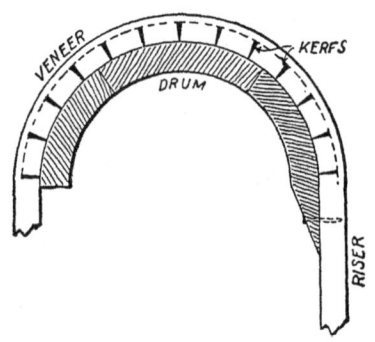

FIG. 17

It will be observed that if the rails were to follow the pitch of the steps the height of each section at the newels would be different.

Fig. 19 shows how to lay out the goose-neck and the easement. The rails for the two intersecting flights are shown to be fixed at a height of 2 ft. 4 in. above the nosing of the steps.

The rail of the top flight strikes the newel at *a* and the rail of the bottom flight at *b*. Draw the horizontal lines at any height desired above *a*. Make *m-o* and *o-n* equal, and from *n* draw a line square to the pitch of the rail to intersect at *w*—the side of the newel. Now take *w* as center to draw the easement curve as shown from *n* to *m*.

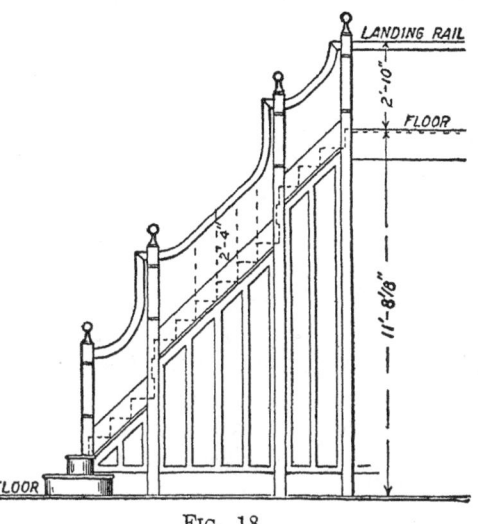

FIG. 18

The goose-neck is shown on the opposite side of the newel aligning with the easement.

The knee is usually made about 5 in. long as shown, and from it lines are dropped to the pitched rail of the bottom flight as

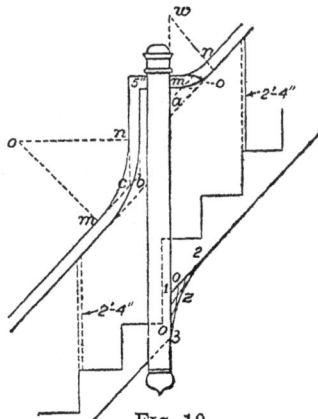

FIG. 19

shown at *c* and *b*, while *c-n* and *c-m* are made equal.

A level line from *n* and a square line to the rail from *m* will intersect at *o*, which will be the center to draw the curves as shown from *n* to *m*.

A drawing of this kind is made full size in practice, and from it is drawn the templates for the easement and goose-neck. It gives also the length of the newel post, and the markings of the grooves for the risers and treads that enter it from all sides.

The method in use to finish the bottom of stringers in examples of this kind is shown at *z*, where an easement is drawn from the bottom of the top stringer to align at the newel with the bottom of the lower flight.

To draw the easement make *1-2* and *1-3* equal; divide the two into equal divisions; intercross lines from one to the other, and the intersecting points will form the curvature of the ease-ment.

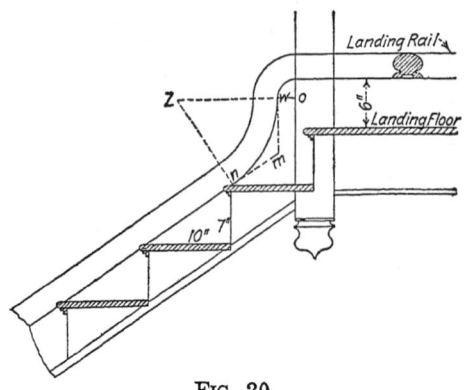

FIG. 20

Two examples of constructed stairways of this type will be found in the last chapter with complete explanation of how such construction are laid out and put to-gether in practice.

In Fig. 20 is shown a method to draw a small goose-neck at the intsersection of a flight and a landing or platform.

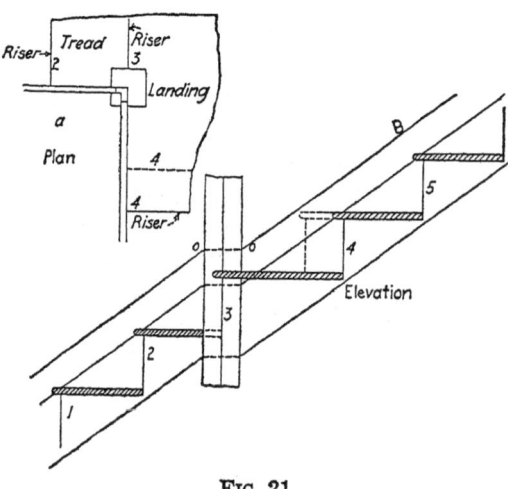

FIG. 21

In this figure the landing rail is shown raised *6* inches above the landing floor, for the purpose of hav-ing it, when in its finished position, high enough for right protection. The usual deter-mined height of the flight rail above the nosing of the steps is *2'-6"*. By raising the land-ing rail *6* inches as shown, the flight rail when in position will be *2'-6"* above the nosing and the landing rail will be *3* feet above the floor.

To draw the goose-neck first determine the location of the landing rail as shown *6* inches above the floor line, draw the line o-w-z as shown; make w-m and m-n equal, and draw the curves as shown from the centers O and Z.

An example of a method to eliminate the necessity of a goose-neck at the intersection of two return flights is shown in Fig. 21. The operation consists in starting the returned upper flight as shown at riser 4 in both plan diagram A and the elevation diagram B, at a specific distance from the newel, as will cause the rails of the two flights to intersect the newel at the same level, as shown in the elevation B at o O.

It will be observed that this example obviates the necessity of constructing an easement and a goose-neck, and thereby a saving of considerable expense.

CHAPTER II

SECTIONS OF PRISMS

The science of handrailing is founded on that special branch of geometry which is used to unfold sections of solids:—primarily the prism and cylinder.

To propound certain methods for laying out the face mold and find the bevels for handrails, while ignoring the fundamental principles whereon such methods are founded; as has been the practice hitherto among writers on the subject; is undoubtedly the cause of so many men of long experience in stairbuilding being deficient in handrailing. Their knowledge being limited, their power of construction is also limited to but very few and simple examples; whereas if properly posted in the knowledge of these principles, they would have in their possession the power to overcome all difficulties encountered, however complex the specific conditions of the example might be.

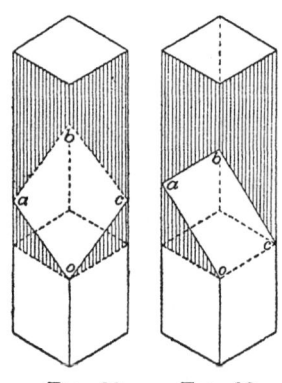

It is the purpose in this chapter to explain thoroughly the fundamental lines in the construction of handrails; not alone the fundamental lines of the specific method contained in this book, but of all and every method published from the time Peter Nicholson, the originator of the science, first published his geometrical problems pertaining to sections of solids, and their application to wreath handrail constructions.

FIG. 23   FIG. 22

Fig. 22 is a view of a right-angle prism revealing a sectional cut made oblique to two of its sides shown at *oa* and *bc* and square to the other two sides shown at *oc* and *ab*, that is, in one direction to its axis. Fig. 23 is a view of a similar prism revealing a sectional cut made obliquely to its four sides; that is, in two directions to its axis.

A view of two cylinders is shown in Figs. 24 and 25. In Fig. 24 there is shown a sectional cut of the same nature as the one

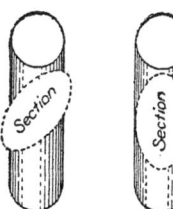
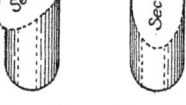

made through the prism in Fig. 22, while in Fig. 25 is shown the same sectional cut as is made through the prism in Fig. 23; that is, the cut made through the cylinder in Fig. 24 is in one direction to its axis, while the cut through the cylinder in Fig. 25 is made obliquely to its axis from all sides of its circumference. In the geometrical method to unfold the straight line sections shown in

FIG. 25   FIG. 24

Figs. 22 and 23 lies the fundamental principle required to unfold tangents of a face mold for a wreath rail, and in the geometrical method to unfold the elliptical sections shown in Figs, 24 and 25 lies the fundamental principle required to unfold the contour curve of the face mold.

A n o t h e r v i e w i s shown in Fig. 26 of a prism or block, having been cut oblique to two of its sides where the co-ordinate planes, the "horizontal" and "vertical," are shown intersected in what is usually defined as the "ground line" and XY

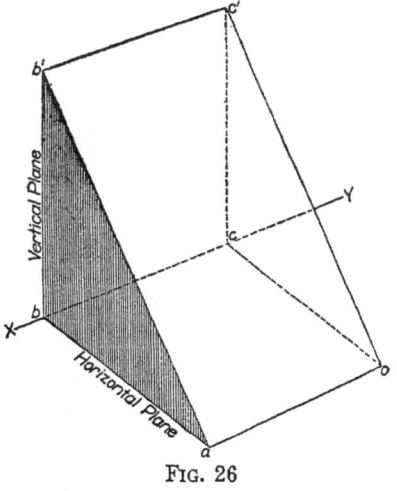

FIG. 26

In this figure are shown three different planes; a, b, c, o being the horizontal; b, b', c, c' the vertical, and the lines b', a, c', o the oblique plane.

Again, in Fig. 27 another of the same kind is shown with an addition of a quarter circle inscribed on the horizontal plane and an equivalent portion of an ellipse drawn on the oblique plane.

By assuming the quarter circle to be the plan of the center line of a handrail, then the portion of the ellipse standing right above it would be the developed center line of the wreath rail, having a pitch equal to the inclination of the oblique plane as shown in Fig. 27 from *a* to *c'*.

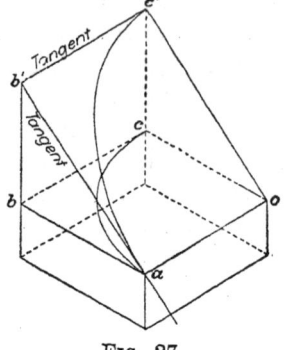

FIG. 27

The relation of this compound figure to handrail construction is graphically shown in Fig. 28, which is another reproduction of the same figure with the addition of a complete curved handrail winding upon an oblique plane and connecting to a newel post on a landing of a stairway.

Having obtained a clear insight as is revealed in these perspective figures into the utility of oblique sectional cuts in the construction of wreath handrails, we will now proceed to explain how to unfold the

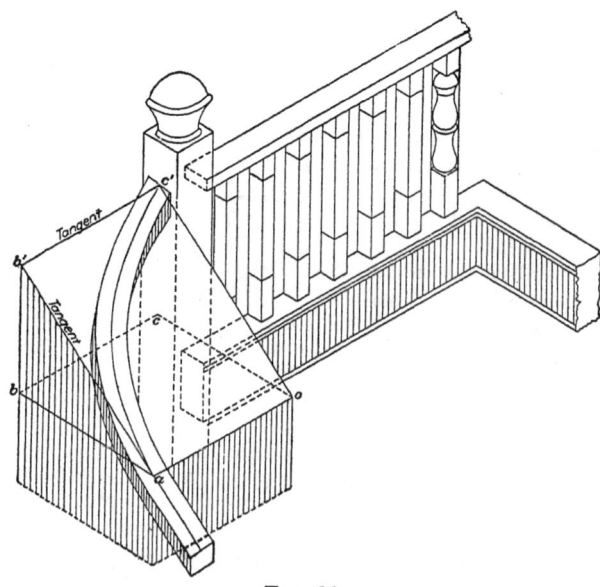

FIG. 28

sections geometrically; that is, how to find the correct size and form of sections.

In Fig. 29 is shown a geometrical drawing of the base of a

square prism, its vertical side, and a section cut oblique in one direction to its axis.

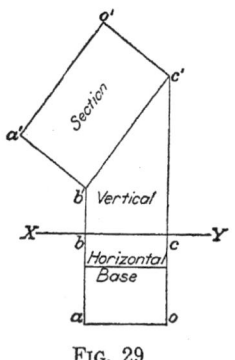

FIG. 29

The line b' c' indicates the inclination or pitch of the cut.

To find the size and form of the section, draw the lines b' a' and c' o' square to the pitch line b' c' and make them equal in length to either side of the base; connect a' o', thus completing the unfolding of the sectional cut made through the pitch line b' c'.

Now compare Fig. 29 with Fig. 30, which is a perspective of it showing it folded into a solid prism cut oblique to the pitch line b' c', the reference letters being the same in both figures.

It will be observed that the method to develop the section as shown in Fig. 29 is merely to draw the lines a' b' and o' c' square to the pitch or inclination of the cut, and the line a' o' parallel to the cut as shown at a' o' and b' c'; the lines a' b' and o' c' to be equal in length to the side of the base or plan.

The section therefore of a cut of this kind will be an oblong figure, its width equal to the side of the base and its length equal to the length of the line indicating the oblique cut. Viewing the section in this light it becomes a very simple matter to determine its size and form—just as simple as it is to determine the size and form of the sloping surface of a "shed roof."

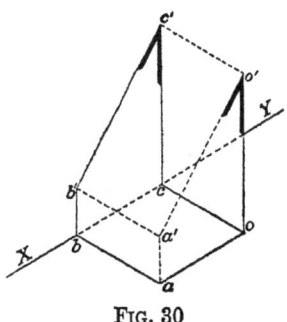

FIG. 30

By comparing the slope of a "shed roof" with the sectional cut shown in Fig. 30 it will be seen that both are alike, the two sloping in one direction.

Reverting now to Fig. 28, where a wreath handrail is shown winding around and above its plan upon a section like the one under consideration, it will be plainly seen how important it is to know of a method to find the size and form of a section.

As shown in Fig. 28 it is the size of the section that determines the length of the wreath as from a to c', and also that the angle of the lines constituting its form as shown at b' determines the direction of the tangents by which in wreath rail construction the joints at each end are worked, to butt square with the rails adjoining, or as shown in Fig. 28, to form an easement in the wreath to butt square to the newel post.

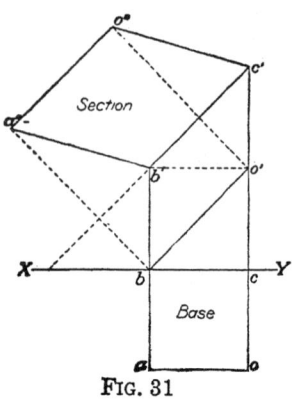

FIG. 31

How to develop the form of a section cut oblique in two directions to the axis of a prism is shown in Fig. 31. Let $o\ a\ b\ c$ below $X\ Y$ be the plan or base of a prism, the line drawn from b on $X\ Y$ to O to be the inclination of the cut made through the side a-o, and the line $b'\ c'$ the inclination of the cut through the side b-c.

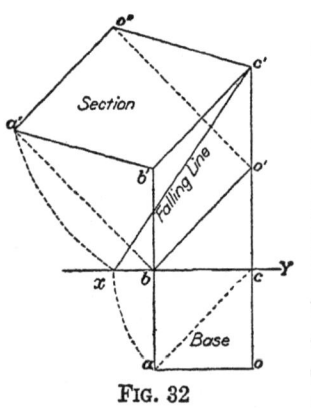

FIG. 32

To find the size and form of the section draw the dotted lines b-a' and $O'\ O''$ square to the inclined line b-O'. Place the point of a compass in b' extend to C' and turn around to cut the dotted lines in O'' and a''. Now connect all the points as shown from b' to a'', from a'' to O'' and from O'' to C', thus determining the size and form of a section cut oblique in two directions to the axis of a prism.

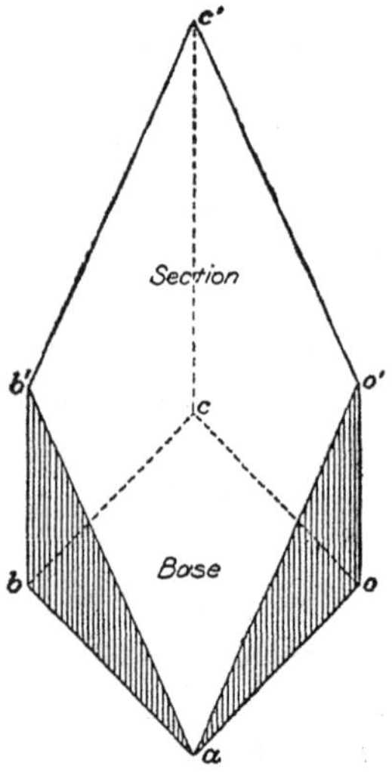

Another method is shown in Fig. 32, where a diagonal line a-c

FIG. 33

across the base is revolved to the line $X\,Y$, as shown by the arc from a to x. From x a line is drawn to c' and revolved as shown by the arc from x to a'. Then all the points in the section are

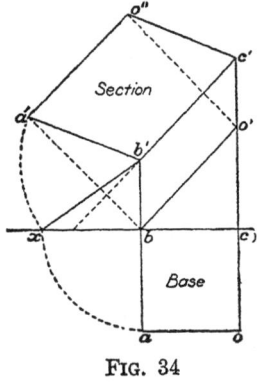

FIG. 34

connected as a'-O''-b'-c'. In Fig. 33 a view is given of the section in position above the base where all points of the section are shown at their respective heights above their correlative points in the base, as b' above b, o' above o and c' above c.

In Fig. 34 is shown how to find the size and form of a section cut oblique to the axis of a prism in two directions, the inclinations being unequal. In this figure it is shown that the cut through the side b-c has a greater inclination than has the cut through the side a-b, as shown from b' to x.

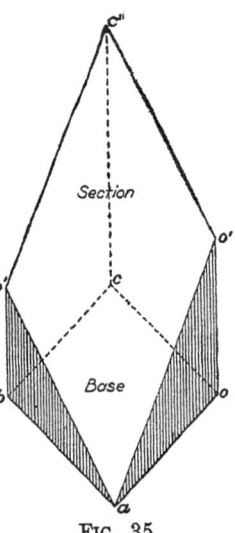

FIG. 35

To find the size and form of the section draw a line from b square to the line $b'\,c'$. Place the point of a compass in b' and extend to x (to get the length of the cut through a-b) and revolve point x to a'. Now connect $a'\,b'$, make $c'\,o''$ parallel to it and connect $o''\,a'$, completing the section.

The block is shown folded in Fig. 35. In Fig. 36 is shown how to find the size and form of a section cut reversely to the one shown in Fig. 34.

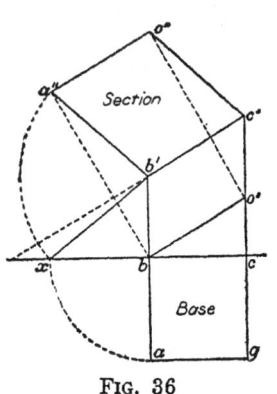

FIG. 36

The cut made through the side $b'\,c'$ in Fig. 36 is less inclined than the cut made through the side a-b as shown from b' to x.

Draw a line from b square to the line $b'\,c'$. Place the compass in b', extend to x, turn over to a''; connect $a''\,b'$, draw a line parallel to it from c' to o'' and a line parallel to $c'\,b'$ from o'' to a'', completing the section as shown outlined by $O''\,a''\,b'\,c'$. In Fig. 37 the section is shown in position above its base.

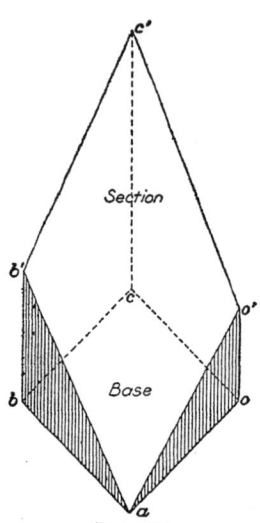

FIG. 37

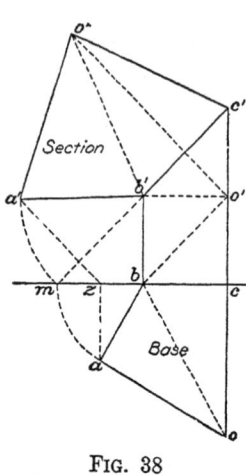

FIG. 38

In Fig. 38 is shown the method of unfolding a section cut obliquely through a prism of an irregular shaped base.

Let o-a-b-c be the outlines of the base and the oblique cut through the sides a-b and b-c equal, as shown from c' through b' to m. Draw a line from a to z and from z a line square to the inclined line $c'\,b'\,m$. Place one leg of the compasses in b' and revolve the other from m to a' as shown by the arc. Connect a' to b'. Again place one leg of the compasses in b' and open out the length of the diagonal line o-b of the base, to cut the line $O'\,O''$. Now connect the points $o''\,a'\,b'\,c'\,o''$, thus completing the outlines of the section.

The section is shown above the base in Fig. 39, where also all points and lines used in Fig. 38 are shown in position relatively to one another

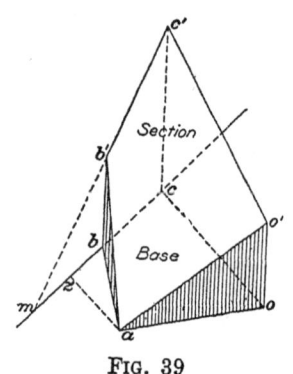

FIG. 39

In Fig. 40 is shown the method of unfolding the section of another irregular base prism.

In this example the oblique cuts through the sides are unequal, the cut through the side *a-b* not being quite as steep as the one through the side *b-c*. To find the size and form of the

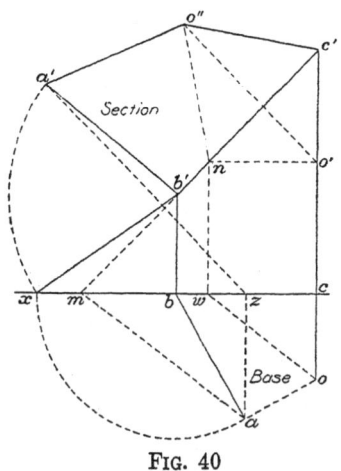

FIG. 40

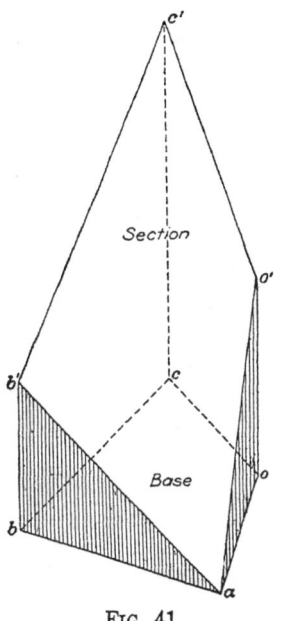

FIG. 41

section draw a line from *a* in the base to *z* and from *z* a line square to the line *b' c'* as shown from *z* to *a'*. Place the compass in *b'*, open out to *x*, and turn around to *a'*, connect *a'* to *b'*.

Now draw a line from *o* in the base to *w* and from *w* up to *n* and from *n* a line across to *o'*. From *o'* draw the line *o' o''* square to the pitch line *c' b'*. Now place the compass in *n*, open it out the length of *o-w* in the base to cut the line *o' o''* in *o''*. Connect *o''* *a' b' c'*, which defines the size and form of the section.

The points and lines of the section are shown in Fig. 41 in position over and above the base points and lines.

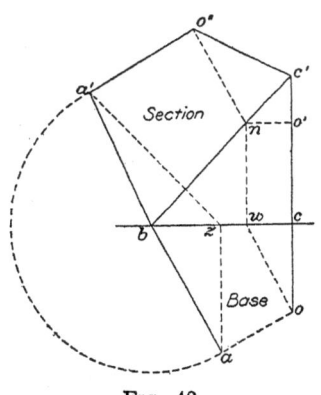

FIG. 42

In Fig. 42 is shown how to find the size and form of the section when it is desired that the line *b-a* be a level line and in Fig. 43 the size and form over the same base when it is desired to have the section level above the line

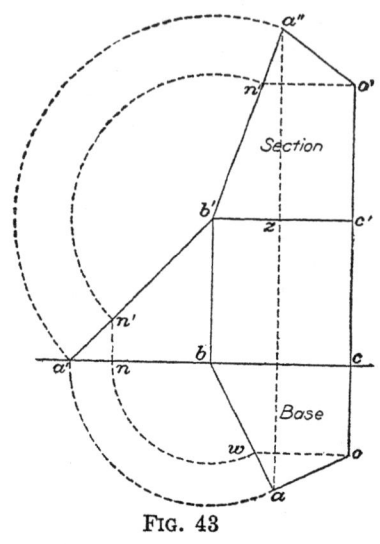

FIG. 43

b-c. The sections as presented in these two figures are the kind handrailers encounter in the execution of wreaths where either the bottom or top tangent is required to be level to form an easement in the wreath.

Referring to Fig. 42 let *o-a″-b-c* represent the size and form of the base, the section to be level over the side *b-a″* and inclining over the side *b-c* equal to the pitch line *b-c′* shown in the figure.

Draw a line from *a* in the base to *z* and from *z* square to the pitch line *b-c* to *a′.*

Place the compass in *b*, open out to *a* in the base and turn around as shown by the arc to *a′* and connect *a′b.*

Now draw a line from *o* in the base to *w* parallel, to the line *a-b.* From *w* draw a line to *n* and from *n* to *o″* parallel to the line *b-a′.* Make *n-o″* equal in length to *o-w* in the base.

Now connect the points *o′ a′ b c* which delineate the size and form of the section as shown in Fig. 44, where it is shown folded over and above its plan.

Note that the section is shown in Fig. 44 to be level above the sides *a-b* and inclined over the other sides.

In Fig. 43 is shown how to find the

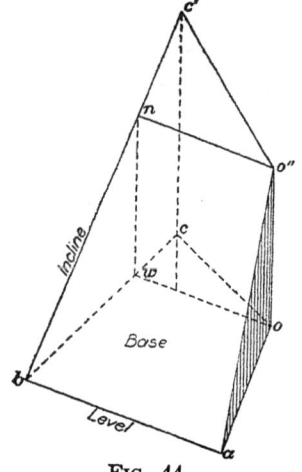

FIG. 44

size and form of a section through the same base prism, when it is desired to have the cut above the side *b-c* level.

Proceed as in all the preceding figures to draw a line from *a* in the base up to *z* and beyond to *a″*. Place the compass in *b* in the base, open it out to *a* in the base, turn around as shown by the arc to *a′*. Now place the compass in *b′*, turn around to *a″* as shown by the arc and connect *a″* to *b′*.

Again from *o* in the base draw the line to *w*, transfer this line also to the section as shown by the arcs from *w* to *n* and from *n′* to *n″*. Now draw a line from *n″* to *o* and connect *o′ a″ b′ c′*, which will define the outlines of the section.

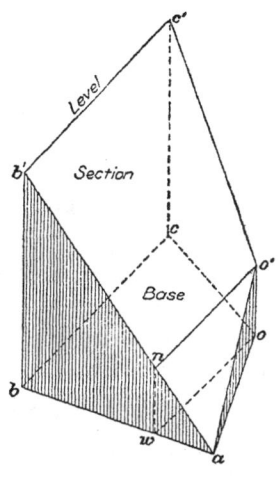

FIG. 45

A view of this section in position over and above the base is shown in Fig. 45 to be a cut level through the side *b-c* and inclined through the other sides.

In the following chapter on "Tangents" as factors in the laying-out of "face molds" the method of developing "sections of solids" as presented in the preceding figures will be seen to be necessary. By means of these sections only it will be possible to find the correct angle between the tangents upon the face mold to square the joints. They are absolutely necessary also to ascertain the correct length of the face mold and even the "bevels" that are required to apply to the joints and tangents to "twist" or square the wreath.

CHAPTER III

TANGENTS

Tangents are used in the construction of wreath handrails to square the joints, and because the wreaths are inclined when in position it will be necessary to find the correct direction of one tangent in its relation to the other; that is, it will be necessary to find the correct angle between the tangents to secure a "square butt" joint with another wreath piece, or with the rails of adjoining flights.

To make the subject of tangents as applied to the construction of wreaths clear and scientifically explicit it will be necessary first of all to know the meaning of the term "tangent." In dictionaries we find it defined as a "straight line touching without penetrating a curved line."

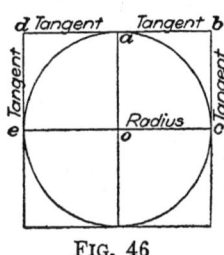

FIG. 46

In Fig. 46 is shown a circle inscribed within a square. Its diameter is a line across it as from e to c. Its radius is a line from its center to its circumference, as o-e or o-a, etc., and the tangents as shown from c to b and b to a are the lines touching the curve of its circumference without penetrating it, as does the diameter and radius. In this figure the tangents are at right angles to one another. In wreath construction we find them often at other angles.

In Fig. 47 are shown tangents standing at an acute angle to one another as at b-a-c and also at an obtuse angle as at e-d-f.

It will be observed that the radius lines o a, o-c, etc., in Fig. 47 are at right angles to the tangents as o-c to the tangent c-b and o-a to the tangent a-b.

Whatever angle there may be between tangents in plan lines of a wreath rail it must always be kept in mind that they are to be at right angles to their respective radius lines; otherwise they will not be tangents to the plan curve.

In Fig. 48 is shown a perspective view of a cylinder inscribed within a square prism, the base of the cylinder representing the

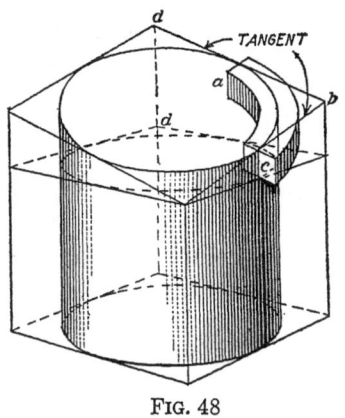

FIG. 48

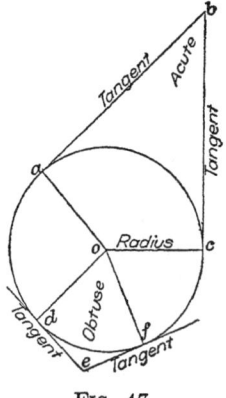

FIG. 47

circle shown in Fig. 46. An oblique cut is shown, made through both cylinder and prism. The curve cut of the cylinder is shown to be the curve of a center line of a wreath, and the cut lines of the square prism the tangents of the same.

The joints of the piece of wreath are shown at *a* and *c* to have been made square to the tangents, indicating the importance of having the correct angle, as at *b*, between the two tangents *b-a* and *b-c*. It is shown here that tangents are essentially necessary as factors in the operation pertaining to the joints of wreaths.

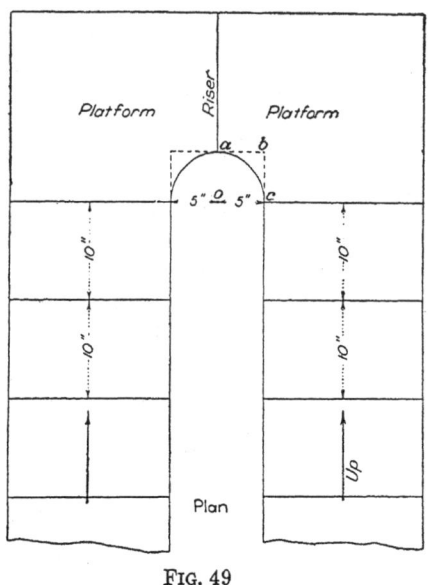

FIG. 49

Knowing now what tangents are, and what use is made of

them in wreath constructions, we will take for an example a cylinder stairway containing two flights, two platforms, and a 10-inch cylinder as shown in plan, Fig. 49. Here it will be seen that the first flight lands upon a platform, then a riser to another platform, and again a second flight to a landing upon the second floor.

It is shown in Fig. 49 that the cylinder curve is inscribed within tangents as a-b and b-c, etc.

To construct a wreath to reach from c to a it will be required, first, to unfold the tangent a-b; second, to find the inclination of the tangents a-b and b-c, and then to find the angle between the two.

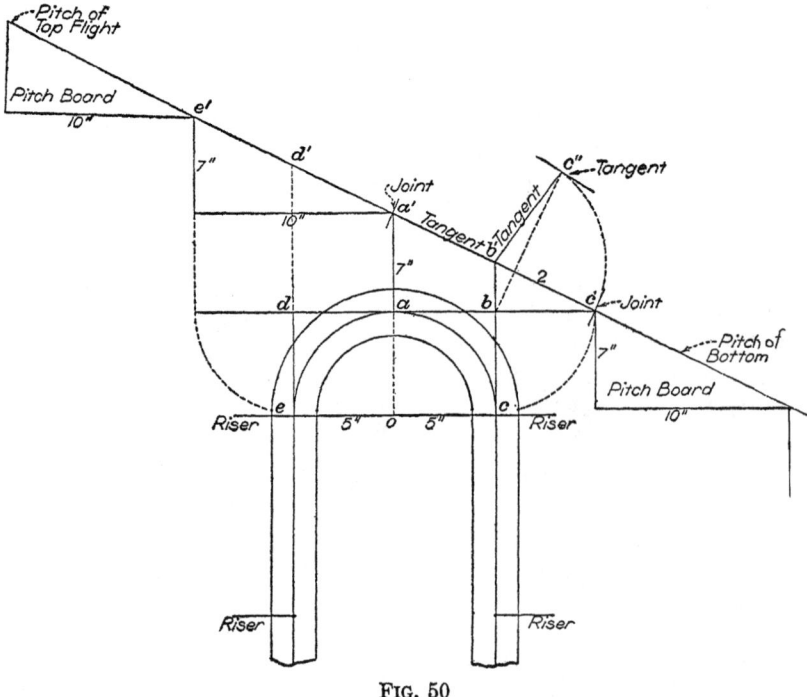

FIG. 50

To unfold the tangent a-b place the compass in b, Fig. 50, open out to c, turn around as shown by the arc from c to c'.

To find the inclination of the tangents, measure from a the height of one riser (the one shown at a in the plan, Fig. 49) as from

a to a'. Now draw a line from a' through b' to c', which indicates the inclination of the tangents a-b and b-c and known generally as the pitch line of the tangents.

It will be observed that the two tangents in this example are equally inclined, a'-b' over and above the plan tangent a-b, and b'-c' over and above the plan tangent b-c.

All that is required now to find the angle between the two tangents is merely to draw a square line to the pitch line of tangents from the corner b, as shown from b through 2 to c'' and place the compass in b', extending it out to c', and turn around to c'', then connecting c'' b'.

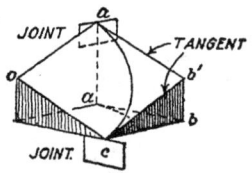

FIG. 51

The angle between the two is shown at b' which gives each one its correct direction to guarantee a true "square butt" joint at the ends a' and c''.

The tangents are shown in position above their respective

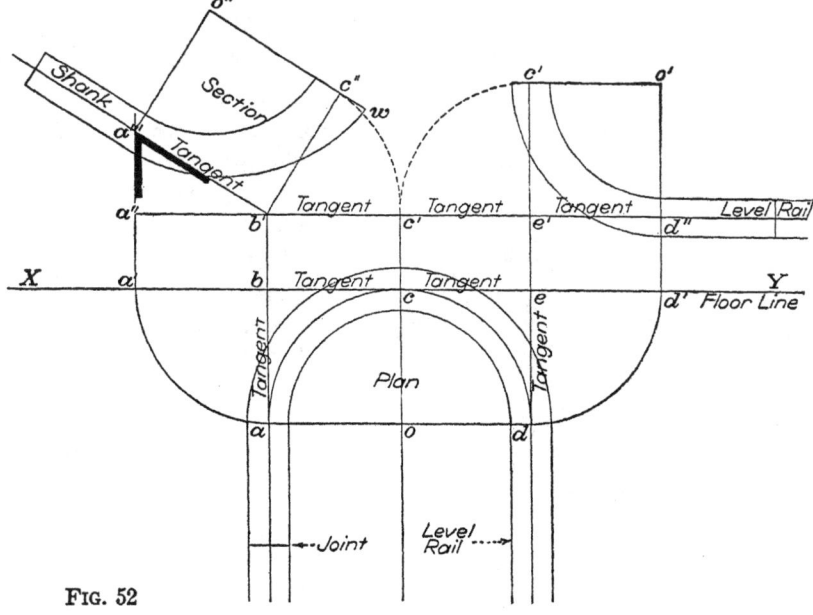

FIG. 52

plans in Fig. 51, showing equal inclination and correct direction to square the joints. Also see Chapter 2 on Sections of Prisms.

It will be observed that the tangents are shown in Fig. 51 to be two lines of a section cut obliquely to two sides of a square prism, emphasizing the fundamental value of a method to unfold sections in the construction of wreath rails.

In Fig. 52 is shown how to handle the tangents in the construction of a wreath winding around a cylinder at the bottom of a stairway from a landing level rail.

The plan tangents are shown at d-e and e-c for the part connecting to the level landing rail, and at c-b and b-a for the part connecting to the pitch rail of the flight. The joint between the two parts is shown at c, the center of the cylinder.

The tangent e-d is shown unfolded by being turned around to d', and the tangent b-a on the other side is shown unfolded by being turned around to a'. They are all now shown to be in line upon X Y, as a-b, b-c, c-e and e-d.

Now erect lines on each point, and draw a line through the center of the level landing rail to cut the vertical lines in d'', e', c', b', a''.

From point b' draw the pitch of the flight as shown to a'', which also will be the pitch over the tangent b-a.

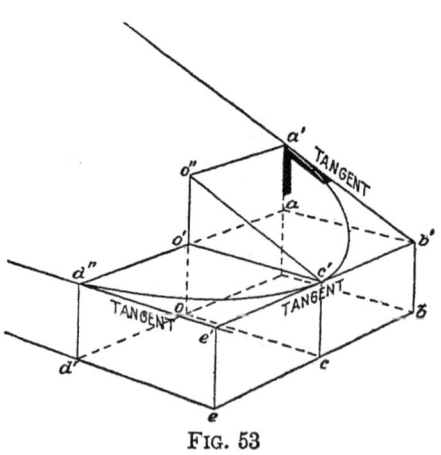

Fig. 53

All the other tangents are shown to be level, aligning with the center line of the level landing rail.

Thus we have found the pitch line of the four tangents, and found also that only one of the four is inclined.

To find the angle between the inclined tangent a'''-b' and the level tangent b'-c' for the piece of wreath connecting to the rail of the flight we need only to draw the square marked section, one side to equal the length of the inclined tangent, the other to equal the length of the level tangent b-c as shown.

The angle at *b* gives the correct direction to each tangent to square the joints at each end. Because the two bottom tangents are level the piece of rail inscribed by them will be a duplicate of the plan curve shown from *d* to *c*.

The four tangents are shown in position above their plan tangents in Fig. 53, where the top tangent *a′ b′* only is shown to incline, the remaining three being level, aligning with the level landing rail. The wreath piece of rail is shown in Fig. 54 in its relation to the tan-

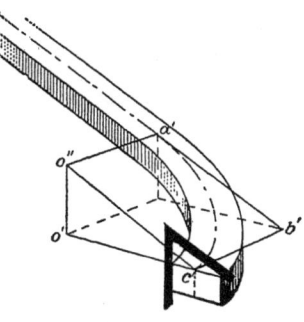

FIG. 54

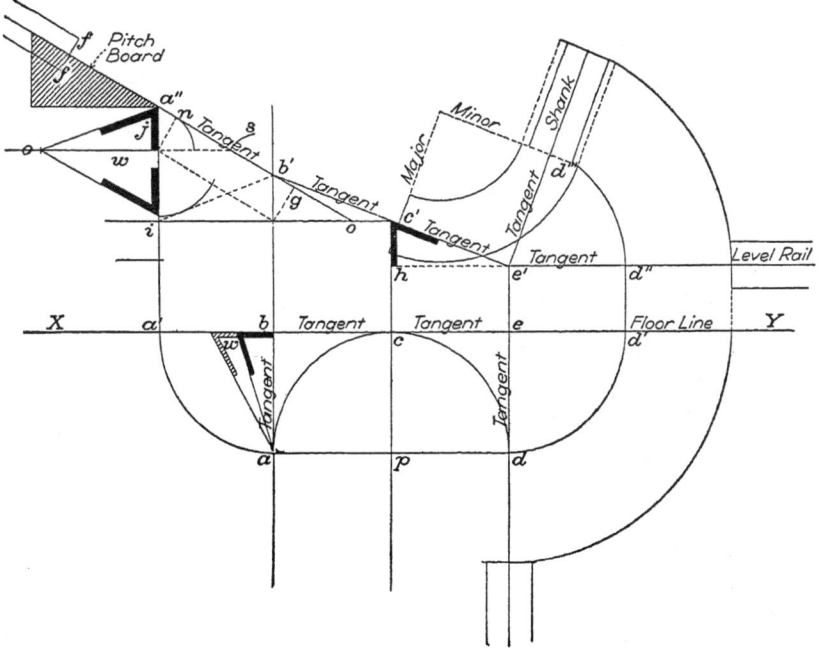

FIG. 55

gents *a′ b′* and *b′ c*, and the bevel in its relation to the operation of squaring it.

In Fig. 55 is shown how to unfold and find the pitch line of the tangents of a wreath rail winding around a cylinder at the bottom of a stairway when the cylinder contains *3* steps, not as in the preceding example, where no steps were placed within the cylinder.

The plan bottom tangent *d-e* is unfolded by being revolved to the floor line, as shown by the arc from *d* to *d'*.

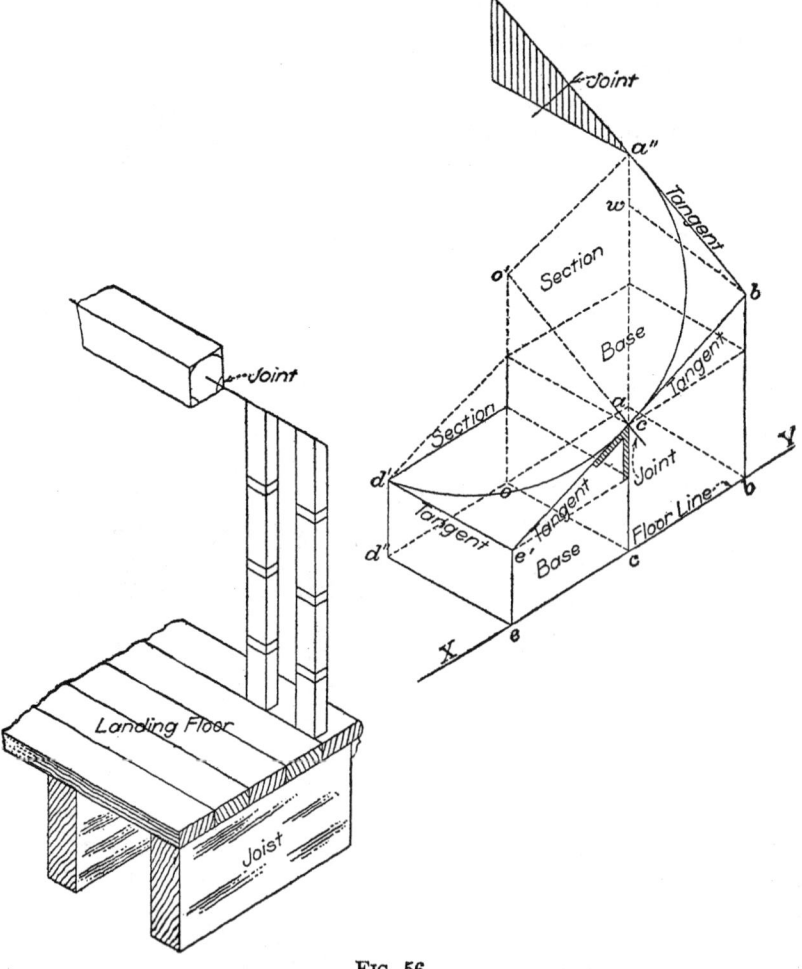

FIG. 56

The upper plan tangent *a-b* is unfolded in the same manner by being revolved to the floor line, as shown by the arc from *a* to *a'*.

Now erect perpendicular lines upon the points a', b, c, e, d' and make the length of the line from a' equal the depth of the three risers that are contained in the cylinder, as shown from a' to a''. Place the pitch board as shown at a'' and draw the pitch of the flight. Produce the flight pitch through b' to O.

From b' draw a pitch line through c' to e' and from e' draw a level line to d'. In this manner the pitch line over all the tangents is determined as shown from a' to b' over the tangent a-b; from b' to c' over the tangent b-c; from c' to e' over the tangent c-e and from e' to d'' over the tangent e-d.

There are three things to be considered as specifically essential to the correct arrangement of pitches over tangents.

First, as shown in Fig. 55 the top tangent a'-b' should, if possible, pitch the same as the rail of the flight because the wreath piece containing this tangent is to be jointed to the rail.

Second, the two middle tangents b-c' and c'-e' must have equal pitch, because the two pieces of wreath are to be jointed at c'.

Third, the bottom tangent e' d' must be level because the wreath piece it belongs to is to be jointed to the bottom level rail. All this is evident when it is considered that the joints of wreaths are made square to the tangents, so as to butt square with the rails adjoining them, and with each other at the center of the cylinder, as shown in Fig. 55 at c'.

A clearer perception of the whole operation will be obtained from an inspection of Fig. 56, where the top tangent a'' b is shown aligning with the pitch of the flight rail, the two tangents b' c' and c' e' aligning with one another, and the bottom level tangent aligning with the level landing rail.

CHAPTER IV

FACE MOLDS

The term "face mold" is applied to the template that is used in the first place to cut out the material from the plank, and after as a guide in the manipulation of "squaring" or "twisting" a wreath rail.

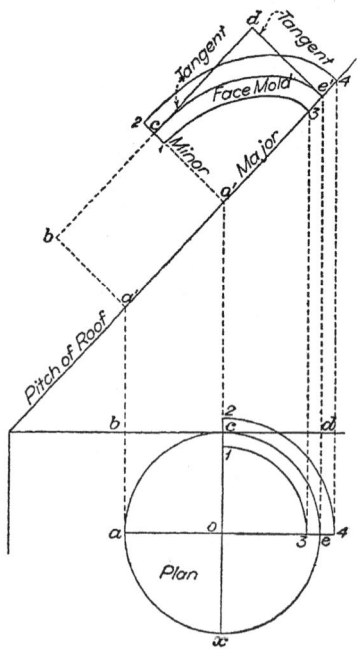

Its curved form in all cases will be a portion of an ellipse, and that because the ellipse only is formed in all cuts made oblique to the axis of a cylinder.

For instance, a stove pipe if made to penetrate a sloping surface, such as a shed roof, will leave a hole that is elliptical in shape. The principle that is involved in finding the true shape and size of such a hole, is one

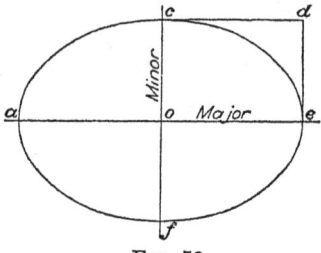

FIG. 57

FIG. 58

of the fundamental principles in the laying-out of a "face mold" for a wreath, the other being the principles already explained in the preceding chapter on "Sections of Prisms," and also in the chapter on "Tangents".

Considering the face mold in this light as being composed of a part of an ellipse, combined with a part of an oblique section cut through a prism, it becomes, to those proficient in the solutions pertaining to the development of sections cut obliquely through the "cylinder" and "prism", an easy matter to lay it out.

Such a solution is shown in Fig. 57, which illustrates the problem of finding the size and form of a hole upon a sloping roof to fit a stove pipe penetrating it.

From the center *o* draw the circle *a-c-e-f* to represent the pipe, and from *a*, *c* and *e* draw the perpendicular lines up to the line representing the slope of the roof penetrating it in *a′ o′ e′*.

Now draw two lines at right angles to one another through *o*, as shown in Fig. 58. Make the line *c-f* equal to the diameter *c-x* of the plan shown in Fig. 57, and the line *a-e* equal to *a′ e′*

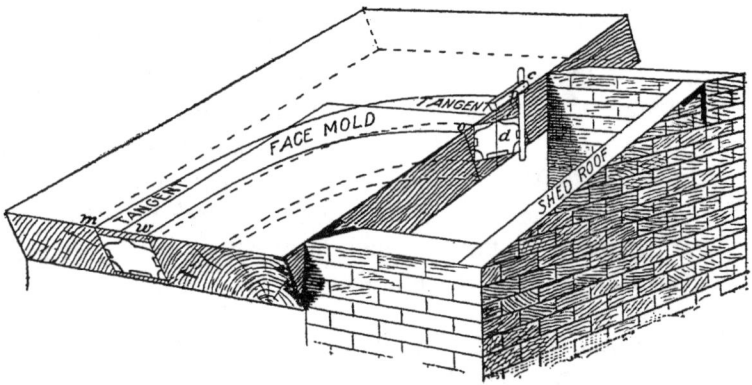

FIG. 59

shown on the slope of the roof in Fig. 57. These two lines will be the axis of an ellipse shown in Fig. 58 drawn through *a-c-e-f*, its form representing the hole upon the roof.

Now consider one-quarter of the plan circle shown in Fig. 57 to be the plan of a wreath rail. Enclose it with the lines *c-d* and *d-e* to represent its tangents, project the points *3* and *4* to the roof as shown. Make *o,-1,-2* equal *o, -1,-2* in the plan. This last line will be the minor axis, and the line of the roof from *o* to *3-e′-4* will be the major axis to draw the face mold for a wreath rail that would have the quarter circle for its plan and the slope of the roof for its pitch.

The lines from *o* to *c* and from *e* to *d* would be the tangents of the face mold as shown.

Fig. 59 represents a view of a shed roof with a wreath rail winding upon its surface, as shown from *M-W* to *P-O*.

In Figs. 60 and 61 are shown the method to draw an ellipse by means of string and pins. Let *B-O-A* in Fig. 60 be the major axis and *D-O-C* the minor, and the points *Z* and *Z* be what is

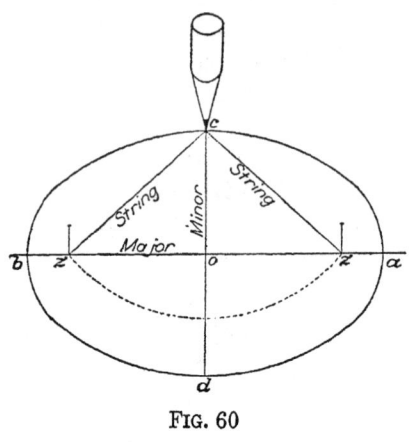

termed the "foci" of the ellipse. To find these points *Z-Z* upon the major axis open a compass out the length of half the major axis as from *B* to *O* or from *O* to *A*, place one point of the compass in *C* upon the minor axis and turn around as shown by the arc to cut the major in *Z* and *Z*.

To draw the curve place pins in *Z* and *Z* on the major and also in *C* on

FIG. 60

the minor. Now fasten a piece of string tight around the pins, replace the pin at *C* with a pencil as shown and turn around. The curve formed will be the ellipse shown.

In Figs. 62 and 63 are shown the method of drawing an ellipse with a straight edge. Draw the lines *b-a* and *c-d* in Fig. 62 to represent the axis and mark upon a straight edge the distance *1-2* to represent the length of half the minor axis and the distance *1-3* to represent the length of half the major axis. Now place the straight edge as shown in Fig. 62 with *2* on the major and *3* on the minor, and mark a dot as shown at *1*. This dot will be in the curve of the ellipse. Proceed to find other dots by changing the position of the straight edge,

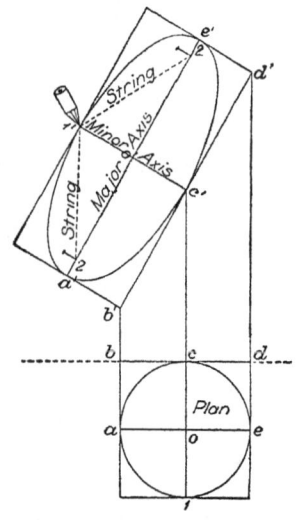

FIG. 61

keeping *2* on the major and *3* on the minor in all the changed positions. A line traced through the dots thus found will delineate the form of the ellipse. The same process is shown in Fig. 63.

A third method to draw an ellipse is shown in Fig. 64 and is known as the "Ordinate method". The lines *1, 2, 3* in this figure are called ordinates, and the way they are used to draw the curve of the ellipse is as follows:

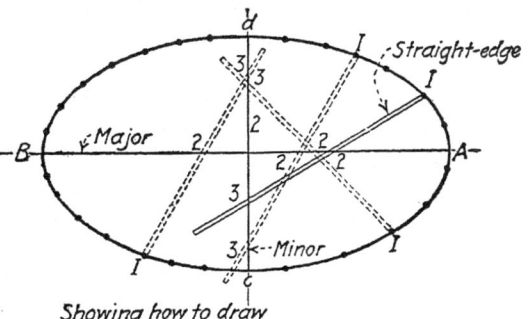

Showing how to draw an Ellipse with a Straight-edge

FIG. 62

Let the pitch line *a-B* represent the length of the semi-major axis, and the line *b o* represent the length of the semi-minor axis. From the plan curve draw the lines *1, 2, 3* parallel to the line *a-c* as shown up to the pitch line, and from the points on the pitch line draw parallel lines to

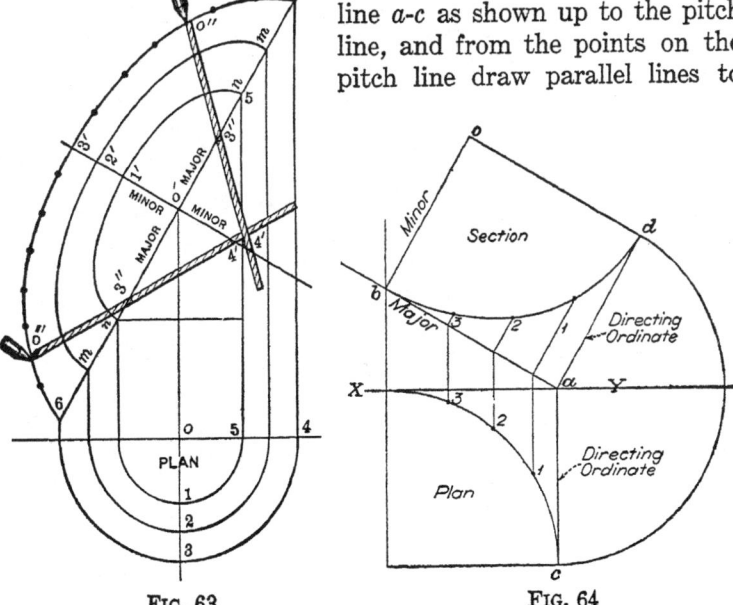

FIG. 63   FIG. 64

a-d; make each one the same length as the lines similarly numbered in the plan; measuring the plan lines from the curve to *X-Y* and those on the section from the pitch line *B-a*. A line

traced through the ordinates *1, 2, 3* upon the section will be a
quarter curve of an ellipse, and if we assume the quarter circle
of the plan to be a center line of a plan rail, then the quarter
curve of the ellipse upon the section would be the center line of
a wreath rail.

There are many other methods to draw the ellipse, but stairbuilders generally avail themselves of the three here described.

In the following figures is shown how the three methods are
applied in the laying-out of face molds.

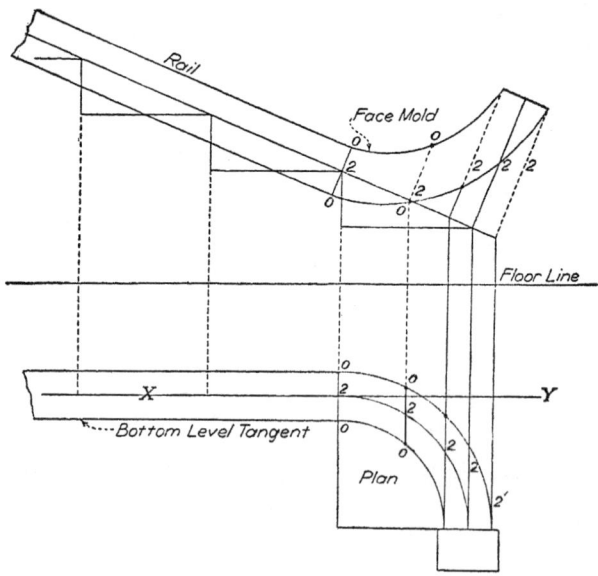

FIG. 65.—Ordinate Method to Lay Out the Face Mold.

The plan in Fig. 65 is that of a rail curving out a full quadrant
at the bottom of a stairway. Above the plan is shown the elevation of the steps and the development of the wreath rail.
The wreath in this example will have an easement so as to butt
at right angles to the newel post.

All that is required to lay out the form of the face mold in this
figure is to follow the explanation of the development of the
quarter circle in Fig. 64, which is merely to make the lines *2, 2*,
etc., upon the face mold equal in length to the lines *2, 2*, etc., in
the plan, measuring the plan lines from *X-Y* and the face mold

lines from the pitch line, then tracing the curves through the points found as shown at o, o and o, o.

In Fig. 66 is shown another case of laying out a face mold by ordinates, the plan of the rail being the same as in Fig. 65, but in this case the wreath rail will not have an easement to butt at right angle to the newel post, and the two tangents therefore will incline equally as shown from c' through b' to n in Fig. 66.

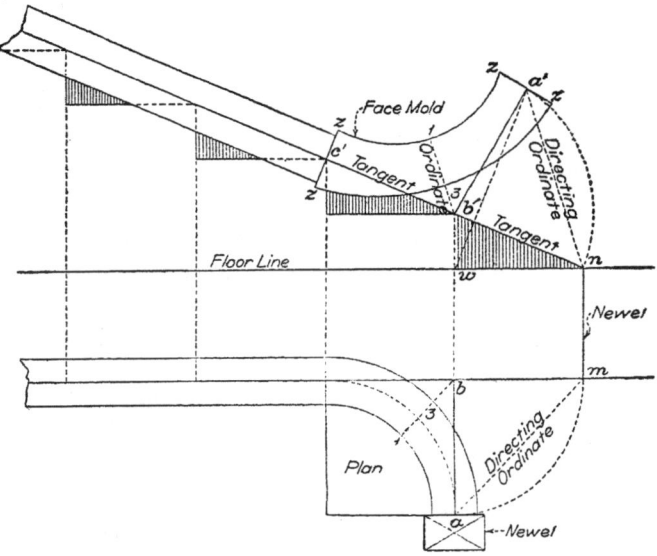

FIG. 66.—Ordinate Method, Two Equally Inclined Tangents.

To lay out the face mold, place one point of the compass in b in the plan, open it out to a and turn around to m as shown. Now draw a line from a to m. This line is the plan "directing ordinate". Erect a line upon m to n and from w; draw a line square to the pitch line of the tangents as shown from w to a'. To find point a' on this line place the compass in b', open out to n (the length of the bottom tangent) and turn around to cut the line from w in a'. Now connect a' to b' and a' to n.

The line a' b' will be the bottom tangent as required upon the face mold in its relation to the top tangent, and the line a' n will be the "directing ordinate" to draw the curves of the face mold.

Now from b in the plan curve draw a line across the plan

curve and parallel to the plan direct ordinate a-m; also draw a line from b' upon the pitched tangents parallel to the ordinate a' n of the face mold. Make b-3-1 upon the face mold ordinate equal to b-3-1 upon the plan ordinate.

The distance between 3 and 1 determines the width of the face mold at this point. Make its width at each end ¼ of an inch wider, as shown at z,z, etc.

Now take a flexible lath and bend it to touch the points z-1-z and z-3-z and scribe the inside and outside curves. The joints at c' and a' are made square to the tangents.

Two other face molds laid out by ordinates are shown in Figs. 67 and 68, but in these examples the plan curves are less than a quadrant, and therefore the plan tangents will be at an obtuse angle to one another, which is usually the case in a turnout at the bottom of a stairway.

In Fig. 67 the problem is to lay out a face mold for a turnout less than a quadrant, the wreath rail to have an easement to butt square to the newel post. To commence, turn the bottom

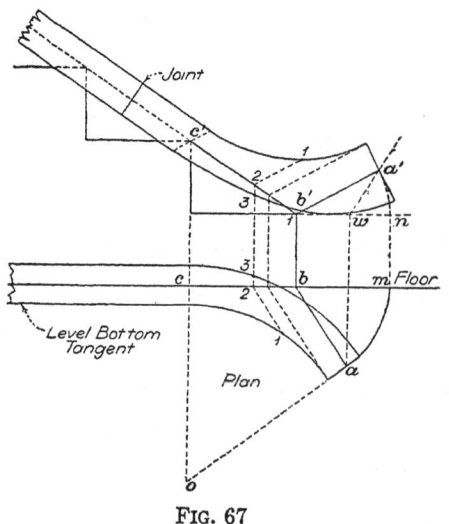

FIG. 67

plan tangent a-b to m, erect m-n. Draw a line from a in the plan to w and from w a line square to the pitch line of the rail to a', connect a' b', which will be the bottom tangent transferred to the face mold. Because the rail is to have an easement to butt square to the newel, this bottom tangent will be a level tangent. It will therefore be the directing ordinate of the face mold, as will also be the plan tangent a-b the directing plan ord nate. Next draw any number of ordinates across the plan rail parallel to the level tangent a-b (the plan directing ordinate) and project them to the pitch line as shown. Now from where the projectors cut the pitch line draw ordinates parallel to the tangent b' a' (the directing ordinate of the face mold) and make them equal in length to those in the plan, as shown at *1-2-3* both in the plan and upon the face mold.

Draw the curves of the face mold as described for the curves in the preceding figures.

In Fig. 68 it is shown how to lay out the face mold for a wreath over the same plan as that of Fig. 67, but with two

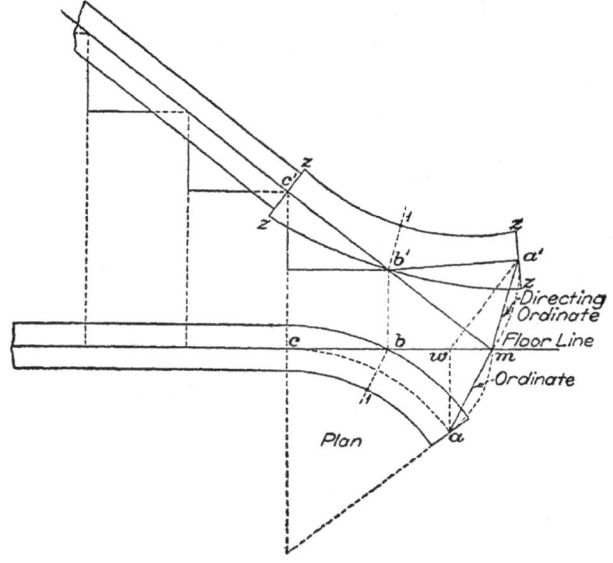

FIG. 68.—Ordinates to Layout Face Molds.

inclined tangents, the wreath to continue without an easement to the newel post.

Revolve the bottom plan tangent a-b to m, and connect a-m, which will be the directing plan ordinate. Draw a line from a to w and from w square to the pitch line c', b', m. Now place the compass in b', open out to m, turn around to a', connect a' b' and a' m. The line a'-b' will be the bottom tangent as required upon the face mold to square the wreath, and the line a' m will be the directing ordinate for the face mold.

Now draw any number of lines desired across the plan rail and parallel to the plan directing ordinate a-m. In this example is used but one line only, shown drawn from *b* crossing the plan rail at *b* and *1*.

Draw also a line from *b* on the pitch line parallel to the face mold directing ordinate *a' m* and make *b'-1* equal to *b-1* in the plan. Now trace the curves of the mold as from *z* through *1* to *z* for the inside curve and from *z* through *b'* to *z* for the outside curve.

All face molds may be laid out by this method, and very often it is found to be the most desirable. The method is very simple and easily memorized, merely to find one directing plan "ordinate" and another one face mold "directing" ordinate. These two lines, as were shown in the preceding figures, are used to give the correct direction to all other ordinates that may be used.

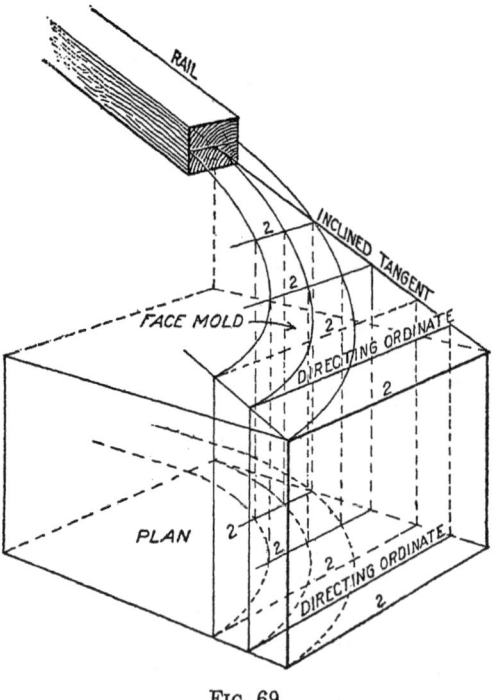

FIG. 69

The view shown of the plan rail and of the face mold right above it, as presented in Fig. 69, will clearly demonstrate the operation.

The plan ordinates *2, 2, 2*, etc., are shown in this figure projected to cut the pitch line, and the ordinates *2, 2, 2*, etc., of the face mold are shown made parallel to the face mold directing ordinate, and each one made equal in length to their correlative plan ordinates. It will be observed that all the ordinates are level lines on plan and on face molds, and that those of the face mold stand over and above their correlative plan ordinates.

In Fig. 69 is shown the operation of laying out the face mold as presented in Fig. 65.

It is shown in Figs. 70 and 71 how to draw the face mold by either the means of a straight edge, trammel or string and pins. In these operations it will be necessary first to find the minor and major axes, and to find the axis it will be necessary also as in preceding figures to find a directing plan ordinate, and a correlative directing ordinate for the face mold. Referring to Fig.

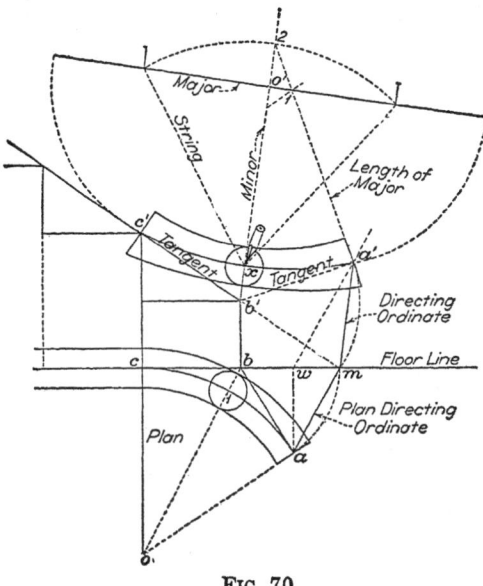

FIG. 70

70, let the plan be the same as in Figs. 67 and 68, namely a turnout curve at the bottom of a stairway.

In Fig. 70 is shown how to lay out the face mold with a string and pins, the rail to continue to the newel post inclining without an easement.

Place the compass in *b* of the plan and revolve the bottom tangent *b-a* to *m* upon the floor line. Next place the compass in *b'* on the pitch line, open it out to *m*, turn around to *a'* and connect *a' b'*, which will be the bottom tangent of the face mold. The plan line *a-m* will be the plan directing ordinate, and the line from *m* to *a'* will be the face-mold directing ordinate.

Now draw a line from *o* to *b* in the plan, parallel to the plan directing ordinate *a-m*. The line from *o* will be the plan line of the minor axis, and that because it is a line drawn from *o*, the center of the plan rail parallel to the plan directing ordinate.

Next project the point *b* to the pitch line as shown from *b* to *b'*, and from *b'* draw a line parallel to the face mold directing

ordinate *m-a'* as from b' to o'. The line b'-o' will be the minor
axis, and point o' will be the center of the elliptical curve of the
face mold.

The length of b' o' is made equal to the line o-b in the plan.
The major axis is to be drawn through o' square to the minor
as shown.

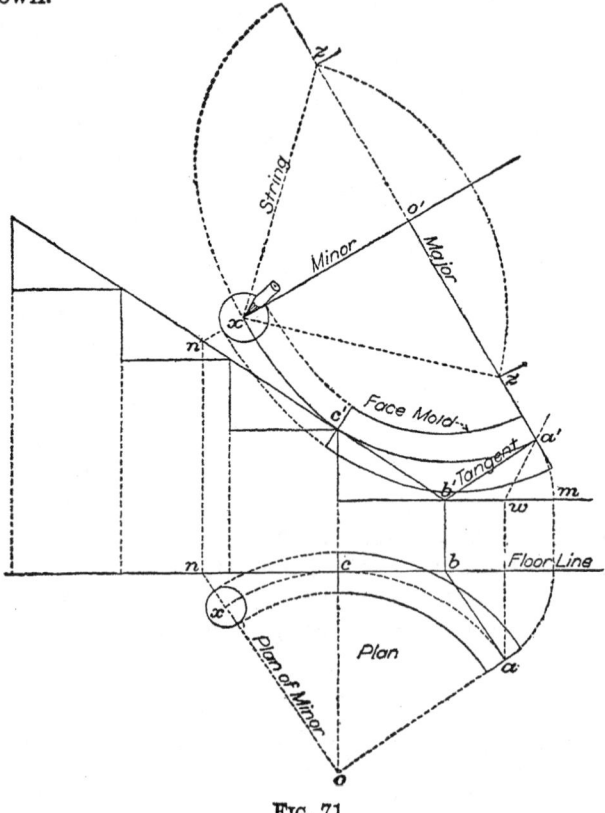

Fig. 71

The next operation is to find the foci—the points on the
major to fix the pins. Open out a pair of compasses the length
of the minor axis *b' o'*, place one point in *a'*, turn around to cut
the major in *I*, and draw a line from *a'* through *I* to *2* on the
minor.

Now place the length of *a' 2* in the compass, fix one point in
x on the minor, and turn around as shown to cut the major

xx, where the pins are shown fixed. Now tie a string to the pins and to the pencil shown upon the minor and sweep the pencil around to form the semi-elliptical curve, a part of which will be the center line of the face mold as shown from *c'* to *a'*.

In Fig. 71 is shown how to lay out the face mold for the same plan where an easement is required to be made in the wreath piece. In this case the bottom tangent will have to be a level tangent. The bottom plan tangent *a-b* in this case will be the plan directing ordinate.

To find the face mold directing ordinate draw a line from *a* in the plan up to *w* and from *w* a line square to the pitch line *c' b'*. Now place the compass in *b'*, open it out to *m*, turn around to *a'* and connect *a'* to *b'*, which will be the directing ordinate for the face mold, and also the bottom level tangent, as it is required upon the face mold in its relation to the inclined top tangent *b' c'* to square the joints.

The minor axis is found by drawing a level line parallel to the plan level tangent *a-b* from the center *o* as shown from *o* to *n*, then up to the pitch line to *n'*, and a line from *n'* parallel to the face mold tangent *b' a'* will be the minor axis. Make its length from *n'* to *o'* equal to *o-n* in the plan and draw the major axis square to it through *o'*. Measure from *o'* to *x* the same length as from *o* to *x* in the plan. Now place the length of half the major axis as from *o'* to *a'* in the compasses, fix one point in *x* and turn around to cut the major in *z* and *z*, fix the pins in *z* and *z*, also the pencil in *x*, tie the string and sweep the elliptical curve, a part of which is shown from *c'* to *a'* will be the center line of the face mold. Observe that the fundamental principle in these operations is to find a directing ordinate or level line in the plan, and draw the plan of the minor axis parallel to it. Then find the directing ordinate for the face mold, and draw the minor axis parallel to that line, making the minor and its plan equal in length, then drawing the major axis square to the minor, and after finding the axis to find the foci for the pins by fixing one point of a compass opened out the length of the major upon the minor, and turning around to cut the major in the points to fix the pins.

For further elucidation of the principle, let Fig. 72 represent the plan, elevation and development of a turnout rail at the bottom of a stairway, the curve in this example to be more than a quadrant and the tangents therefore to be at an acute angle to one another in the plan.

The plan tangents are shown at *a-b* and *b-c*, the tangent *a-b* to incline and the tangent *b-c* to be level to form an easement, as shown at *b* upon the falling mold.

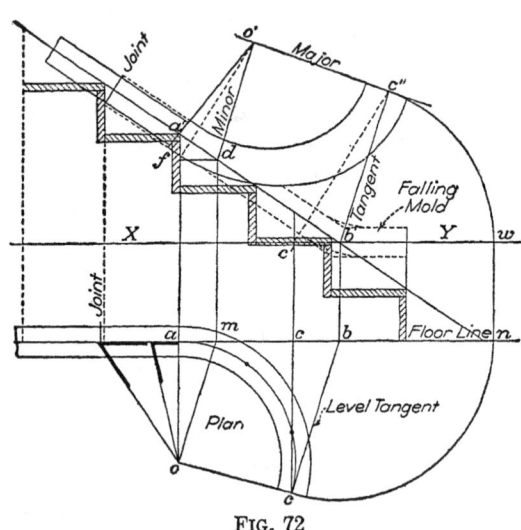

FIG. 72

In this case the level plan tangent *b-c* will be the plan directing ordinate.

Now draw a line from *o* parallel to the plan directing ordinate *b-c*, as shown from *o* to *m*.

The line *o-m* will be the plan of the minor axis.

The next process is to transfer these two lines to the face mold. Upon *b* and *m* erect perpendicular lines to the pitch line of the flight, as shown from *m* to *d* and from *b* to *b'*. Now revolve the plan level tangent *c-b* to the floor line, as shown by the arc from *c* to *n*. Upon *n* erect a line to *w*, a point on *X-Y* indicating the height of the wreath rail above the floor line when in position.

Now place the compass in *b'* on the pitch line, open out to *w* and revolve point *w* to *c''*. Connect *c''* to *b*. This line will be the bottom tangent of the face mold, and because the tangent is level it will be also the directing ordinate of the face mold.

To find the minor axis draw a line from *d* to *o'* parallel to the directing ordinate *b'c''*, and make *d-o'* equal in length to its plan line *o-m*. The line *d-o'* will be the minor axis, and a line drawn through *o* square to the minor will be the major axis. Now the curves may be drawn by either the ordinate, straight-edge, string and pin, or the trammed method. The same face mold is drawn in Fig. 73 with but one ordinate only, which is shown

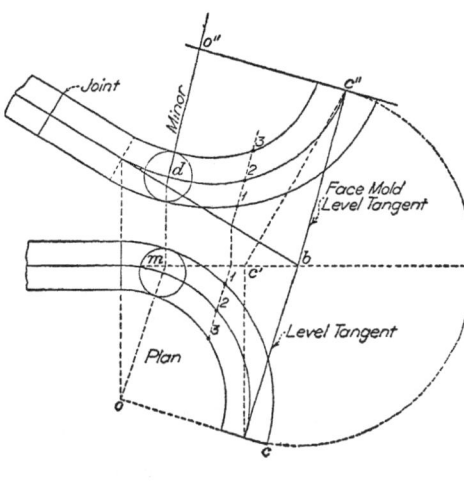

at *1, 2, 3* in the plan to be paralle to the plan level tangent and in the face mold to be parallel to the face mold level tangent, both of these lines being the "directing ordinates", and that because they are level lines.

It is shown in Fig. 74 how to draw the face mold for the same plan curve when the wreath rail

FIG. 73

to continue to the newel without an easement. In this example the face mold curves are shown drawn with string and pins, all the remaining lines by the method as presented in the preceding figures of transferring "ordinates" or "level lines" from the plan to the face mold.

The bevels to square the wreath are shown in this figure at *w* and *w*, which will be thoroughly explained in another chapter.

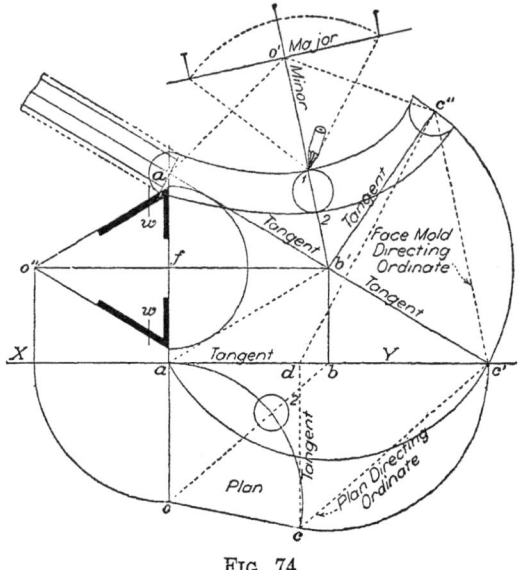

FIG. 74

In Figs. 75 and 76 it is shown how the material for the wreath is treated preparatory to its twisting. In Fig. 75 it is shown

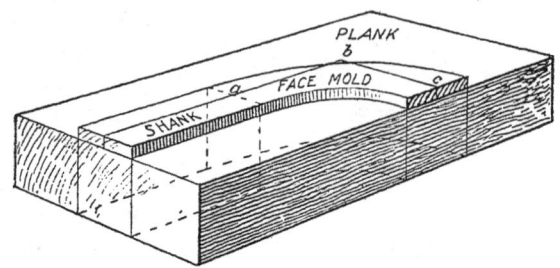

FIG. 75.—How to Cut Out the Material for the Wreath From the Plank.

cut out of the plank square to the surface of the plank, and in Fig. 76 the face mold is shown applied to both the surfaces in positions determined by the bevels.

In this case there is only one bevel to be applied as shown at the end c. The position of the face mold on both top and bottom face of plank is shown to be determined by the lines a and b of the bevel.

FIG. 76. How to Apply the Face Mold to Twist the Wreath

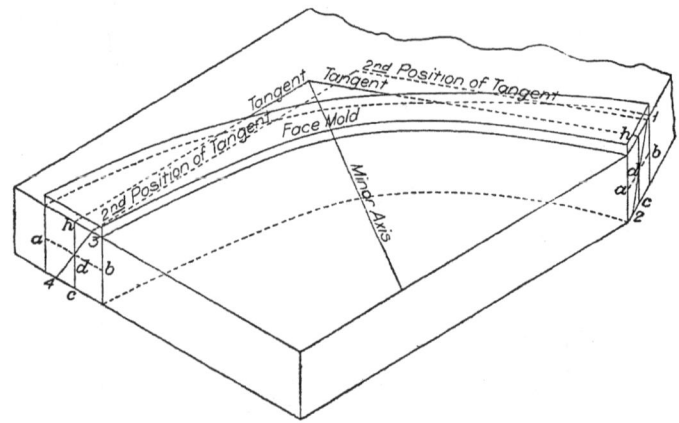

FIG. 77.—Isometric View, Showing Method of Applying Face Mold to Plank for Purposes of Cutting the Material for the Wreath.

In Figs. 77 and 78 the same operation is shown where two bevels are applied.

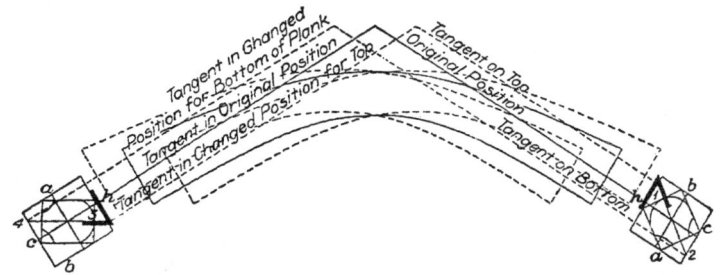

Fig. 78.—Diagram Illustrating Method of Applying Face Mold to Trace the Outlines of the Wreath Preparatory to Squaring its Verticle Sides.

Current Practice in Laying Out Face Molds

In the following figures is shown the method generally practiced by qualified stairbuilders to lay out the face mold. Fig. 79 represents a plan and elevation of a stretchout curve less than a quadrant, the pitch of rail to continue without an easement as shown at *1, 2, 3, 4.* The face mold is laid out as shown in Fig. 80. The line *1-2-3-4* in Fig. 80 represents the pitch line *1-2-3-4* in Fig. 79. To draw the mold drop a line from *2*; place the compass in *3*, open out to *1*, turn

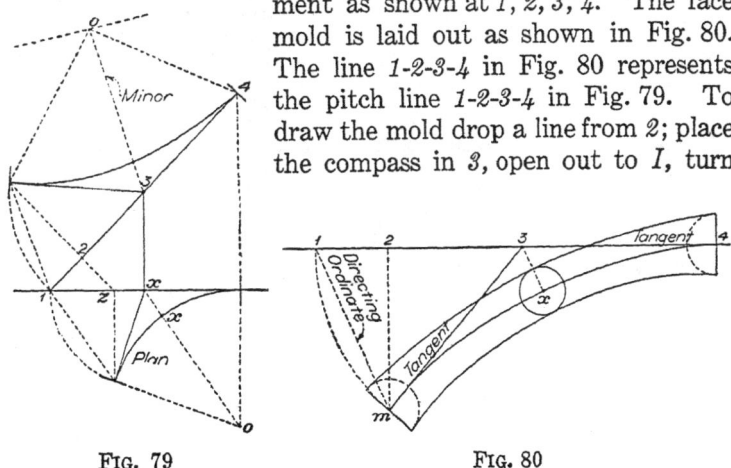

Fig. 79   Fig. 80

around as shown to *m*, connect *m-1* and *m-3*. Now make *3-x* equal *x-x* in Fig. 79 and draw the curve from *m* through *x* to *4*, which will be the center line of the wreath rail.

The width of the mold at x will be the same as that of the plan rail, and at 4 and m, about a quarter of an inch wider, the exact width may be found from the bevels.

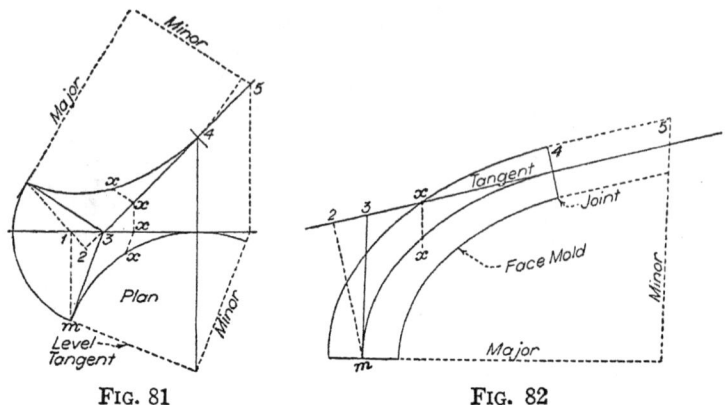

FIG. 81   FIG. 82

Fig 81 has the same plan as Fig. 79, but the bottom tangent is to be level in Fig. 81. To draw the face mold reproduce the pitch line of the tangents as shown at $2, 3, x, 4, 5$ in Fig. 82. From 2 drop a line perpendicular to m and make m-3 equal in length to the bottom plan level tangent 3-m, shown in Fig. 81. Make x-x equal x-x in Fig. 81 and draw the curve from m through x to 4.

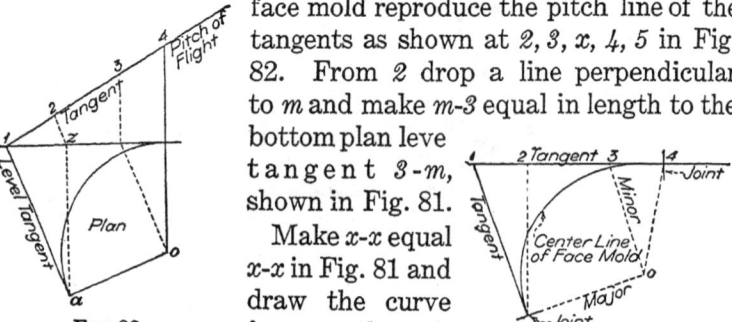

FIG. 83   FIG. 84

The same operation is shown in Figs. 83 and 84 for a plan curve more than a quadrant.

CHAPTER V

WREATH RAIL BEVELS

What is meant by "bevels" in handrailing is the angle of inclination of the oblique plane; the wreath rail is assumed to wind upon its surface over and above its plan curve.

The use made of the bevels is to "square" or "twist" the wreath, so that its sides will be vertical at all points throughout its whole course of winding.

In order to make the nature of bevels as clear as possible, the following figures are presented as being the most efficient for the purpose.

Fig. 85 illustrates a center line plan for a wreath, the curve being less than a quadrant, also the plan tangents, bevel and the inclination of the tangents.

The tangents as shown from a'' to b'' and from b'' to c'' are inclined equally; therefore, the bevels to square the wreath will be equal, but owing to the two tangents being inclined the bevel must be used at the two ends of the wreath.

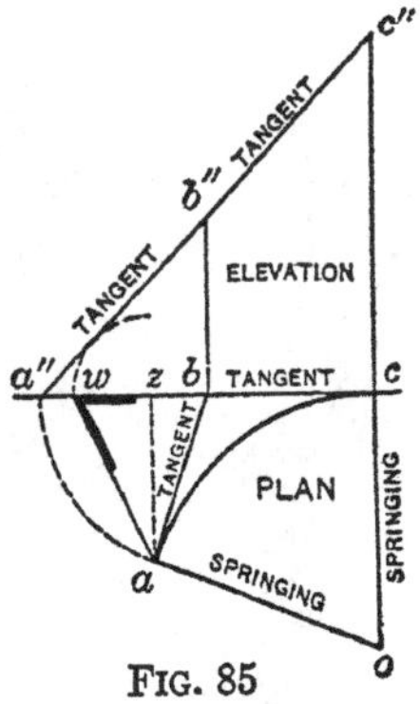

FIG. 85

The bevel is shown at w, having been found by placing the compass in z, opening it out to touch the tangent a'' b'', and turned to w, then connecting w to a.

In Fig. 86 is shown all the plan lines of Fig. 85 and the inclined tangents a'' b'' and b'' c'' in position, also the center line of the wreath over and above its plan curve, and upon the inclined plane before mentioned.

It will be observed that the tangents in this figure form two sides of a section cut obliquely through a prism, and that this section cut is what constitutes the oblique plane, the angle of which constitutes the bevel to square a wreath.

How to develop sections has been already explained in the chapter on "Sections," and the relation of tangents to the sections in the chapter on "Tangents." It will therefore suffice here to state that the angles of inclination of sections or bevels as applied in wreath rail constructions are determined by the tangents.

In Fig. 85 the tangents a'' b'' and b'' c'' are shown to incline equally. The tangents in some cases are found to incline unequally and in others one tangent only is inclined, the other being level, etc.

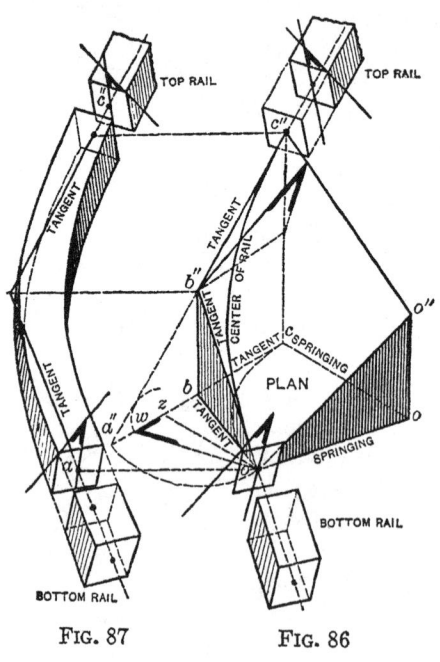

FIG. 87　　　　FIG. 86

The variations of necessity will cause the sectional planes to have different angles of inclination, and to find these angles is the problem of "bevels" in wreath rails.

In Figs. 86 and 87 the bevels are shown applied, and in Fig. 87 the wreath piece also is shown after it is "squared" or "twisted" so as to have its top horizontal and its sides vertical when in position upon its plane of ascension, winding around its plan curve from the lowest point a to the highest point $c.''$

A better insight into the nature of bevels may be had from Figs. 88, 89 and 90, in which Fig. 88 represents a plan and elevation of few steps adjoining a quarter-turn curve. The pitch of the two tangents g-e and e-c, as shown, are equal, and equal also to the pitch of the two flights.

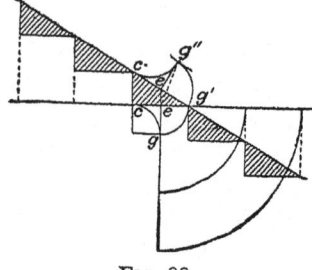

FIG. 88

Fig. 89 represents the plane of the tangents, the bevels upon the plane indicating its angle in two directions, showing graphically their similarity to the top common rafter bevel.

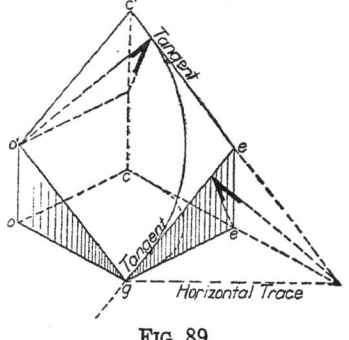

FIG. 89

In Fig. 90 is shown a perspective of the steps, the plan of the section and the bevels applied to the wreath in its winding position over and above its plan.

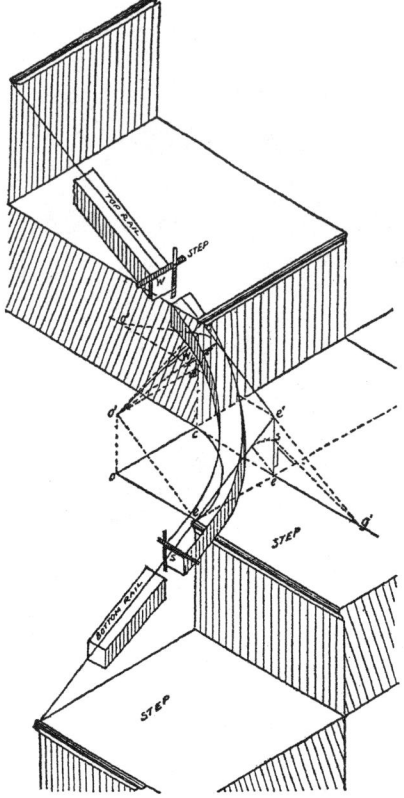

FIG. 90

The method to square the wreath by means of the bevels is shown in Figs. 91, 92, 93.

The material or plank to make the wreath piece is shown in Fig. 91. The face mold is placed upon its surface to mark the form, then the form is marked and cut out square to the face of the plank, as shown at z and z.

In Fig. 92 is shown the bevels applied to each end of the piece, and in Fig. 93 how the wreath appears after it is squared or twisted.

One method to find the correct bevels is shown in Figs. 94 and 95. In Fig. 94 the tangents a' b' and b' c' are shown to incline equally.

Place the compass in b, and open out to touch the tangent a' b' as shown, after which turn around to n and connect

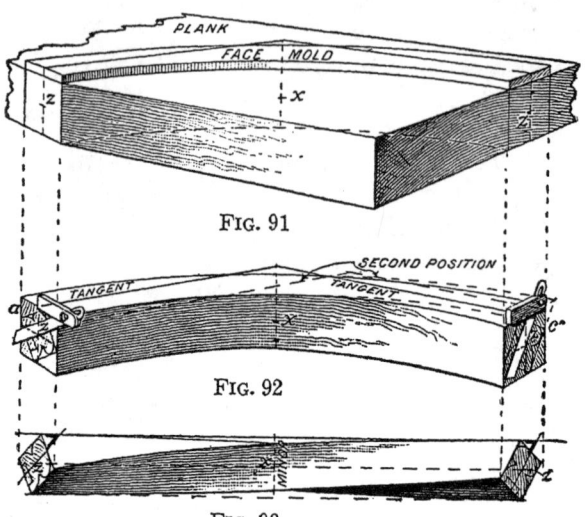

FIG. 91

FIG. 92

FIG. 93

n-a'. The bevel will be found at n for the two tangents because the two are equally inclined.

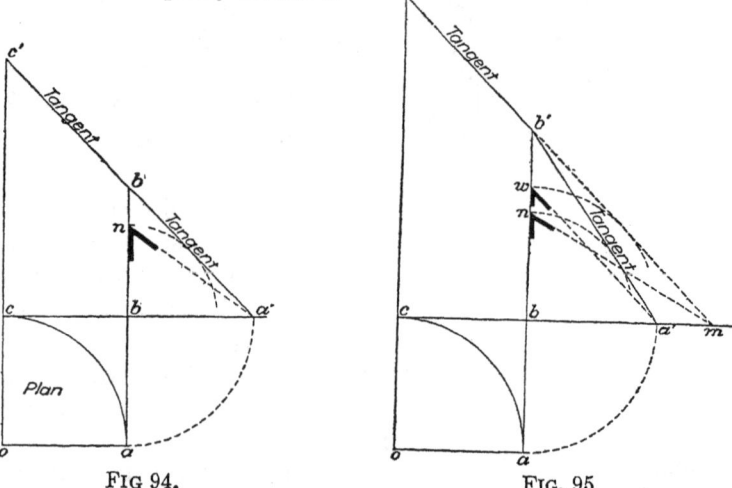

FIG 94.

FIG. 95

In Fig. 95 the tangents are shown to differ in pitch, the bottom tangent a' b' being steeper than the top tangent b' c'. To find the bevel produce the top tangent as shown to m and as in Fig. 94, place the compass in b, open out to touch the bottom tangent a' b', and turn around to n, connect n to m. The bevel shown at n is the one to apply to the end a' of the bottom tangent.

Place the compass again in b, open out this time to touch the top tangent b' c' continued, and turn around to w, connect w to a. The bevel w is to be applied to the end c' of the top tangent.

A second method to find the bevels is shown in Figs. 96 and 97. The tangents in Fig 96 are equally inclined. From b draw the line b-o' parallel to the pitch of the tangents. Place the compass in b' on the pitch line, open out to a' and turn around as shown by the arc to c; connect c

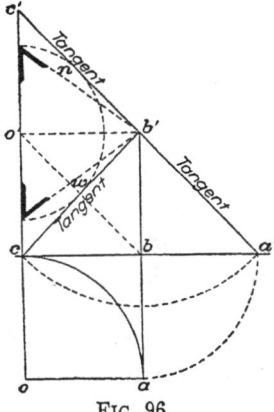

Fig. 96

to b'. The line c-b' represents the bottom tangent b-a' in a second position.

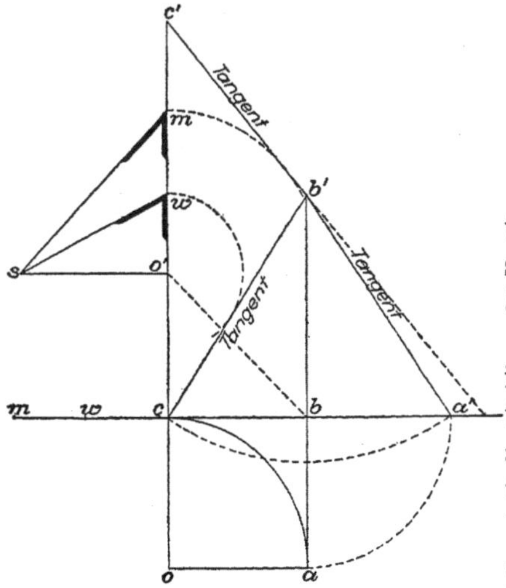

Now place the compass in o', open out to touch the tangent c-b' and turn around as shown. Note that the curve touches the bottom tangent c-b' at w, and also the top tangent b'-c' at n, showing the tangents to be equally inclined and that consequently the same bevel will apply to both tangents.

In Fig. 97 the same method is applied in a case where the tangents are inclining unequally, the bottom one having more inclination than the top one, a similar case to the one shown

Fig. 97

in Fig. 95. From *b* draw a line to *o'* parallel to the pitch of the top tangent *c'-b'*, and as in Fig. 96 revolve the bottom tangent *b' a'* to *c*, connect *c* to *b'*, thus fixing the bottom tangent

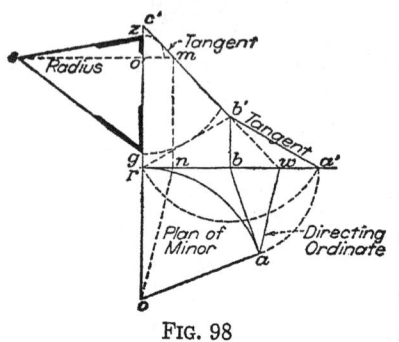

in a second position. Now place the compass in *o'*, open out to touch the bottom tangent *c-b'* and turn around to *w*. Again, place the compass in *o'*, open out to touch the top tangent *c' b'* and turn around to *m*.

Now draw a line from *o'* to *s* equal in length to the radius of the plan curve, as

FIG. 98

o-a or *o-c* and connect *s* to *w* and to *m*. The bevel *m* is to be applied to the end *c'* of the wreath and bevel *w* to the end *a'*. Note that the bevels assume the form of right angle triangles; that their altitudes equal the distance from point *o'* to the tangents, and that the base is equal to the radius of the plan curve.

Fig. 98 illustrates the manner in which this method is applied to find the bevels for a wreath over a curve less than a quadrant, while Fig. 99 illustrates the application of a method to find the bevels for a wreath over a curve more than a quadrant.

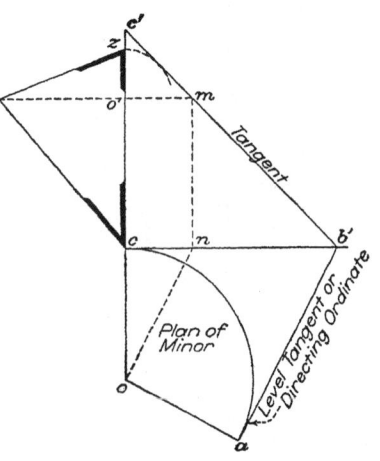

FIG. 99

The inclination of the tangents *a' b'* and *b' c'* in Fig. 98 is shown to be reversely to the tangents as shown in Fig. 97, the bottom one *a' b'* being less inclined in Fig. 98.

To find the bevels, find first the plan directing ordinate shown in the figure to be the line *a-w*, then draw a line from *o* (the center of the plan curve) parallel to the directing ordinate as shown from *o* to *n*. From *n* erect a line to cut the pitch of the top tangent *b' c'* in *m*, and a line as shown from *m* to *s;* make *o', s* equal the radius of the plan curve. Now place the compass in *o'*, open out to touch the top tangent, and turn around to *z*. Again, place the compass in *o'*, open out to cut the bottom tangent in its second position as shown at *r' b'* and turn around to *g*. Now draw a line from *g* to *S* and from *z* to *S*.

The bevel *g* belongs to the bottom end *a* of the wreath and the bevel *z* to the top end *c'*.

The same process to find the bevels is shown in Fig. 99. The directing ordinate in this figure is the plan tangent *a-b*, and that because it is a level tangent. The tangent *b' c'* is shown to incline.

The problem here therefore is to find the bevels for a wreath winding around a curve more than a quadrant having its bottom tangent level, and its top tangent inclining, a condition of tangents always occurring where an easement is to be made at the bottom of a stairway.

To find the bevels draw the plan of the minor axis as shown from *o* to *n* parallel to the bottom tangent *a-b'* (the directing ordinate). Upon *n* erect a line to *m* and from *m* a line through *o'* to *S*, the distance from *o'* to *S* to equal the radius of the plan curve.

Now place the compass in *o'*, open out to touch the top tangent, and turn around as shown to *z*, connect *z* to *S* and the bevel at *z* will be the one required to apply to the top end *c'* of the wreath.

Again, connect *c* to *S* and the bevel at *c* will be the one to apply to the bottom end *a* of the wreath.

The section shown cut through the prism in Fig. 100 indicates the plane whereon the wreath shown in Fig. 99 is winding over and above its plan curve, as shown from its lowest point *a* to its highest point *c'*. A study of Fig. 100 will be of great benefit to understand the method of operation as shown in Fig. 99 to find the bevels. It will be observed that bevel *z* determines the inclination of the plane in one direction, and bevel *c* in another direction, which as already mentioned is the problem to be solved in finding bevels for wreath rails.

A third method to find the bevels is shown in Figs. 101 to 105 inclusive, which considered from the viewpoint of universal adaptability to all cases of wreath rail construction is undoubtedly the most simple, the most easily memorized and consequently the most serviceable known.

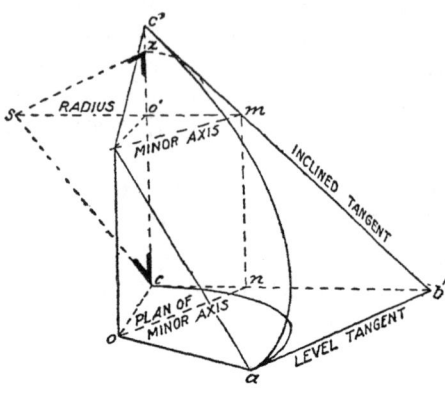

FIG. 100

Its simplicity consists in the fact that only two lines need to be understood, and manipulated in the operation.

It is applicable to all cases of wreath rail that may possibly occur in the practice of the stairbuilder, either for wreaths winding around a quarter turn curve or a curve more or less than a quarter turn. These two lines in all cases constitute the base and altitude, respectively, of the triangle containing the bevel. The base line of the bevel triangle will be found in the plan and in all cases where the plan tangents are at a right angle to one another, which will always be the case where the plan curve is a quarter turn, the line will be the radius of the plan curve, or, in other words, the length of either one or the other of the plan tangents.

The altitude line of the bevel triangle in all cases invariably will be a line indicating a distance from a certain fixed point in the plan to the tangents or lines parallel to them in the elevation.

The fixed point just mentioned is shown at b in Figs. 101 to 105 inclusive, where the side plan tangent a b intersects the crown plan tangent c b. In all other cases the "fixed point" in the plan from which to measure the distances to the elevation tangents will be found by drawing a perpendicular line to the crown tangent b c from the point a in the plan to z as shown in Figs 106 to 114, inclusive. It may be interesting to remark at this point that the operation of finding bevels in wreath construction is justly regarded as the most difficult of any to accomplish. It is due to the varied conditions of the oblique planes upon which the wreaths are assumed to rest while winding above and around their plan curves from one end of the cylinder to the other. The planes are so varied and numerous as to make it an impossibility for any one not thoroughly proficient in the science of solid geometry to find the correct bevels unless they are made acquainted with a method that is applicable to any and all conditions the planes may assume. The nature of the planes mentioned has been already explained, so that for those readers who have grasped the prinicples involved in connection with them, and their application in the construction of wreath rails, the method presented herewith to find the bevels will be readily understood.

In Figs. 101 and 102 is shown the most simple examples of wreath construction. The plan of the center line of rail in both diagrams as indicated from a to c is a quarter turn.

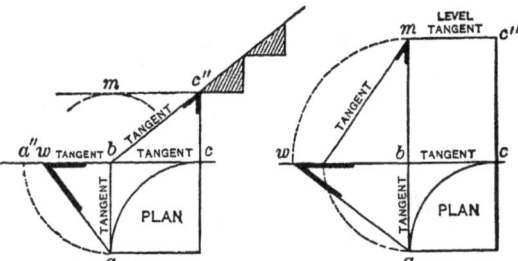

FIG. 101.—Finding Bevels for a Bottom Level Tangent and an Inclined Top Tangent.

FIG. 102.—Finding Bevels for a Top Level Tangent and a Bottom Inclined Tangent.

In Fig. 101 the tangent $a\,b$ is shown to be level and the tangent $b\,c$ to be inclined, as represented over and above it from b to c''.

To find the bevel place one leg of the dividers in the point b and the other to touch the line $c''\,m$, as indicated by the arc m. The bevel is shown at w to be composed of an altitude $b\,w$ equal to the distance from b to m and of a base $a\,b$ equal to the plan tangent $a\,b$.

Note that at c'' is shown exactly the same bevel. It has the same altitude $b\,m$ and the same length of base $b\,a$ or $b\,c$. Note also that it equals the top angle of the pitch board, and that this invariably is the case where one tangent is level and the other inclined of a wreath over and above a quarter turn plan curve, such as we encounter when dealing with a cylinder placed at the junction of a level landing and a flight.

In Fig. 102 is shown an example of a wreath with the tangents reversed. In this case the bottom tangent a b is inclined and the top tangent c'' m is level. To find the bevel proceed as shown in connection with Fig. 101 by placing the compass in b; extend it to touch the line c'' m; turn over to w and connect w with a.

These two examples represent wreaths over a cylinder placed at the junction of a flight and a level landing—Fig. 101 at a bottom landing and Fig. 102 at a top landing.

From the explanation just given it will be observed that for wreaths having tangents in the position represented in the diagrams the bevels are found in the angle formed between the inclined tangent and a vertical line as shown at c'' in Fig. 101 and at m in Fig. 102; also that they are to be applied in each case to the level tangent. One bevel only is required, owing to the plane being inclined in one direction only. The method demonstrated in these two figures to find the bevels is applicable in determining the bevels in all cases of wreath construction, as will be shown in the examples following.

In Fig. 103 we have a case where the two tangents have the same inclination. Place the compass in b; extend it to touch the tangent at x; turn over to w and connect w with c. The bevel will be found at w, and is composed of an altitude equal to the distance from b to the tangent at x and a base equal as in the two preceding figures to the plan tangents a b and b c.

Now, let it be understood that because the two tangents for the wreath represented in this figure are inclined, it calls for two bevels to square it—one to be applied at each end— and further, because the two tangents are inclined equally the two bevels also will be equal, so that in reality it will be necessary to find only one bevel, as, for example, the one shown at w in Fig. 103. This same bevel is to be applied to each end of the wreath, and in all cases where the plan tangents, as in this example, stand at right angles to one another, the bevels are to be applied reversely.

In Fig. 104 is represented a case of tangents inclining unequally. Here the bottom tangent is much steeper than the top one. By reason of the fact that the two tangents incline unequally, it will be necessary to find two unequal bevels—

one for each end. Apply the same method to find them as in the preceding examples by placing the compass in b, opening it out to touch the upper tangent extended and strike the arc w m. By connecting w with c, the bevel which is to be applied to the top tangent is found at w. The reason why this bevel is to be applied to the top tangent is because its altitude represents the distance from the point b to the top tangent continued as shown by the arc at m.

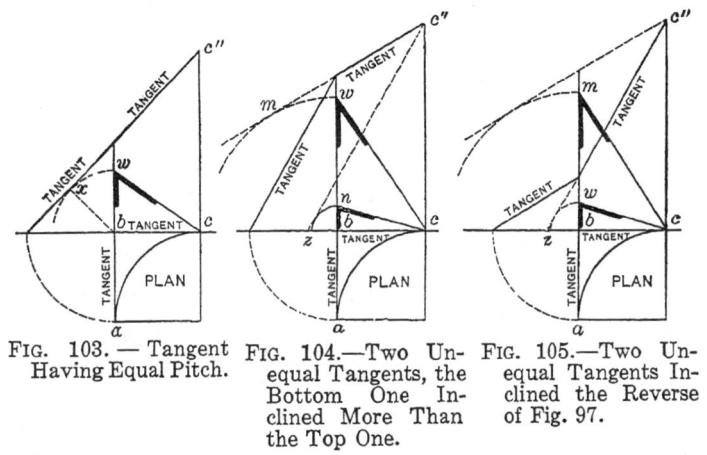

FIG. 103. — Tangent Having Equal Pitch.

FIG. 104.—Two Unequal Tangents, the Bottom One Inclined More Than the Top One.

FIG. 105.—Two Unequal Tangents Inclined the Reverse of Fig. 97.

To find the bevel to apply to the bottom tangent place the compass again in b, open it out to touch the dotted line drawn parallel to the bottom tangent from c'' to z as shown by the arc $n\,z$, and connect n with c. The bevel is found at n. It is to be applied to the bottom tangent because its altitude represents the distance from b to the line drawn from c'' parallel to the bottom tangent, as indicated by the arc described.

Many stairbuilders and some of considerable experience are often puzzled to know to which tangent the bevels belong. In this connection it should be remembered that the bevel in all cases belongs to the tangent from which its altitude is taken.

A position of tangents just the reverse of those in Fig. 104 is presented in Fig. 105, where the top tangent inclines much more than the bottom one. The same method of finding the bevels will apply in this case as in all preceding examples.

It may be well to remark here that the preceding examples represent all the variety of position tangents may possibly assume in actual practice. Inasmuch, however, as they all represent tangents over a quarter turn plan curve, and that other kinds of plan curves are often met with in practice, even if the tangents over the latter kind do assume the same relative position to one another as do the tangents in the preceding examples, the problem of finding bevels will be incomplete unless due notice be taken of the method for finding them over either a plan curve less or more than a quarter turn.

In the diagrams which follow it will be shown that the same method of operation as heretofore explained is applicable to all conditions of plan and elevation of tangents. When a plan curve of a wreath is less than a quarter turn the plan tangents will form an obtuse angle with one another; that is, an angle greater than a right angle, as for example, that formed between the tangent $a\ b$ and $b\ c$ in Fig. 106. The plan curve in this example as from a to c is shown to be less than a quarter turn.

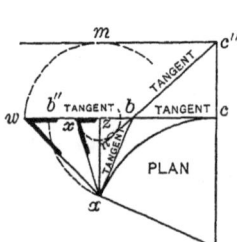

FIG. 106.—Finding Bevels for Bottom Level Tangent and an Inclined Top Tangent Over an Obtuse Angle Plan.

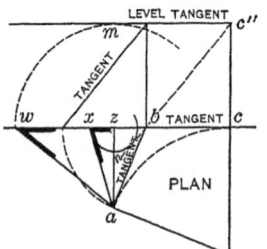

FIG. 107.—Finding Bevels for a Top Level Tangent and an Inclined Top Tangent Over an Obtuse Angle Plan.

To find the bevels for a wreath over a curve less than a quarter turn where the plan tangents will form an obtuse angle, as in Fig. 106, the method heretofore explained will apply. The elevation of the bottom tangent $a\ b$ is shown at $b\ b''$ to be a level line, and the elevation of the tangent $b\ c$ is shown from b to c'' to be inclined.

Place one leg of the compasses in z, open out the other to touch m and turn over to w, making the dotted arc shown, and connect w with a. The bevel will be found at w, and it is to be applied to the bottom level tangent a, b. Again place one leg of the compasses in the same point z, open out the other to touch the top tangent c'' b, continued in n; turn over as shown by the dotted arc to x and connect x with a. The bevel will be found at a and is to be applied to the top tangent c'' b.

We have the same plan for the curve and tangents in Fig. 107, but the elevation of the tangents is reversed. The top tangent in this diagram is level and the bottom one inclined.

We find the bevels in this case as in all the other examples. Place one leg of the dividers in the point z, open out the other to touch the top tangent continued in m and turn over to w. Connect w with a, and the bevel found at w is to be applied to the top level tangent at the end c''.

To find the bevel for the bottom inclined tangent draw a line from c'' through b continued as shown to n parallel with the inclined tangent. Now place one leg of the compasses in z, open out the other to touch the line b n and turn over as indicated by the arc to x and connect x with a and the bevel is found at x. It will be observed that the method of finding the bevels as shown in this diagram is similar to the one in Fig. 106, and that the similarity is due to having the same condition of tangents in the two diagrams—namely, one level and one inclined. It matters not that the condition is reversed in the two figures, as it does not alter the nature of the plane upon which the wreaths in each case are assumed to be resting. The principle is that if we have the same plane we will also have the same bevels, because the bevels in wreath construction merely indicate the angle of inclination of such planes. It is something similar to a top bevel of a common rafter intersecting a ridge pole.

In Fig. 108 we again show the same condition of plan curve and plan tangents, but the two tangents as shown from c'' through b'' to a'' in the elevation are equally inclined, and therefore require only one bevel which will have to be applied to both ends of the wreath.

To find the bevel place one leg of the compasses in the point z, as in all the preceding diagrams, open out the other to touch the bottom tangent, as indicated by the dotted arc, turn over to w and connect w with a. The bevel is found at w.

The elevation of the tangents in Fig. 109 shows them to be unequally inclined over the same plan as that shown in Fig.

108. To find the bevels place one leg of the compasses in z, extend the other to reach the top tangent continued in m, turn over to w and connect w with a. The bevel shown at w is to be applied to the top tangent at c'' owing to its altitude, $z\,w$ having been measured from z to the top tangent continued to m, as shown by the dotted arc $m\,w$.

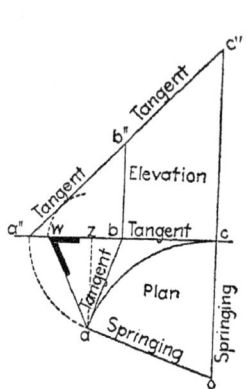

FIG. 108.—Equal Inclined Tangents Over an Obtuse Angle Plan.

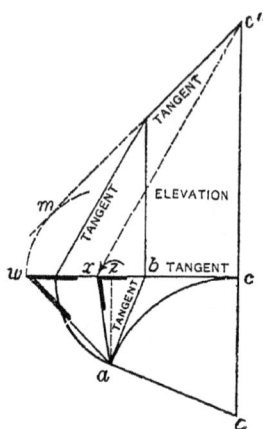

FIG. 109. — Obtaining Bevels for Unequal Tangents Over an Obtuse Angle Plan.

To find the bevel for the bottom tangent it is necessary to draw to it from c'' a parallel line as shown by the dotted line $c''\,x$. Measure its altitude from z to this line by placing one leg of the compasses in z, extending the other to touch the line as shown by the arc and turning over to x. The bevel is found at x by connecting x with a, and it is to be applied to the bottom tangent; that is, to the end a of the wreath.

As any further explanation of the method to find the bevels would simply cause unnecessary repetition, we present the diagrams, Figs. 110 to 114, inclusive, merely as illustrations of the varied relative conditions, the plan, and elevation tangents of a wreath are liable to assume in actual practice. The reader should be able to understand these figures and find the bevels for each example if he has paid due attention to the explanatory particulars accompanying the preceding figures.

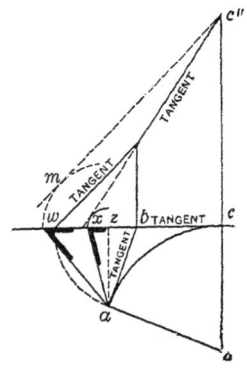

FIG. 110.—Finding Bevels for Tangent the Reverse of Those Shown in Fig. 102.

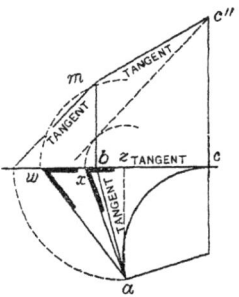

FIG. 111.—Finding Bevels for Unequal Tangents Over an Acute Angle Plan Tangent and a Plan Curve Greater Than a Quarter Turn.

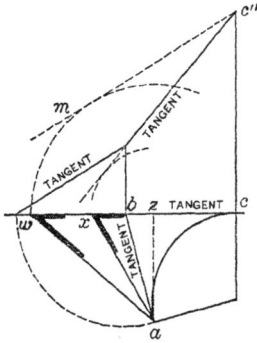

FIG. 112.—Finding Bevels Reversely Inclined to Those in the Previous Figure.

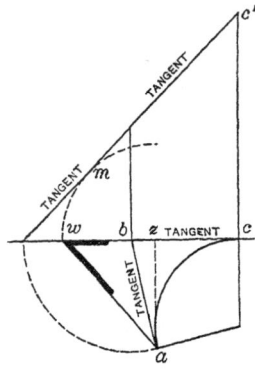

FIG. 113.—Finding the One Bevel Required for Two Equally Inclined Tangents Over an Acute Angle Plan Tangent.

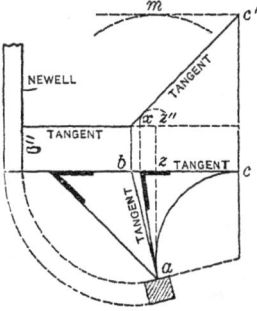

FIG. 114.—Showing How to Find Bevels for Tangents Over an Acute Angle Plan and a Curve Greater Than a Quarter Turn, the Top Tangent Being Inclined and the Bottom Tangent Level.

CHAPTER VI

ARRANGEMENT OF RISERS IN AND AROUND A CYLINDER

An important item in stairbuilding is the correct arrangement of the risers in and around a cylinder. If incorrectly arranged the effect will be felt in the greatly increased labor attending the construction of both the stringers and rails. In cylinders containing a number of risers it will be best to place the risers at equal distances, and start the first riser 2 or 3 inches outside the springing line.

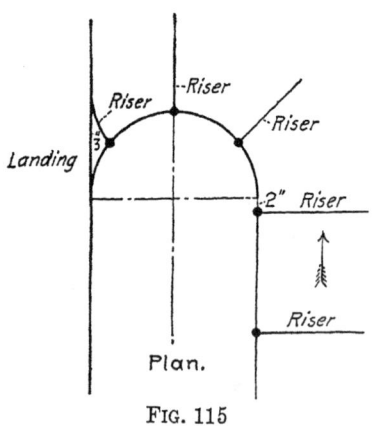

Fig. 115

Where a cylinder is placed at either top or bottom of a stairway and to contain 3, 4 or more risers, the one next to the landing should be placed at least 2 in. within the cylinder, and the remaining risers at equal distances as shown in plan, Fig. 115.

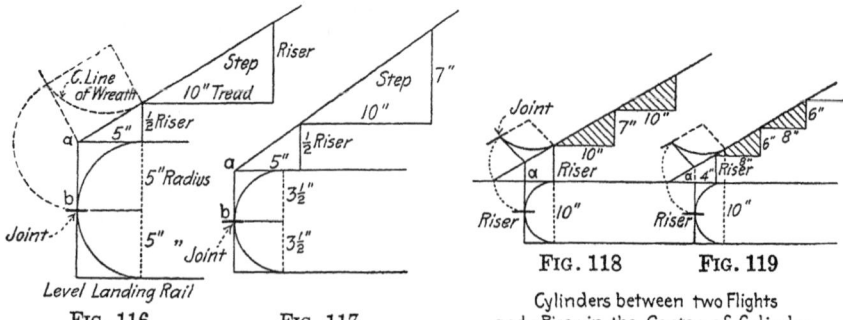

Fig. 116   Fig. 117   Fig. 118   Fig. 119

Cylinders between two Flights and a Riser in the Center of Cylinder.

FIGS. 116, 117, 118, 119.—How to Arrange Risers Around the Well-hole.

70

In what is known as level landing stairways, where a cylinder is placed at the intersection of two returning flights upon a level landing, the best arrangement is for the diameter of the cylinder to be equal to the width of the treads and the risers to be in the springing as shown in Fig. 116. Where a variation happens between the width of the treads and the diameter of the cylinder, as occasionally it does in practice, the best arrangement will be to fix the risers half a tread from point a, as shown in Fig. 117, obtaining by so doing the same condition of tangents as in Fig. 116; namely, one inclined and one level. When a riser is placed in the center of a cylinder at the intersection of two returning flights the best arrangement is the one shown in Fig. 118. The diameter of the cylinder is shown in this figure to be equal to the width of the tread, and the first risers placed in the springing, resulting as shown in having two equally inclined tangents for the wreaths. To obtain the same result where the diameter of the cylinder and the width of the tread are different the first

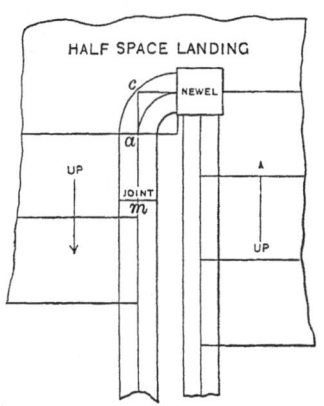

FIG. 120.—Partial Plan Showing Method Where a Small Curve is Placed at Bottom of Return Flight.

riser as shown in Fig. 119 should be placed at a distance of half a tread from point a.

In Fig. 120 is shown the best arrangement for a curve at the bottom of a return flight. The radius of the curve is made equal to half the width of the tread, and the riser placed in the springing resulting as in Figs. 116 and 117 in having one tangent of the wreath rail inclined and one level.

Fig. 121 demonstrates the advantage of the preceding arrangements. The triangle in this figure represents the pitch board. Point c is placed in its center and the part not shaded represents the width of the plain rail. On the long edge of the pitch board the width of the face mold is determined. The line b-d represents the level tangent and the line d-n the inclined tangent as required upon the face mold. The curves may be drawn by either method in practice. The bevel is shown at the top end of the pitch board in Fig. 121, and it is shown applied to the bottom end of the wreath piece in Fig. 122.

To further demonstrate the advantage gained in proper arrangement of risers in and around cylinders the following figures are presented representing an entrance hall stairway.

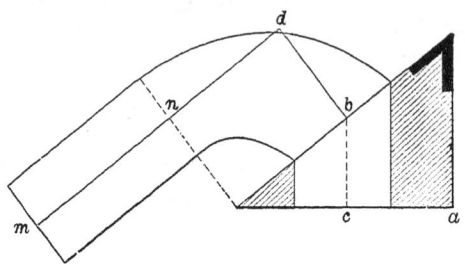

FIG. 121.—Method of Drawing a Face Mold for Figs. 116 and 117.

A perspective view of such a stair is shown in Fig 123, and in Fig. 124 is shown the plan and elevation of the cylinder shown at the intersection of the main and return flights.

The arrangement of the risers in and adjoining the cylinder, as presented in this figure, is similar to those presented in Fig. 124. On both sides of the cylinder the risers are placed at a distance equal to half a tread from point c and the same upon the crown tangents also, resulting as shown by the elevation of the tangents in having the same pitch over the tangents as that of the adjoining

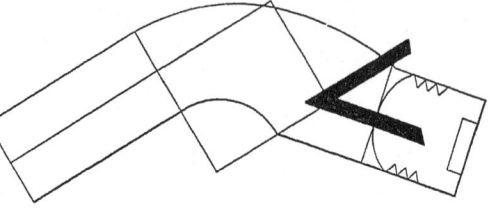

FIG. 122.—Bevel Shown Applied to Wreath.

flights. With this arrangement the problem of drawing the face mold and finding the bevels becomes to be a very simple matter as shown in the figure.

The wreath part of the scroll as shown in plan Fig. 125 is merely a quadrant curve, the drawing of the face mold for which is the simplest of all in the realm of wreath construction. It is here shown to have been drawn by the means of ordinates. To twist the wreath it calls for but one bevel only, and that found at the top angle of the pitch board similar to the one shown in Fig. 121.

Figs. 126 and 127 are here presented to show the simplicity attending the drawing of face molds where tangents are equally

FIG. 123.—Scroll Curve at the Bottom and a 20″ Cylinder Between the Returning Flights Upon the Landing.

inclined as in Fig. 124 over the intersecting cylinder. The points 1, a, 2, c, d, Fig. 126 are taken from the elevation line of the tangents in Fig. 124. The same face mold is shown drawn from the pitch board in Fig. 127, the operation being the same as in Figs. 124 and 126.

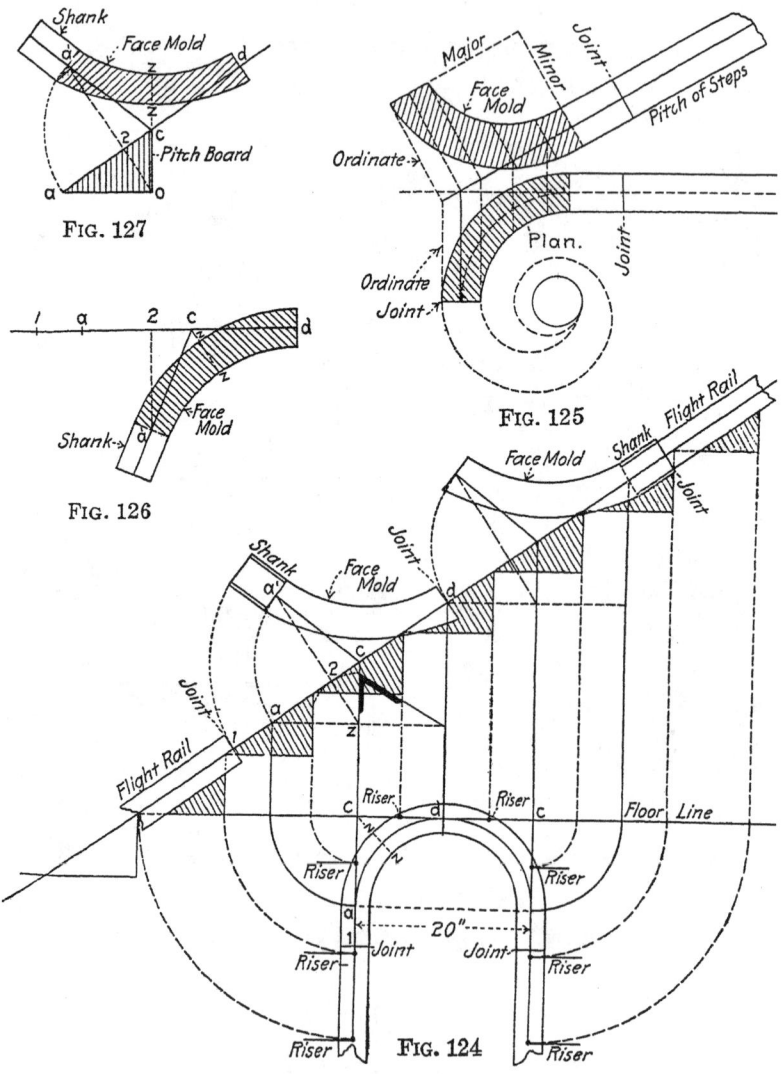

FIG. 127

FIG. 126

FIG. 125

FIG. 124

A Simple Method to Reduce Treads Adjoining a Cylinder Placed Between Two Returning Flights

Where a staircase is limited in run space it becomes necessary to crowd a number of winders in the cylinder, causing the pitch over the cylinder to be much in excess of the pitch over the adjoining flights.

To remedy the abruptness at the intersection of the two pitches the method shown in Fig. 128 will be found of value.

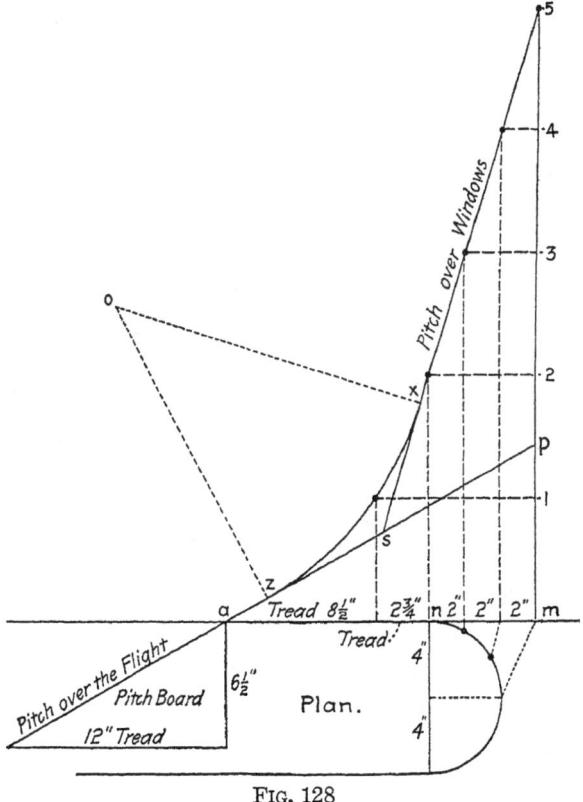

FIG. 128

It consists as shown in reducing the width of few treads adjoining the cylinder.

In Fig. 128 it is determined to reduce only two treads; therefore place the pitch board as shown at a distance less than the width of two treads from the cylinder and prolong the pitch to p.

Make n m equal to the stretch out of half the cylinder and upon m erect the line m, 5 equal in length to 5 risers.

From point 5 draw a line to s a point half way between a and p.

Make s z and s x equal; draw a line from z square to z s; and a line from x square to x s.

These two lines will intersect in O which will be a center to draw the curve as shown from z to x.

Now draw level lines from *1, 2, 3* and *4*, to cut the pitches and curve; and lines also from the pitches and curve down to the line a, n, m.

Upon this line will be found the exact width of the treads reduced adjoining the cylinder; and also the winders within the cylinder as shown.

It will be observed that by this method the abruptness at s'

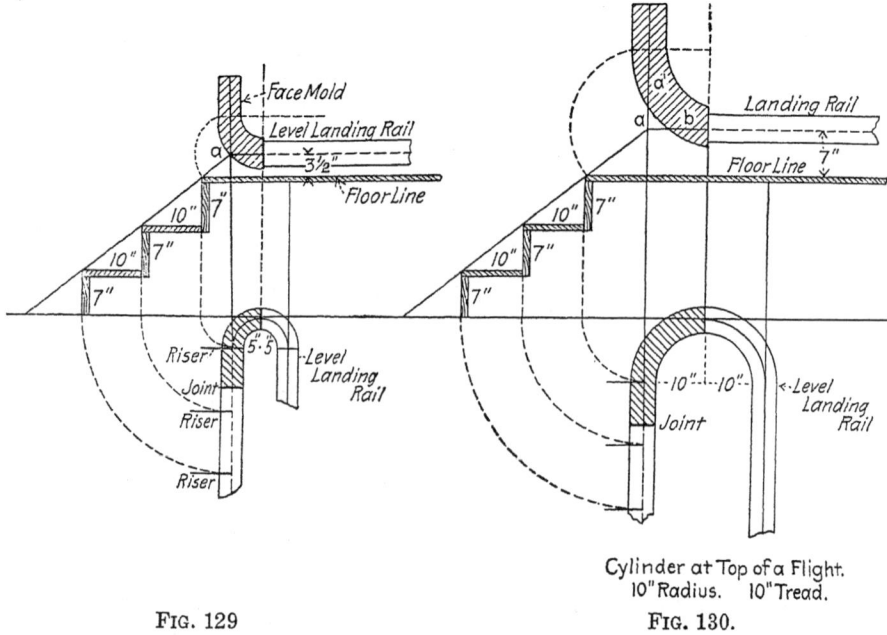

FIG. 129

Cylinder at Top of a Flight.
10" Radius.   10" Tread.
FIG. 130.

between the two pitches is done away with; and that the top edge of the stringer and also the rail will follow the nosing of the steps.

Lowering or Raising a Landing Rail

Where a cylinder is placed at either top or bottom of a flight the right arrangement will be for the diameter of the cylinder to equal the width of the tread; as shown in Fig. 129, where the level landing rail is shown to be at the height of $3\frac{1}{2}$ inches above the floor line.

By this arrangement, the rail above the landing when in position will be $\frac{1}{2}$ a riser higher than the flight rail will be above the nosing of the steps.

In Fig. 130 the cylinder being 20 inches in diameter as shown will cause the landing rail to be at the height of 7 inches above the floor line which is $3\frac{1}{2}$ inches too high when in position.

The method to lower the landing rail in an example of this kind is shown in Fig. 131. A line is drawn $3\frac{1}{2}$ inches above

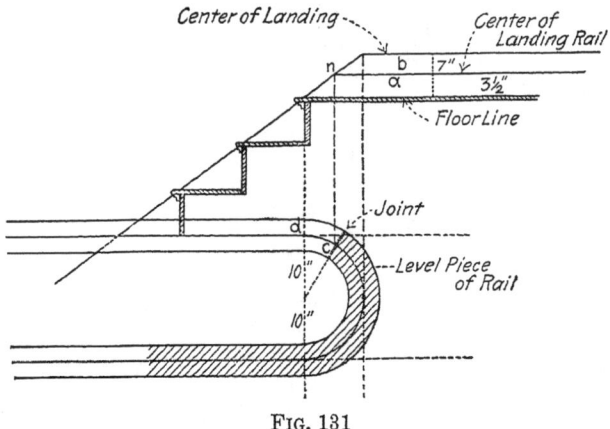

FIG. 131

the floor line as shown from n through a; and from n drop a line to cut the plan of rail as shown at c.

The shaded portion of the plan rail by this operation will be level; leaving the remainder of the curve as shown from c to d for the wreath.

In Fig. 132 the same operation is shown where a small cylinder is used.

In this case the width of the tread is 10 inches and the diameter of the cylinder only 5 inches resulting in the necessity of raising the landing rail instead of lowering it as in Fig. 131. The

operation as shown is to draw a line *3½* inches above the floor
line to intersect the pitch of the flight as shown at *b″* and to drop
a line from *b″* as shown to *a*; and from *a* a line to *b* in the plan
curve of the rail; thus fixing the joint and the length of the
wreath piece; as shown from *b* to *d*.

It is shown in Fig. 132 how to draw the center line of the
wreath.

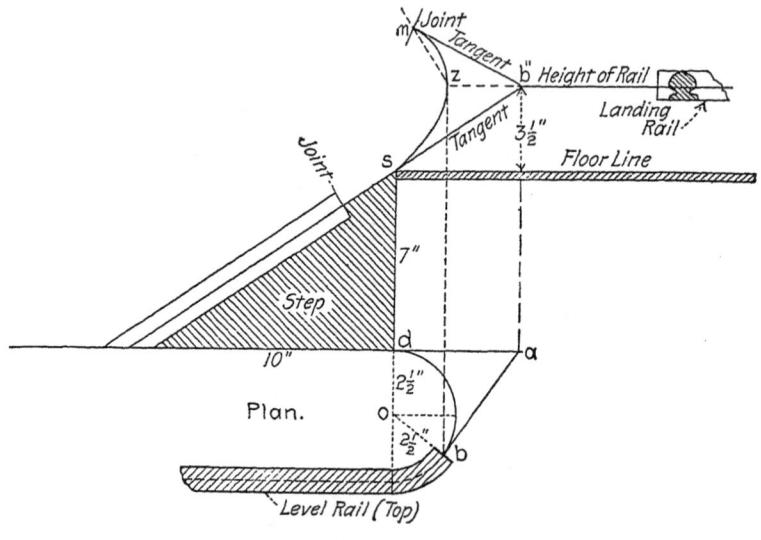

FIG. 132

From *b* in the plan a line is drawn up to *z*: through *z* and
square to the pitch of the flight is drawn the line *z, m*.

By connecting *m* and *b″* the angle between the two tangents
m, b″ and *b″, s* is determined.

The length of *m b″* is equal to the plan tangent *a, b* because
the two are level tangents.

The same method of operation is shown in Fig. 133 where a
cylinder is placed at the bottom of a flight.

As in Fig. 132 the diameter of the cylinder is only *5* inches
where the width of the tread is *10* inches.

Produce the pitch of the flight as shown through *s* to *b″*; intersecting the line marked tangent; which is the center line of the
landing rail; standing as shown *3½* inches above the floor line
as required.

Now from b in the plan draw a line to z: from z draw a line square to the pitch of the flight to m; connect m, b'' and make it

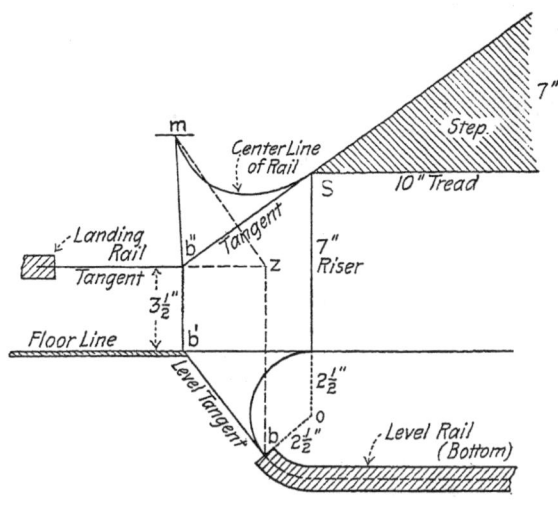

FIG. 133

equal in length to the plan level tangent b' b.

How Cylinders are Constructed

Cylinder is a term used in stairbuilding for a curve fixed at the intersection of two flights and intersection of flights and landings.

In Fig. 134 is shown a method of building one of a small diam-

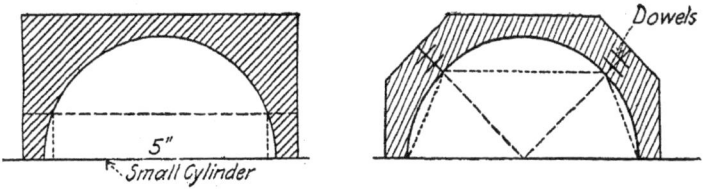

FIG. 134   FIG. 135

eter (4, 5 and 6 inches). In Fig. 135 for building one of larger size; and in Fig. 136 one larger still.

It is shown at *a* in Fig. 136 how the cylinder is connected to the stringer by being halved and screwed; and in Fig. 137 by means of a dovetail and wedges; as shown at *b*.

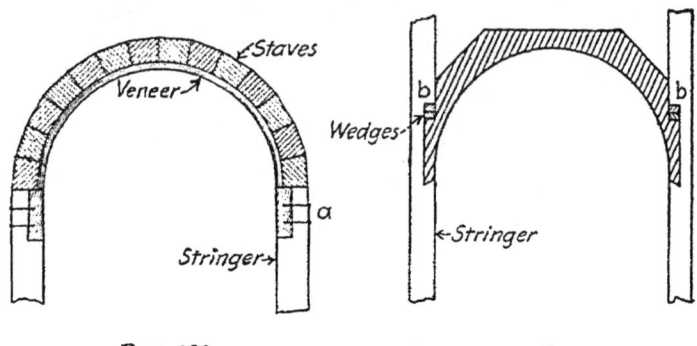

FIGS. 136   FIG 137

CHAPTER VII

A STRAIGHT FLIGHT OF STAIRS

Fig. 138 illustrates a stair so limited in run and height that a riser *8* in. deep meets the conditions of satisfactory stepping. Take *8* in. on the compasses, and step along the story rod to find how many times it takes *8* in. to reach from floor to floor—a total height of *8* ft. *8* in. This process proves that *13* risers *8* in. in depth are required, and this method is the most common among stairbuilders to determine the number of risers. A better method is to reduce *8* ft. *8* in. to inches, which equals *104* in. divided by *8* in. gives the number of risers.

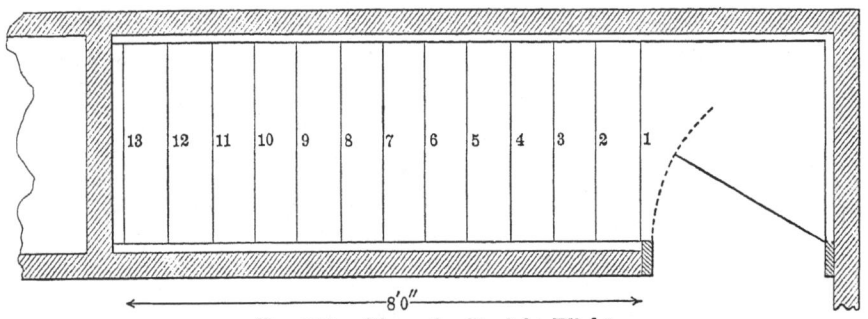

FIG. 138.—Plan of a Straight Flight.

Fig. 139, representing the elevation of the stairs illustrated in the plan, Fig. 138, shows that a flight having 13 risers requires *12* treads; this is one less than the number of risers, and the result of including the landing on the second story among the number of treads. The flight begins with a riser, and ends with a riser, thus calling for one more riser than tread—an item that should be always considered in laying out stairs.

To lay out the treads, divide the 8-foot space allotted for the total run by *12* either with the compasses or by simple division. *8* ft. reduced to inches equals *96* in., and *96* in. divided by *12* equals *8* in., the width of the tread. In this example the treads and risers are the same—that is, *8* in.

To ascertain if this relative proportional dimension of treads and risers guarantees a safe, easy stepping, one rule is to divide the width of the riser into the number *66*, as follows: $66 \div 8 = 8\frac{1}{4}$ in.   This is the exact width of a tread for a riser *8* in. deep.

Another rule is to make twice the depth of the riser, and once the width of the tread equal *24* in.   For example, assuming the

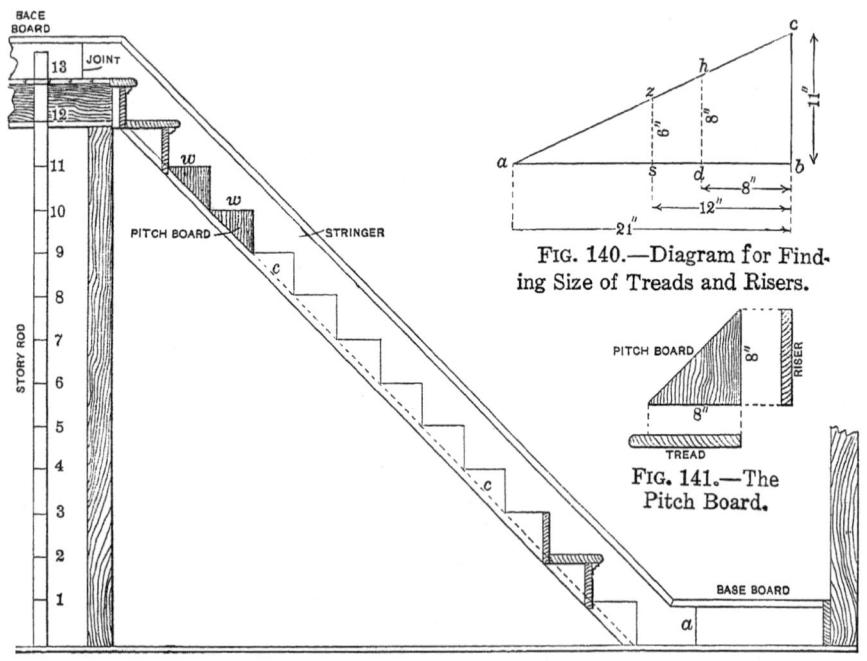

FIG. 140.—Diagram for Finding Size of Treads and Risers.

FIG. 141.—The Pitch Board.

FIG. 139.—Elevation of the Straight Flight.

riser, as in Figs. 138 and 139, to be *8* in., twice *8* equals *16*, and *16* subtracted from *24* leaves *8*—the exact proportional dimension of the tread for an *8*-in. riser, according to this standard rule.

Still another rule is illustrated in Fig. 140, of the diagrams. Here the base of the triangle *a b c* is made to equal *24* in., and the altitude *b c* to equal *11* in.   From *b* on the base line, measure *8* in. to *d*, to indicate the width of the tread; at *d*, erect the line *d h*, cutting the long edge of the triangle in *h*.   Then the line *d h* is the exact relative riser for a tread *8* in. wide.

Again measure from *b* on the base line, *12* in. to *s*.   At *s* erect the line *s z*; this line *s z* indicates the relative proportional depth of a riser for a tread *12* in. wide, etc.

Any one of these rules is considered safe to follow in obtaining relative dimensions of treads and risers, but the first is considered the most satisfactory.

The next process is to get out a templet known as a "pitch board," for laying out the form of the steps on the stringers. The templet is shown in Fig. 141, in the form of a right-angle triangle, the base representing the width of the tread, *8* in., and the altitude, the depth of the riser, *8* in.

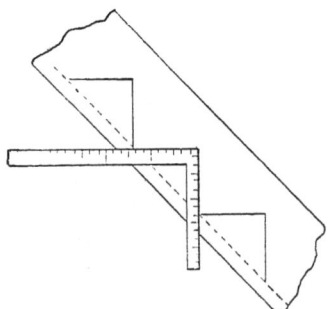

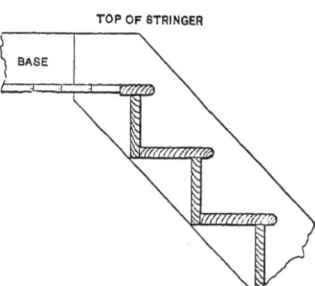

FIG. 142.—Laying Out Steps on Stringer with Steel Square.

FIG. 143.—Showing How Stringer is Cut at Top to Fit Floor.

Fig. 139 shows how the pitch board is applied to the stringer. The line *c c* in the illustration is gauged at a distance of 1¼ in. from the bottom edge, and the pitch board is applied to this line, and indicated by the shaped steps, *w, w*; the long edge is placed against the line, and the pitch board moved along the stringer as many times as there are steps required.

Fig. 142 illustrates a very common method of laying out the steps on a stringer, with the steel square. Take *8* in. on the blade, and *8* in. on the tongue; apply to the line *c c* of Fig. 139, and move the square along the stringer as many times as required, to complete the number of steps contained in the flight. To save time, this method is usually employed for rough hemlock stringers.

In Fig. 143 the stringer is cut at its top end to fit the floor, and to connect with the baseboard on the landing. Fig. 139 shows at *a* how the stringer is cut at the bottom end to fit the floor and to connect with the baseboard.

CHAPTER VIII

A FLIGHT WITH WINDERS AT THE BOTTOM

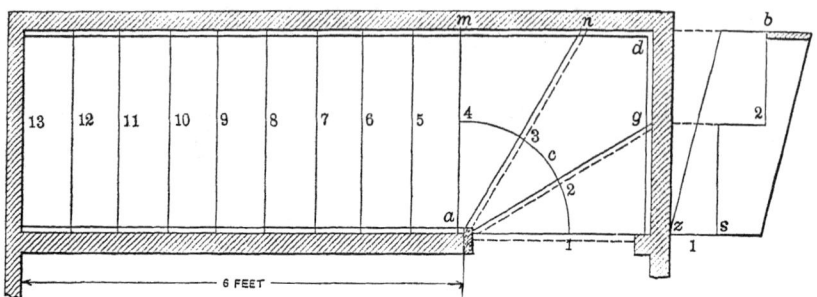

FIG. 144.—Flight of Stairs with Winders at the Bottom.

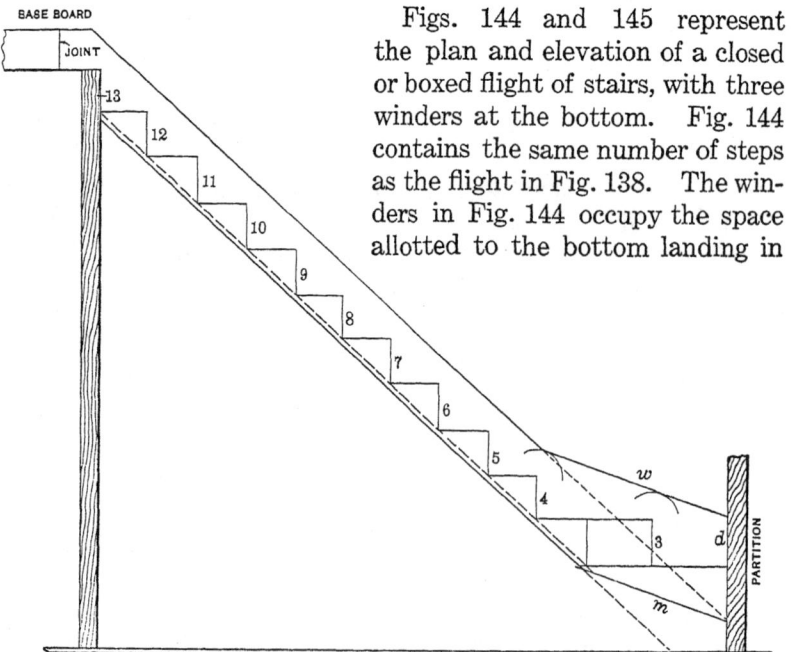

Figs. 144 and 145 represent the plan and elevation of a closed or boxed flight of stairs, with three winders at the bottom. Fig. 144 contains the same number of steps as the flight in Fig. 138. The winders in Fig. 144 occupy the space allotted to the bottom landing in

FIG. 145.—Elevation of Flight of Stairs Shown in Previous Figure.

Fig. 138; a gain equal to the width of the landing is procured in the run of the flight, by this manipulation of the winders.

In order to lay out the winders, place one leg of the compasses at the outside end of the riser *4*, at *a*; extend the other leg *14* in., and describe the curve *c*. Divide this curve into three equal divisions, and through the points draw the lines of the winders from *a* to the stringer. The dotted lines indicate the addition to each winder for the nosing. In this process the winders must be laid out full size on a drawing board, or on the floor. From the drawing, the form and correct size of each winder is obtained.

Fig. 145 shows how to lay out the wall stringer for the winders, by measuring from riser *4* to riser *3* the distance *m n* on the plan of stringer in Fig. 144, and from *3* measure to *d* the distance shown by *n d* in the same figure. Place one point of a pair of compasses upon the nosing of riser *4*, and extend the other point, illustrated by the arc, to the top edge of the straight stringer; repeat upon riser *3*, and draw the line *w* as shown upon the arcs, and the line *m*, parallel to the line *w*.

Fig. 144, at the right, shows the method of laying out the short stringer to receive the first and part of the second winder. Draw riser *1* from *Z* to *S* and riser *2* from *g* to *2*; make the distance from *S* to *2* equal the width of first winder, and the distance from *2* to *b* equal the portion *g d* of the second winder. Make the height of the stringer at *b* equal to the height at *d*, of the long stringer in Fig. 145.

CHAPTER IX

A PLATFORM AND NEWEL STAIRWAY

The plan of a newel and platform stairway containing three flights, four newels, and two curved steps at the bottom of the first flight, is indicated in Fig. 146.   The rail having easements

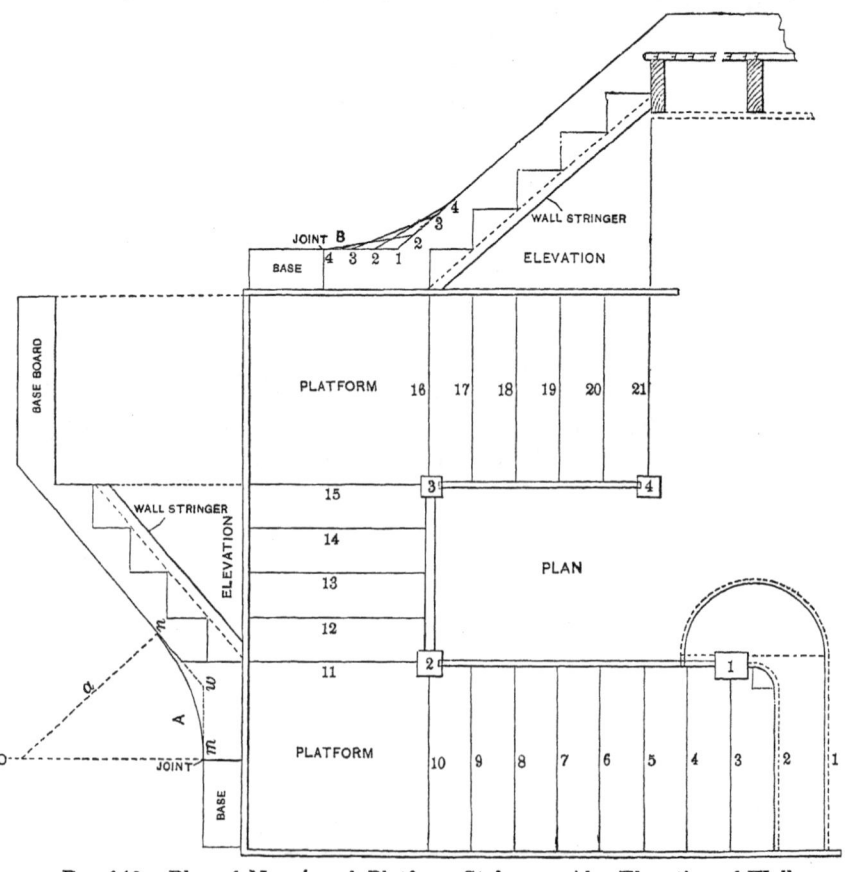

FIG. 146.—Plan of Newel and Platform Stairway; Also Elevation of Wall Stringers.

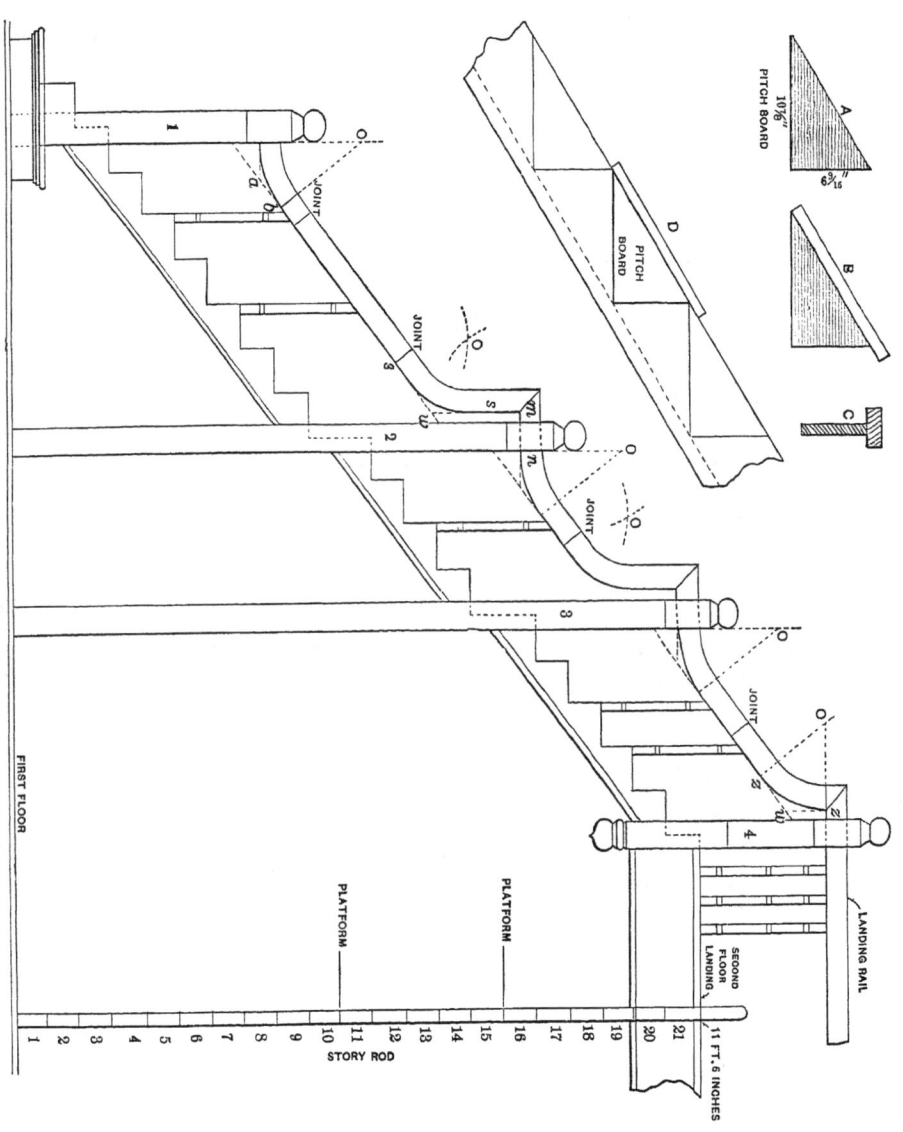

FIG. 147.—Elevation of Newel and Platform Stairway, Showing Pitchboard and its Application.

and goosenecks is illustrated in the elevation, Fig. 147. The type of stair presented in these figures may be seen in all sections of the country, usually in reception rooms of residences.

In constructing a stair of this kind special care must be taken to secure the correct relative dimensions of the treads and risers for the steps. The risers should never be more than 7 in. in height; a *6* or *6½*-in. riser is preferable. Having determined upon the size of the riser, it is placed on the compasses, and the story rod is divided into the number of risers required to reach from the first to the second floor. The story rod in this example indicates a total height of *11* ft. *6* in. from floor to floor in Fig. 147. If the compasses indicate *6½* in. for the assumed risers, by stepping the story rod its full length, it is found that *21* risers are required to reach from the first to the second floor, and also that a *6½*-in. riser, *21* times, is just a trifle too small to cover the distance between floors, as indicated on the story rod. By trying the stepping on the rod with the compasses expanded a little over *6½* in. we find the exact dimension of the riser, and also find the number required. This method is presented here to show how stairbuilders generally find out in practice the dimension of the riser. The better way is to divide the total length on the story rod by the assumed required dimensional riser.

In the flight in Fig. 146 the total height on the story rod is *11* ft. *6* in., or *138* in. Dividing *138*, the total height, by *21*, the number of risers, we find the exact depth of the riser to be 6. 9-16+ in.

To find the relative proportional dimension of a tread for this riser, one rule is to double the depth of the riser, and deduct the dimension from the figure *24* as follows: 6. 9-16 × 2 = 13⅛; 24 — 13⅛ = 10⅞ in., the exact width of a tread for a riser 6. 9-16 in. deep.

The pitchboard for the steps is shown at *A* in Fig. 147, and at *B* a fence is nailed to the pitchboard; while *C* represents *s* sectional view of the pitchboard and fence. At *D* the pitchboard is applied to a cut and mitered stringer. The fence is placed against the upper edge as a guide, and the pitchboard is moved along as many times as there are steps required to be marked on the stringer.

In Fig. 147 the newels *2* and *3* reach down from the stairs to the floor line; an arrangement considered necessary in order to support the two platforms shown in Fig. 146. The newel marked *4* is finished at the top landing with a drop a little below the ceiling line, and indicated in Fig. 147. The latter figure also shows how the easements and goosenecks are laid out. From *a*, below the easement of the bottom flight, a level line is drawn to the newel post, and the length of this line measured on the rail to *b*. From *b* a line is drawn square to the pitch of the rail to *o*, the center from which the curve of the easement from *b* to the newel is described. The easements for the rail over the second and third flights are described by the same method. The easements in all cases should be described before the goosenecks, because, as shown in Fig. 147, the height of the gooseneck is determined by the intersection of the easement with the newel. The easement of the rail over the second flight connects with newel No. 2 at *n*.

To describe the gooseneck for the rail over the bottom flight proceed as follows: draw the lines of the knee shown at *m* in continuation of the lines representing the top and bottom of the easement on the rail over the second flight at *n*. From *m* draw a line parallel to the newel to *w'*, measure from *w* to *s* on this line, and to *s* on the straight rail, equal distances. Place one leg of the compasses in *s* on the line *w m*; extend the other leg to *w*, and draw the arc shown at *o*. Again place one leg of the compasses in *s* on the straight rail, and with the same radius draw the arc intersecting the other arc in *o*. From *o* as center, describe the curve of the goose neck indicated from *s* on the rail to *s* on the line *w m*.

Another method of laying out the gooseneck curve is shown over the upper flight connected with newel No. 4. The center, *o*, is found for this method, by drawing a level line in continuation of the bottom of the landing rail, and another line from *z* on the pitch rail and square to it to intersect the level line in *o*. Taking *o* as center, the curve may be described with the compasses, from *z* to *z*.

In Fig. 148 the risers are tongued into a groove on the under side of the tread, and the tread is tongued into a groove made on the face of the riser. At *A* and *B* the tread and riser are shown separately. Templets representing these sections are prepared by the stairbuilder, to be used by the mill man as patterns, in running the stuff through the machine.

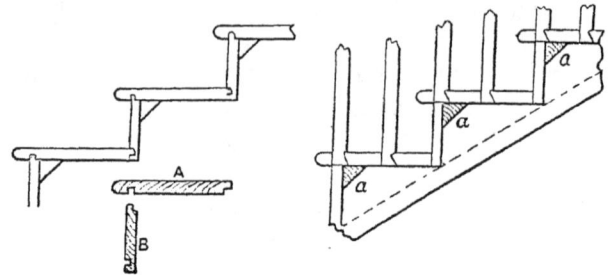

FIGS. 148 and 149.—Showing How Treads, Risers and Balusters Are Fastened.

Fig. 149 represents a sectional view of a few steps indicating the method of dovetailing the balusters into the treads and also at *a, a,* etc., the blocks that are placed behind the risers and under the treads for the purpose of reinforcement.

The manner in which the treads are prepared to receive the dovetails on the balusters, and the cut on the nosing to miter with the return nosing, which is to be nailed on the finished end of the treads to cover up the dovetails, is clearly indicated in Fig. 150. Fig. 151 presents the under side of a step showing the

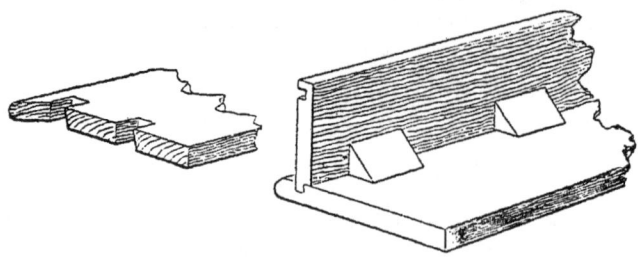

FIGS. 150 and 151.—Showing Framing of Ends and Underside of Step.

method of placing the blocks indicated at *a* of Fig. 149.

At *B* on the stringer of the upper flight, Fig, 146, a method of treating the intersection of the stringer with the base board is shown. The figures *1, 2, 3, 4* on the stringer and *1, 2, 3, 4* on the base are equal divisions. Draw a line from *2* on the stringer to *4* on the base, also one from *3* on the stringer to *3* on the base, and one from *4* on the stringer to *2* on the base. The intersection of these lines forms a curve tangential to both stringer and base.

At *A* on the wall stringer of the middle flight there is another method of treatment in use by stairbuilders. Measure from *w* to *m* and *n* equal distances; draw the line *m o* square to the base line, and the line *n o* square to the pitch line of the stringer. These lines intersect at *o*, the center point from which to describe the curve with the radius *o n* or *o m*. Either of these methods may be used at the top landings of the flights.

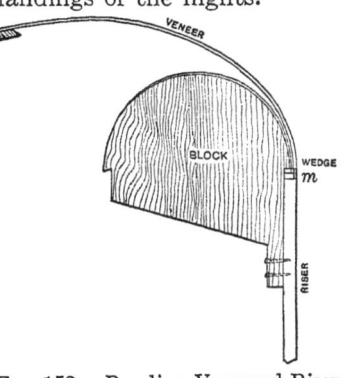

Fig. 152 is a view of a prepared semi-circular curved block, to bend the veneered riser shown to be the first riser on the plan, Fig. 146. A section through the block indicating the method of its construction is presented in Fig. 153; Fig. 154 is a view of the block for a quarter circle turn for bending the second riser, shown in Fig. 146.

Finding the exact distance between the saw cuts or kerfing

FIG. 152.—Bending Veneered Riser over Curved Block.

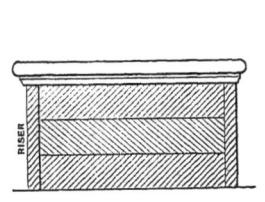

FIG. 153.—Section of Block Showing Construction.

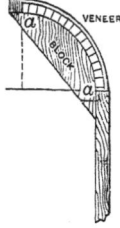

FIG. 154.— Block for Bending Second Riser.

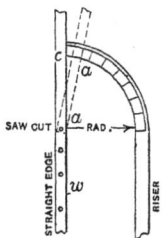

FIG. 155.—Showing How to Find Distances Between Kerfing Lines.

lines is illustrated in Fig. 155. The letter *w* in this figure indicates a straight edge made of material equal in thickness to that of the riser. At *a* there is a saw cut made to a depth within about 3-16 of an inch of the opposite face. The straight edge is nailed fast from *a* to *w*, then the part from *a* to *c* is gradually moved in the direction of *a*, until the cut at the lower *a* is closed. The distance shown between *c* and *a* on the curve indicates the space between the saw cuts or kerfing lines.

CHAPTER X

THE CONSTRUCTION OF A PLATFORM NEWEL AND A STRETCHOUT CURVE AT THE BOTTOM OF A STAIRWAY

Platform Stairway

Fig. 156 is a plan of a platform and newel stairway, composed of *5* flights and *3* platforms; the first two flights have turned out stringers and swell steps.

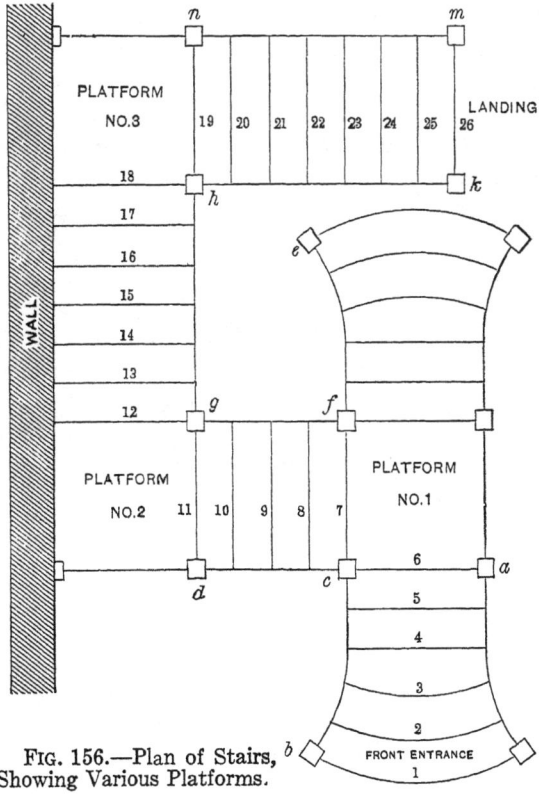

FIG. 156.—Plan of Stairs, Showing Various Platforms.

93

These flights meet at the same platform, No. 1, and from this platform the stairs turn at right angles, landing on platform No. 2, and turn again at right angles to platform No. 3, and finally from this point reach the landing at the second story. The structure contains 26 risers, but as they are distributed in the manner shown, and each small flight has a resting platform, the exertion in ascending and descending is reduced to a minimum.

With such a plan as this the only possible way of spoiling the work is in misproportioning the treads and risers and in varying the pitch of the flights. The method used for proportioning the treads and risers is immaterial, for the many different plans of procedure show practically the same results. The construc-

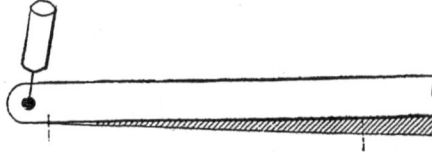

FIG. 157.—The Pitch Board.

tion under consideration is placed in a public building, where the run is not restricted, and a 12-inch tread would have been a better arrangement than the 10-inch tread decided upon.

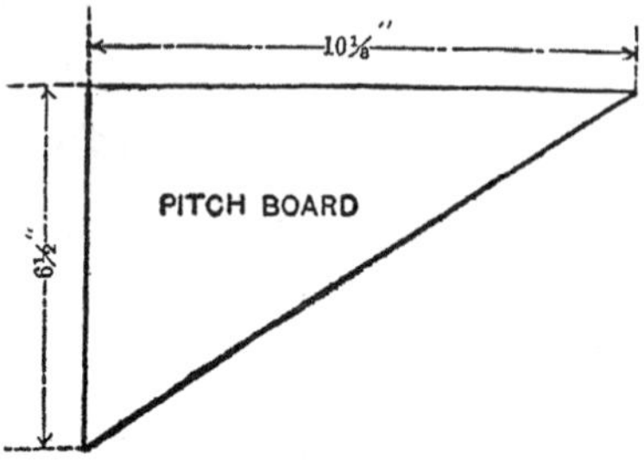

FIG. 158.—Tread and Wedge Templet.

To find the best proportional riser for a tread of 10 inches, divide 66 by 10, which gives 6½ in. for the width of the riser. In laying out the pitch board, Fig. 157, it is necessary to know the exact height between floors; in this instance it is 14 feet 1 in., or 169 inches. Dividing this by 26, the number of risers, the quotient is 6½ inches, the width of the riser. To find the proportional tread, divide 66 by 6½, obtaining as a result 10 2-13 in. for the width of the tread, or a little over 10⅛ inches.

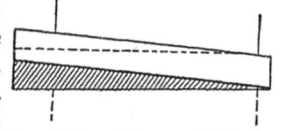

FIG. 159.—Riser and Wedge Templet.

Lay out a pitch board of 1-inch stuff, having one edge measuring 10⅛ in., the width of the tread, the other edge 6½ inches, the width of the riser. This triangle is used as a templet on the face of the material intended for stringers, and to mark the outlines of the treads and risers. A plan view of it is shown in Fig. 157.

Two other templets are needed to mark the thickness of the treads and risers, combined with the size of the wedges. These are indicated in Figs. 158 and 159 respectively, while in Fig. 160 the pitch board and the two templets are shown applied to the stringer; *2* in this figure shows the pitch board, and *3* the two templets applied to mark the outlines of the "housing" or "grooves," and at *4* the groove is housed.

Fig. 161 is a stringer grooved and the wedges in place. It contains eight risers and seven treads, the number of treads and risers contained in the top flight of the stairway, in Fig. 156,

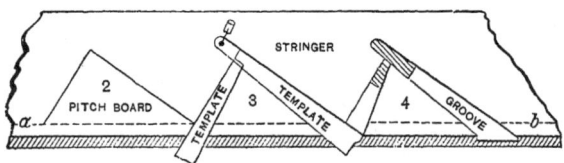

FIG. 160.—Showing Application to Stringer of Pitch and Templets.

FIG. 161.—View of Stringer Grooved and Wedges in Place.

from platform No. 3 to the landing at the second story. A small tenon is added to the length at each end, to enter the newels. This treatment applies to all the stringers.

The elevation of the newel post at the first flight, connecting with the stretchout stringer, and the complete bottom flight of stairs, appear in Fig. 162. To find the exact length of the newel, and the location of the squares opposite the point where the rail and the stringer intersect it, let the length of the short baluster be *2* ft. *2* in. from the nosing to the bottom of the rail, and continue the line representing the bottom of the rail to the center of the newel, at *b*. From *2* draw the level line *2 c*, and from *c* upward mark the thickness of the rail, as indicated. From the floor line to *a* the height of the riser is 6½ in.; from *a* to *b* the length, *2* ft. *2* in., of the short baluster; from *b* to *c*, a length equal to *7* in., representing the height of the rise in the rail decided upon for a suitable easement, and from *c* to the top of the rail, *3* in. These items added together equal *3* feet 6½ in., the exact length of the newel from the floor to the top of the rail.

The location of the squares on the newel to receive the stringer and the rail are shown by the shaded parts in the diagram, and are opposite the rail and stringer, respectively.   In the

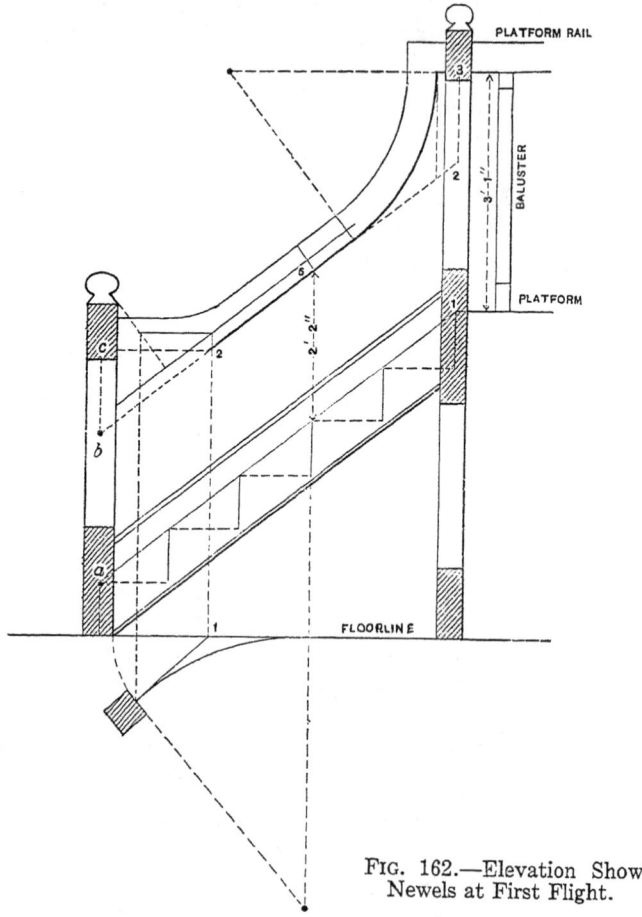

Fig. 162.—Elevation Showing Newels at First Flight.

diagram there is also another newel, reaching from the floor to the first platform, the plan of it indicated at *a*, in Fig. 156.   In Fig. 162 it is shown reaching from the floor to a little above the platform rail.   The height from the floor line to *1*, the line of the platform, is the space of six risers, each *6½* in., equaling *3* feet *3* in.   From *1* to *2* is *2* ft. *2* in., the length of a short baluster; from *2* to *3* is *11* in., and from *3* the thickness of the rail.   Adding these items together gives *6* ft. *7* in., the full length of the newel, from the floor line to the top of the platform rail.

The baluster between the platform floor and the platform rail is *3* ft. *1* in. long, made up, shown in the diagram, from *1* to *2*, with an addition of *11* in. from *2* to *3*. This *11* in. is determined by the method shown in Fig. 163, and should be carefully considered, as it defines a very important item in the construction of platform stairways—namely, the securing of similar "easements" and "goosenecks" for the rails of all the flights that the stairway may contain. Fig. 163 represents a partial elevation of two adjacent flights with a newel between, a case similar to the one shown at newel *c* in Fig. 156. The nosing line of the bottom flight cuts the center of the newel at *2*, and that of the upper flight at *o*, a distance above *2* equal to the width of one riser, *6½* inches.

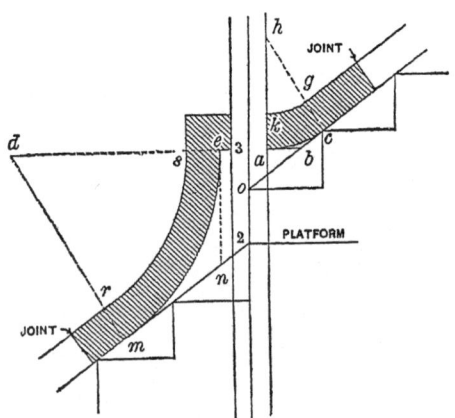

FIG. 163.—Partial Elevation of Two Adjacent Flights, with Newel Between.

If the upper rail had been arranged to run straight to the newel, the under side of it would cut the center of the newel in *o*; but if an easement is determined upon, then the rail must be raised as shown from *o* to *3*, or to any other point indicated. In this case, by fixing the point *3*, at a distance of *4½* inches from *o*, the best results are obtained, one of which is a suitable length for the platform baluster, Fig. 162.

Any addition to the height of point *3* increases correspondingly the height of the platform rail, and therefore the length of the platform baluster. Another very desirable result of this arrangement is the satisfactory limit it gives to the height of the "knee" in the gooseneck, a point common to the easement of the upper rail and of the gooseneck of the lower rail, shown in Fig. 163.

To draw the easement in Fig. 163, make *b c* equal *b a*, and from *c*, at right angles to the pitch of the rail, draw the line

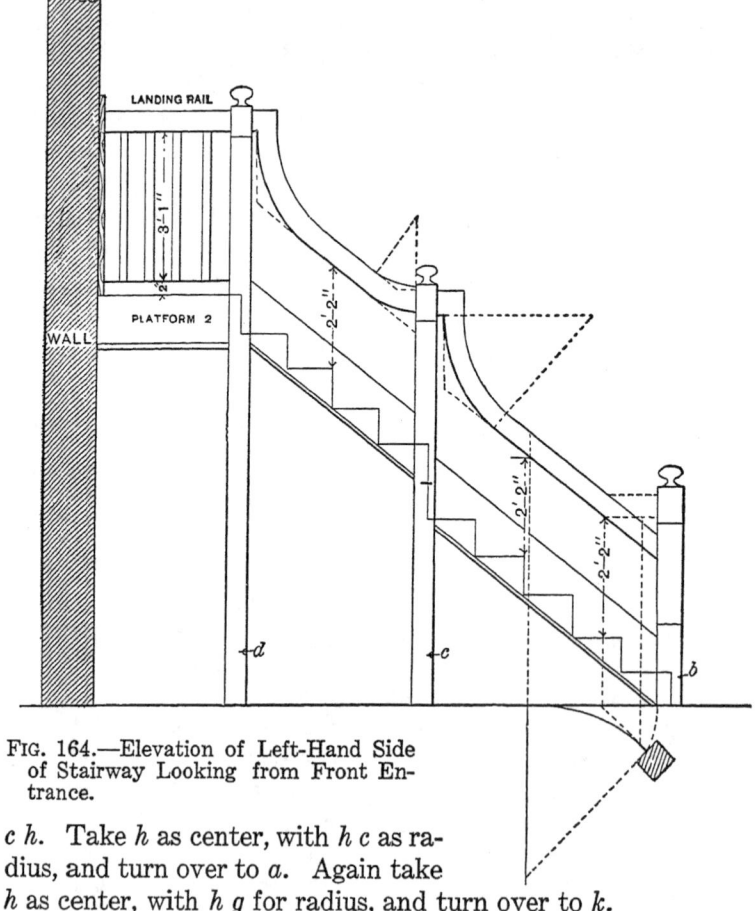

LANDING RAIL

PLATFORM 2

WALL

FIG. 164.—Elevation of Left-Hand Side of Stairway Looking from Front Entrance.

c h. Take *h* as center, with *h c* as radius, and turn over to *a*. Again take *h* as center, with *h g* for radius, and turn over to *k*.

To draw the templet for the gooseneck proceed as follows: draw the line *3 d* at right angles to the newel; from *e* draw the line *e n* parallel to the newel; make *n m* equal *n e*, and from *m*, square to the pitch of the rail, draw the line *m d*. Take *d* for center, with *d m* as radius, and turn over to *e*; again take *d* for center, with *d r* as radius, and turn over to *S*. The templets are the shaded portion of the diagram and extend a trifle beyond the curves, to make a better joint with the straight rails. Fig. 164

is the elevation of the left-hand side of the stairway, looking from the direction of the front entrance, the newels indicated in Fig. 156, at *b*, *c* and *d* respectively.   The platform baluster here is also *3* ft. *1* in. long, the same length as those on platform No. 1. Fig. 165 presents the elevation of the newels marked in Fig. 156, at *e*, *f*, *g*, *h* and *k*, and of the stringers and rails between them.   Fig. 166 represents the elevation of the newels *m* and *n* of Fig. 156, and of the stringer and platform No. 3.   The baluster on this platform is also *3* ft. *1* in. long.

The balusters under the landing rails, shown in Figs. 165 and 166, are only *2* ft. *8* in., the height desired for the landing rail at the second-story floor.   This treatment calls for a gooseneck of different form and dimensions from those previously described.   To form the templet in Fig. 167, a few steps are drawn adjacent to the landing newel, and also a line to represent the floor at the second story.   From this line measure *2* feet *8* inches, the length of the baluster, thus fixing the height of the landing rail.   From the nosing line of one of the steps, measure *2* ft. *2* in., the height of the short baluster, and draw the lines to represent the rail of the flight.   The rest of the work is similar to that explained in connection with Fig. 163.

Fig. 168 shows the plan of the platform joist, where the one marked *a* is kept back a certain distance from the newel post.

Fig. 169 is the elevation of the platform, as well as an elevation of one of the carriers that support the flight; the upper end of the flight is sustained by the joist *a* of Fig. 168, thus indicating the necessity of keeping this joist back, as stated above.

Fig. 170 shows the plan of the curved rail from the center *o*. The plan tangents are *a b* and *b c*, respectively.   The tangent *a b*, at *2 c* in Fig. 162, is a level tangent, while the tangent *b c*, shown from *2* to *5* in Fig. 162, is inclined; the inclination is that of the flight, represented in the pitch board.   From *b*, in Fig. 170, draw the line *b c''*, with the pitch board   This line represents the elevation of the plan tangent *b c*.   From *a* draw the line square to *n c*; through *n* and square to *b c''* draw the line *m n a''*. Place one leg of the compasses at *b*, extend the other to *a*, and describe the arc indicated by the dotted line *a a''*.   Connect *a''* with *b*, and the line represents the bottom level tangent, required on the face mold, while *b c''* represents the other tangent of the face mold. Draw the joint at a'' square to the tangent $a''\,b$, and the joint at c'' square to the tangent $b\,c''$.

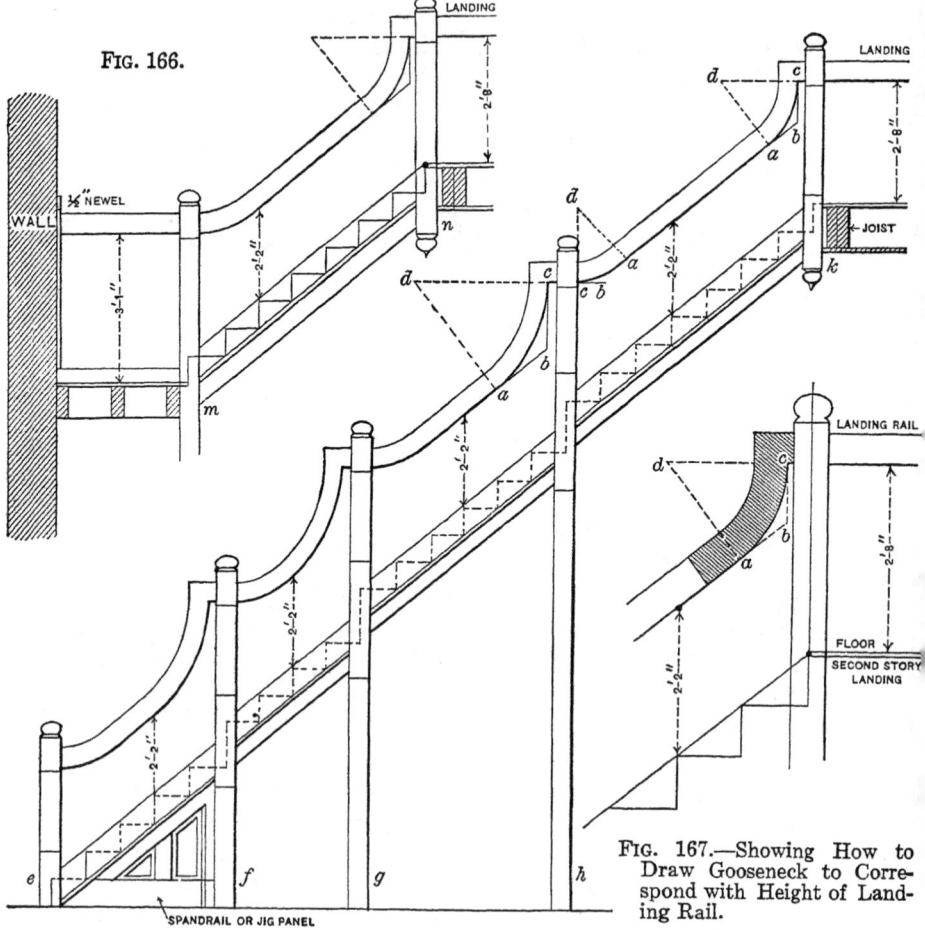

FIG. 166.

FIG. 167.—Showing How to Draw Gooseneck to Correspond with Height of Landing Rail.

FIG. 165.—Elevation of the Newels Marked on the Plan Fig. 156 at e, f, g, h, k.

Draw the curves of the mold by means of a single ordinate. The line *2 3*, which is drawn parallel to the plan level tangent a b, is the plan ordinate, and the line *4 5*, which is made parallel to the level tangent $a''\,b$, is the ordinate across the face mold.

The principle used here is to make the two ordinates the same length—that is, *2 3* to equal *4 5*.   This operation makes it pos-

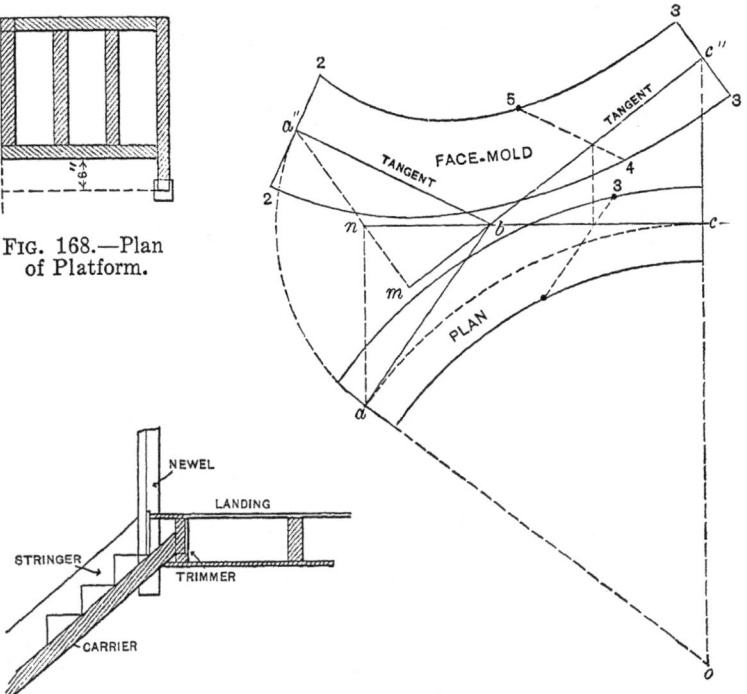

FIG. 168.—Plan
of Platform.

FIG. 169.—Elevation of Platform
Shown in Previous Figure.

FIG. 170.—A Very Simple Method of
Drawing Face Mold for the Stretchout Wreath.

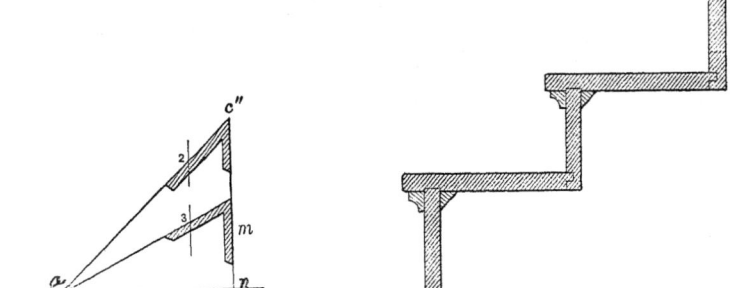

FIG. 171.—Bevels to Square
the Wreath.

FIG. 172.—Section through Stairs.

sible to locate the points *4* and *5*, which are contained in the curves of the mold.

To find the width of the mold at each end, refer to the bevels shown in Fig. 171. Make *a n* Fig. 171 equal *a n* of Fig. 170, and *n m* equal to *n m* of the same figure; connect *m a*; the bevel is at *m*, and is applied to the end *c″* of the mold.

Again make *n c″* equal to *c c″* of Fig. 170, and connect *c″ a*. The bevel is at *c″* and is applied to the end *a″* of the mold.

Draw the line *2* and *3*, at a distance from the line *n m c″*, equal to half the width of the rail on each side of *a″*, in Fig. 170. Place the distance *c″ 2* of Fig. 171, as shown at *a″ 2* of Fig. 170. On each side of *c″* of Fig. 170, place the distance *m 3* of Fig. 171, indicated by *c″ 3*, in Fig. 170.

CHAPTER XI

A STAIRWAY CONTAINING A STRETCHOUT CURVE AT THE BOTTOM; A 10-INCH CYLINDRICAL WELL HOLE, CONTAINING TWO FLIGHTS, AND A QUARTER TURN CURVE AT THE TOP LANDING

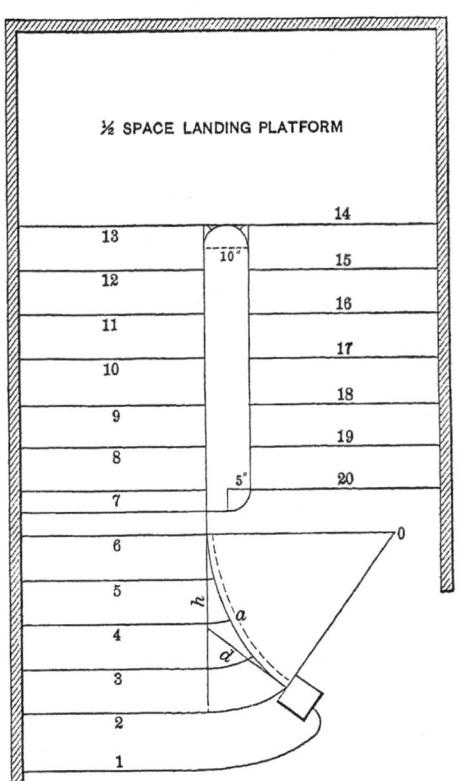

FIG. 173.—Plan of Cylinder Stairway Containing Stretchout Curve at the Bottom, a 10-in. Cylindrical Well Hole and a Quarter Turn at the Upper Landing.

Fig. 173 represents the plan of the stairway. It contains a turn-out curve at the bottom; a *10*-inch cylinder well hole; and a quarter-turn curve at the upper end of the second flight connecting with the landing of the second floor.

The total hight between floors is *11* ft. *8* inches; equaling *140* inches; which, by being divided by 7, the assumed width of the riser, indicate that *20* risers will be required to reach from the first floor to the second floor.

The first flight is shown in the figure to contain *13* of these risers; and the second flight therefore will contains the remaining *7*. To find the best proportional tread for a *7*-inch riser, multiply *7* by *2,* and subtract the product *(14)* from the number *24,* as follows: $7 \times 2 = 14 + 24 = 10.$

Now make a pitchboard of the following dimensions; *7*-inch riser and a *10*-inch tread.

The method of laying out a pitchboard is explained in connection with Figs. 166, 167 and 168 for the stairway shown in

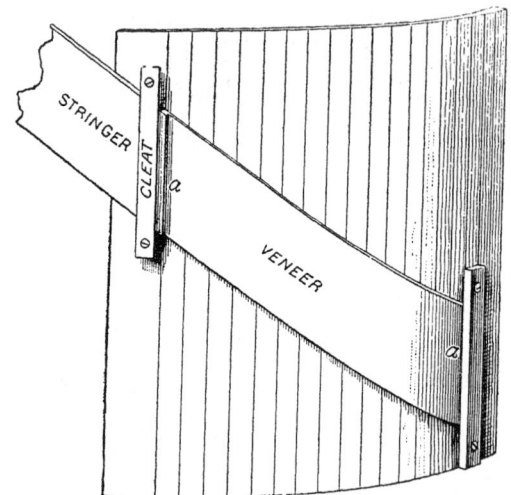

FIG. 174.—Stringer Fixed on Drum for Bending.

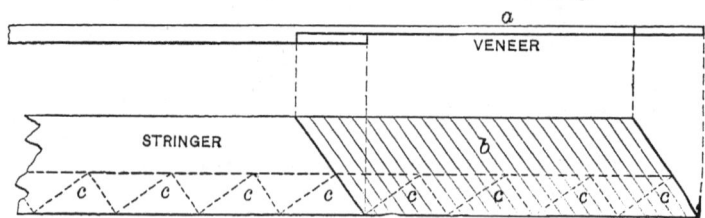

FIG. 175.—View of Stringer Prepared for Bending.

Fig. 164, and the method of applying the pitchboard to a cut and mitered stringer is shown in Fig. 165.

Fig. 174 shows a drum and stringer prepared for bending the portion of the stretchout curve at the bottom of the first flight. The drum is made to coincide with the curve in Fig. 173 at *a,* where the dotted curve shows the outside face of the stringer.

The stringer is placed on the drum, Fig. 174, and held securely by means of cleats, and the space on the stringer from a to a' is tightly filled with narrow strips called "keys," glued to the veneer. The stringer is left on the drum for the keys to set, after which it is cut for the treads and risers.

Fig. 175 shows how the stringer is prepared for bending; an edge view of the veneered portion is at a, while b is the back face of it, the lines indicating the direction which the keys

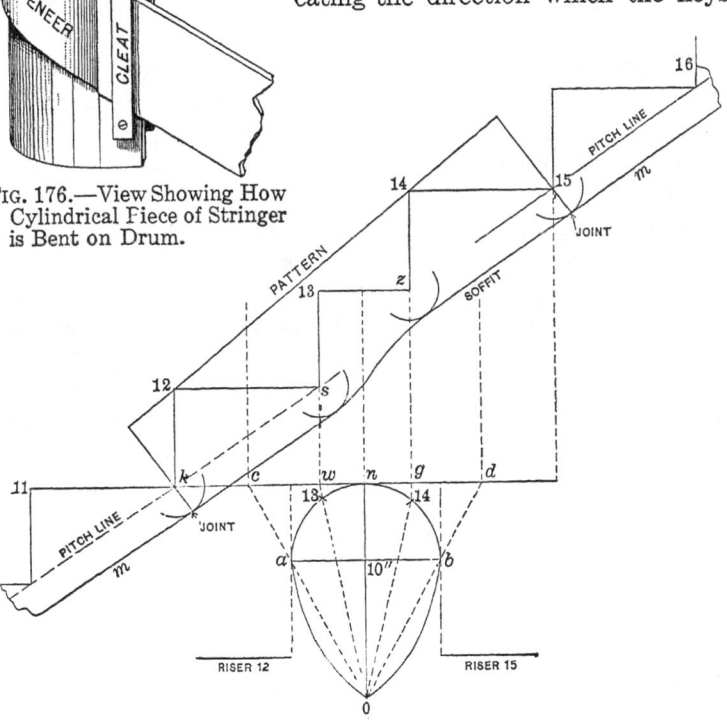

Fig. 176.—View Showing How Cylindrical Piece of Stringer is Bent on Drum.

Fig. 177.—Pattern to Bend Around the Concave Face of the Cylinder to Mark for Cutting Treads and Risers.

assume, when placed on the veneer in the space from a to a in Fig. 174. The stringer is marked for the treads and risers at c, c, c, and c, in Fig. 175, before it is placed on the drum.

Fig. 176 is another drum and a piece of a stringer bent around it. This one is for the *10*-in. cylinder of the well hole. The process of preparing and bend ng the stringer is the same as that just described for the portion illustrated in Figs. 174 and 175, except that for this piece of a stringer it is necessary to lay out a pattern or templet of its true form.

The manner of laying out the pattern is illustrated in Fig. 177, viz., describe the semicircle *a n b*, with the radius of the cylinder, which represents the concave face curve of the well hole stringer; then with *a* and *b* for centers and *b a* for radius, describe the arcs crossing at *o*.

From *o* draw a line through *a* to *c*, and also one through *b* to *d*. The distance from *c* to *d* indicates the stretchout length of the semicircular curve *a n b*. Again draw a line through the points *13* and *14*, to *w* and *g* respectively. Draw the perpendicular lines from *c w*, *n g* and *d*; upon the line drawn from *w*, set off from *w* the height of two risers at *s* and *13*. From point *13* draw the line *13 z*; and from *z* measure the height of one riser to *14*, and draw the line *14, 15*. Again from *s* draw a line to *12*, and set off

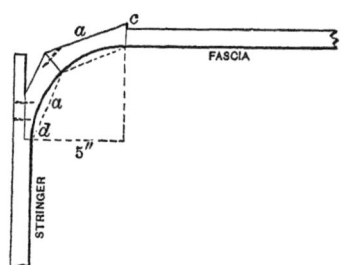

FIG. 178.—Stringer Cylinder for the Quadrant at Landing on Second Floor Connecting to the Landing Face.

from *12* to *h*, the height of one riser; from *h* draw the line *h 11*, and drop a riser as shown from *11*. Draw the pitch of the bottom flight through *h* and *s*, and the pitch of the upper flight from *15* and *16*. Draw the lines *m* and *m* parallel to the respective pitch lines. Take the distance from *15* to this line on the compasses, and placing one leg in *s*, draw the arc. Again place one leg in *z*, and draw another arc; draw a free hand curve to touch the arcs, thus forming the soffit of the cylindrical stringer. Draw a line through *14* and *12* and square to it draw lines from *15* and *h*; thus completing the pattern.

Fig. 179 represents the plan, elevation and pitch of tangents for the stretchout curve shown in Fig. 173, where it is shown that the curve contains the risers *3, 4, 5*, and *6*.

To draw the elevation and pitch of tangents, draw the pitch

of the flight as shown through n to c and from c draw a level line to the newel.

This level line is the elevation of the level plan tangent, $s\,d$ and the pitch line $c\,n$ is the elevation of the plan tangent $h\,d$. Draw s, w, a, and from a draw the line $a\,b$ square to the pitch line $c\,n$.

To find the bevels, make $s\,w$ in diagram D equal to $s\,w$ in Fig. 179, and $w\,b$ in the diagram equal to $a\,b$ in Fig. 179. Draw

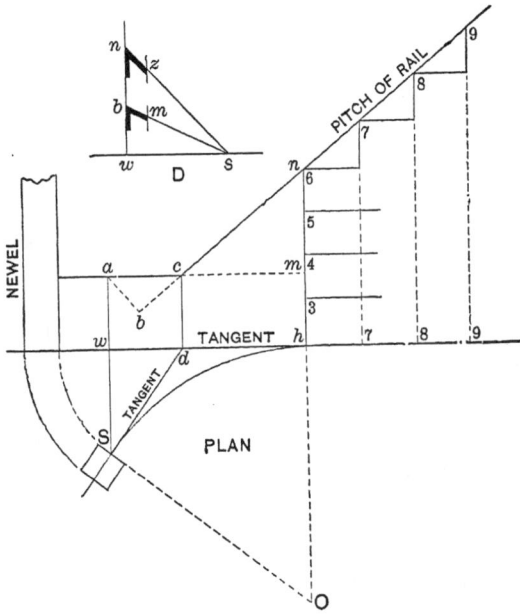

FIG. 179.—Plan and Elevation of the Stretchout Curve and Tangents.

a line from b to s in the diagram, and the bevel at b is the one required to apply to the end n of the face mold in Fig. 180. To find the bevel to apply to the end s of the mold in Fig. 180, make $w\,n$ in diagram D equal to $m\,n$ in Fig. 179, and draw a line from n to s. The bevel at n is the one required.

Fig. 180 shows how to lay out the face mold. Draw the plan of the stretchout rail from s to h; and parallel to the level tangent line $s\,d$, draw the dotted lines 4, 4, etc., across the plan of the rail in Fig. 180. From the points where these lines cut the ground line at *2, 2,* etc., draw perpendicular lines to cut the pitch line *c n* at *2', 2',* etc.; and from the points *2'* on this line, draw lines parallel to the line *s c* of the elevation shown by *1' 3, 1' 3',* etc., and make each line equal in length to its correlative lines on the plan of the rail. Through the points *1', 1',* etc., trace the inside curve of the face mold, and through the points *3', 3',* etc., trace the curve of the outside of the mold. The method just described is known as the "ordinate method," and is the most simple one for laying out the face mold.

Fig. 181 shows how to lay out the face mold by means of pins and strings, and is probably the most common method practiced by stairbuilders. Draw the plan of the center line of the rail,

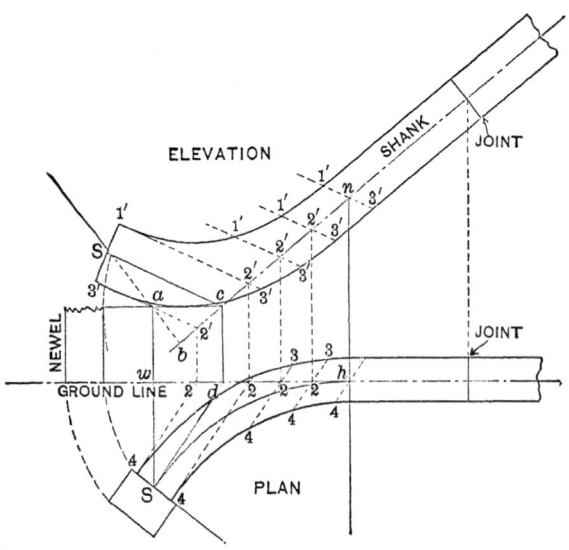

Fig. 180.—Laying Cut Face Mold by Means of Ordinates.

and the tangents *s d* and *d h*. From *d* and *h* draw the line *d c* and *h n*; connect *c n*, and prolong indefinitely to locate *b* and *5*. From *s* on the plan, draw the line *s w a*; with *d* for center, and *d s* as radius; revolve point *s* to *g*; upon *g* erect the line *g s'* and connect *s' a c*, and draw a line through *a* from *b* square to the pitch line *c n*. From *c* as center revolve point *s'*, to cut the line previously drawn from *b* through *a* in *s'*, and connect *s''* to *c'*, thus determining the angle *c* between the tangents required on the face of the mold to square the joints. On each side of

s'', at *6* and *7*, set off the distance $n\ z'$, taken from the bevel n in diagram D, Fig. 179, thus determining the width of the mold at the end s''. Again on each side of n, place the distance

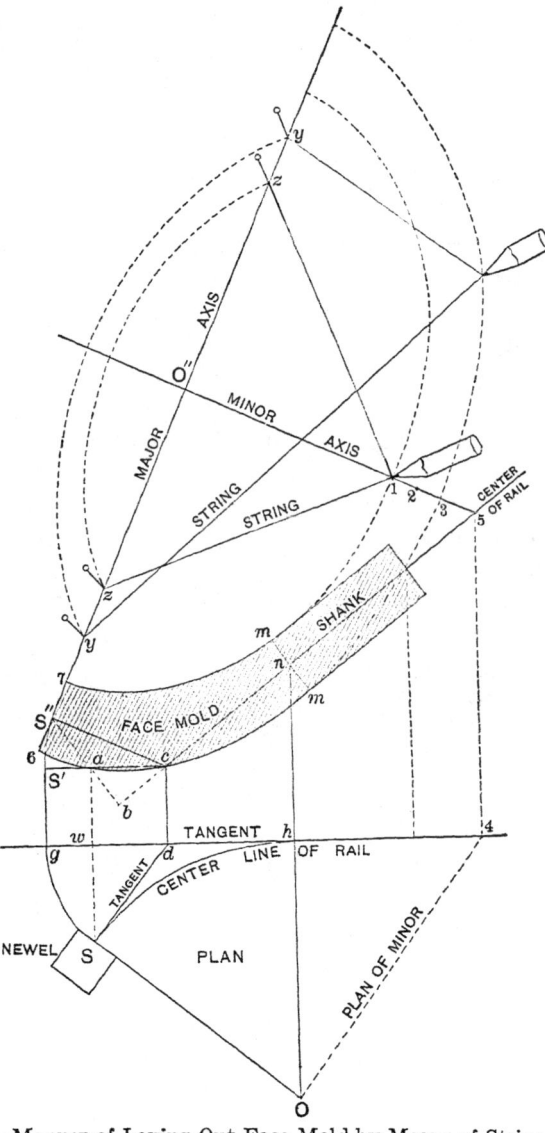

FIG. 181.—Manner of Laying Out Face Mold by Means of String and Pins.

$n\, m$, equal to $b\, m$ in diagram D, Fig. 179; this is the width of the mold at the end n.

To find the major and minor axes of the ellipses that contain the inside and outside curves of the mold, draw a line from o in Fig. 181 to 4, parallel to the level tangent $s\, d$, and at 4 erect the line $4\,5$. From 5 draw the line $5\,o''$, parallel to the line $c\, s''$, making it equal in length to the line $o\,4$, the line of the minor axis. Through o'', and square to the line $o''\,5$, draw a line to s''. The line $5\,o''$ is the semi-minor axis and the line $o''\,s''$ is the semi-major axis of the ellipses that contain the curves of the face mold. Measure from o'' along the semi-minor axis to 2, a distance equal to $o\,s$, the radius of the center line of the rail. On each side of 2, measure to 1 and to 3, a distance equal to one-half the width of the rail.

To find the points of the major axis in order to insert the pins for the inside curve, take the distance $o''\,7$ of the major axis in the compasses, and the point 1 on the minor for center, and describe the dotted arc cutting the major axis in z and z, respectively. Again, take with the compasses the distance $o\,''6$ shown on the major, and from point 3 on the minor describe the dotted arc cutting the major in y and y, the points on the major at which to insert the pins to hold the string to describe the outside

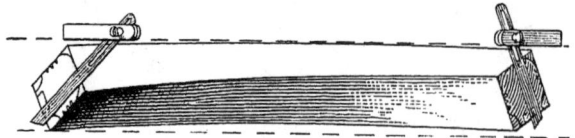

Fig. 182.—Showing Appearance of Wreath for the Stretchout Curve After it is Squared and the Bevels Applied.

curve. Fasten the string tight to the pins at z and z on the major, stretch it out to 1 on the minor, place the pencil, and sweep the inside curve all around from 1 to 7. Again, fasten the string to the pins at y and y, extend it to 3 on the minor axis, and sweep the outside curve from 3 to 6.

The face mold in the diagram is a very small part of these ellipses, extending only from $m\, m$ at the end n, and to $6\,7$ at the end s'' of the mold. The remainder of the curves are drawn to prove that the face mold for a wreath is merely a portion of certain ellipses, and to emphasize the necessity of knowing how to find the axis of the ellipses containing the curves of the face mold under all conditions of the wreath construction.

Fig. 182 is a view of the wreath after it is squared, and the bevels applied to each end, and directed towards the inside of the wreath.

The method of laying out the wreath for the *10*-in. cylinder

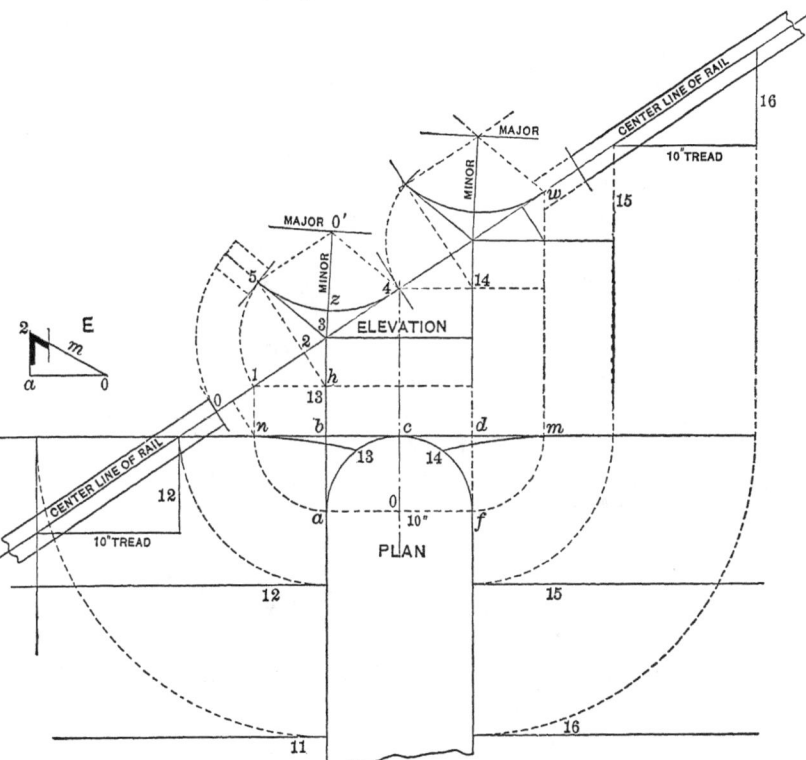

FIG. 183.—Plan, Elevation and Development of Tangents and Center Line of Rail for the 10-in. Cylinder of the Well Hole.

of the well hole in Fig. 173, connecting the two flights at the half-space landing platform, is shown in Fig. 183 of the diagrams. Draw the plan of the center line of rail, and the elevation of the steps adjoining the cylinder, of the bottom and upper flights, shown at *12* and *16* in Fig. 183. Over these steps draw lines to represent the pitch of the straight rail of the two flights, and continue the center line over and above the cylinder. The same pitch is over the cylinder as over the straight flights, a condition due to the diameter of the cylinder, *10* in. being equal to the width of the *10*-in. treads of the adjoining flights.   Place the compasses in *b*, extend to *a*, turn around to *n*, and on *n* erect the line *n 1*.   Again place the compasses in *d*, extend to *f*, turn around to *m*, and erect the line *m, w*.   Upon *c* erect the line *c 4*.   From *h* draw the line *h 2-5*, square to the pitch line; and placing the compasses in *3*, extend to *1*; draw an arc to *5*, and connect *5* with *3*.   Draw a line from *5* to *0'* parallel to the line *3 4*, and draw a line from *4* to *0'* parallel to the line *3 5*.   Connect *0' 3*, the minor axis, and through *0'* and square to the minor axis draw the major axis, and measure from *0'* to *z* on the minor axis, a distance equal to the radius *0 a* of the plan.   Take a flexible lath, bend to touch the points *4, z 5*, and trace the curve of the center line of the wreath.

The same process is employed for the development of the central line of the portion of wreath that winds over and above the bottom quadrant of the cylinder, and for the development of the central line of the upper portion of the wreath that winds over and above the plan quadrant *c f*.

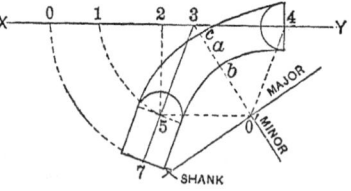

FIG. 184.—Laying Out Face Mold for 10-in. Well Hole Cylinder Rail.

Fig. 184 shows how the face mold for the two portions of wreath is laid out, viz., drawing the straight line *X Y*, and transferring to it the points *0, 1, 2, 3, 4*, from the pitch line in Fig. 183.   From *2* draw the line *2 5* square to the line *X Y*, and place the compasses in *3*, extend to *1*, and draw an arc to *5;* connect *3 5*, and extend to *7*. From *5* draw the line *5 0*, parallel to the line *3 4*.   From *4* draw the line *4 0*, parallel to *3 5*.   Connect *3* and *0';* this is the minor axis.   Draw the major axis square to the minor axis through the point *0'*.   Make *0' a* on the minor axis equal to the radius *0 a* in Fig. 183, and on each side of *a* measure a distance equal to half the width of the straight rail, thus determining the width of the face mold on the minor axis, which in all cases of the face mold developments is to equal the width of the straight rail.   To find the one bevel necessary, shown in diagram E of Fig. 183, make $O\,a$ in the diagram equal to the radius $O\,a$ of the curve; make $a\,2$ equal in length to the line $h\,2$ in the elevation, and connect 2 to O. The bevel is found at 2, and it is applied to both ends of the wreath. Draw the short line at m in the diagram, across the bevel at a distance from the line $a\,2$, equal to half the width of the straight rail. Take the distance $2\,m$, along the long edge of the bevel, on the compasses, and draw the semi-circles shown in Fig. 184, at 4 and at 5. The diameter of these semicircles indicates the width of the mold at each end.   To draw the curves take

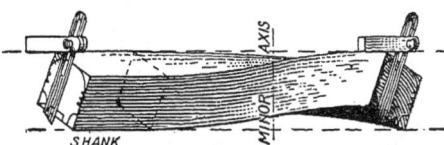

FIG. 185.—View Showing How Bevels Are Applied and Wreath Squared.

a flexible lath, bend it to touch the semi-circles at each end and the point b on the minor axis for the inside curve of the mold, and again bend it to touch the semi-circles and the point c for the outside curve. Draw the shank from 5 to 7, thus completing the development of the face mold. Fig. 185 is a view of the wreath after it is squared and the bevel applied to each end.

Fig. 186 shows how to get out the curved rail for the 5-in. quarter turn at the upper end of the top flight, connecting with the level rail of the landing on the second floor. From O draw the curves of the quarter turn rail; revolve point a to m on the ground line, and upon m erect the line $m\,n$. Upon b erect the line $b\,b'$, and upon c the line $c\,c'$. Draw the elevation of the steps 19 and 20 adjoining the quarter turn, and upon the apex of these steps draw the center line of rail of the flights to b'. From b' through c draw the center line of the level landing rail, and from b' as center, $b'\,c'$ as radius, revolve point c' to s. From s draw the line $s\,O'$ parallel to $n\,b'$, the line $n\,O'$ parallel to the line $b'\,s$, and these two lines square to the pitch line $n\,b'$. The bevel for this wreath is at b', and the development of the center line of the rail from n to s.

A very simple method to lay out the face mold for the wreath is illustrated in Fig. 187. Draw the square $O'\,n\,b'\,s$ equal to the developed tangents $O'\,n\,b'\,s$ of Fig. 186. Make the mold at n the same width as that of the straight rail, and at the end

s make *s z* equal to the distance *b' z*, shown on the long edge
of the bevel in Fig. 186. Bisect *n b* in *2*, and make *2 1* and *2 3*
equal to *2 1* and *2 3* shown across the plan rail in Fig. 186.
Also make *s. z* and *s. z* equal *z, b'* shown upon the bevel in Fig. 186.
Bend a lath to touch the points *z, 1,* and *a* in Fig. 187, and
trace the outside curve of the mold. Again bend the lath to

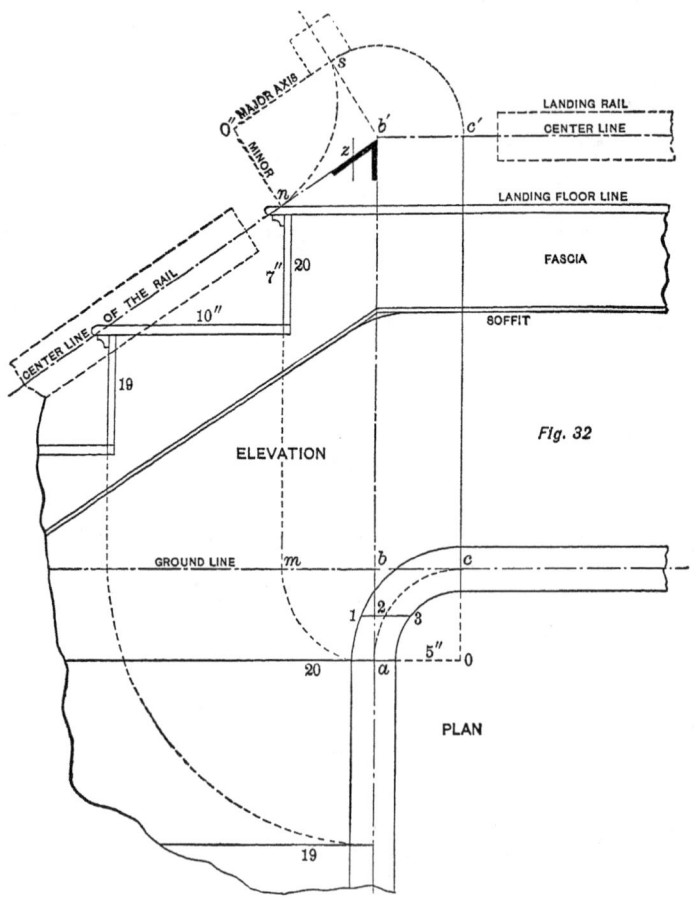

FIG. 186.—Plan and Elevation of a Few Steps Connecting the Quadrant
Turn and the Second Floor Landing.

touch the points *z, 3,* and *a,* and trace the curve for the inside of the mold. The bevel is applied to the end *s* by holding the stock parallel to the joint, and the blade directed

toward the outside. A bevel is not required at the end n, as it is on the minor axis. The face mold is applied to the plank in Fig. 188, and the wreath cut square to its face, along the lines $a\ b$, etc. At the end s the bevel is applied and a section of the rail is drawn to indicate how the wreath is twisted by means of the bevel.

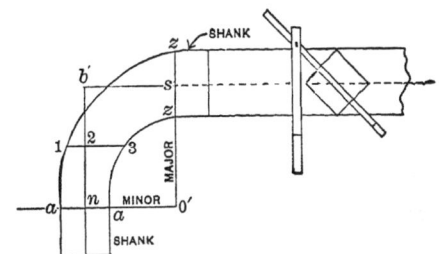

Fig. 187.—Method of Laying Out Face Mold
with Ostandier

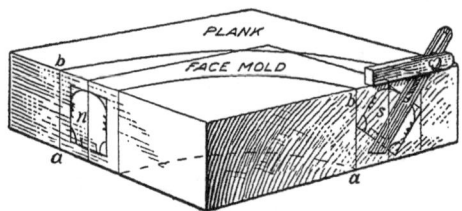

Fig. 188.—Face Mold Shown Applied to Plank.

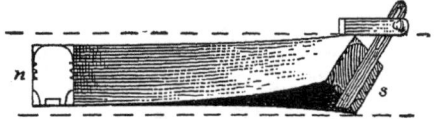

Fig. 189.—Showing the Wreath Squared
and the Bevel Applied at One End.

At the end n a bevel is not required. The wreath, squared, with a bevel at end s, and without one at end n, appears in Fig. 189.

CHAPTER XII

SHOWING A METHOD TO CONSTRUCT A SCROLL WREATH

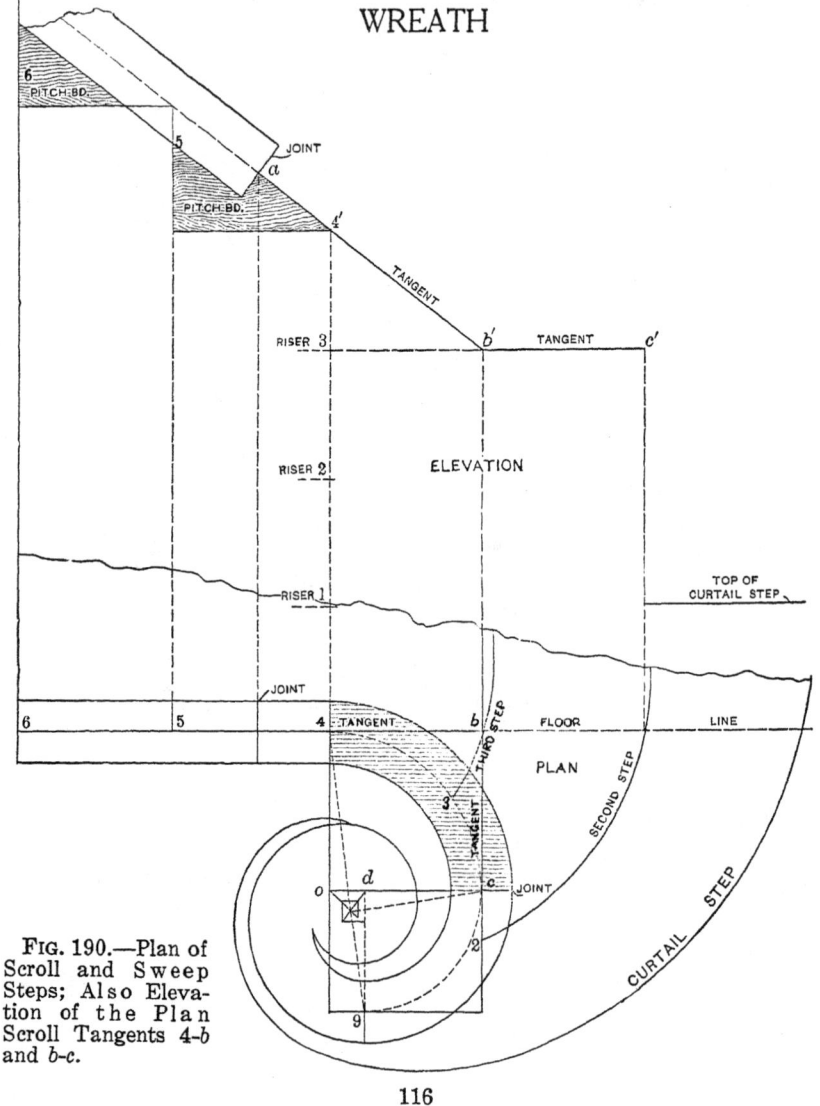

FIG. 190.—Plan of Scroll and Sweep Steps; Also Elevation of the Plan Scroll Tangents 4-*b* and *b-c*.

A partial plan and elevation of a stairway starting with a scroll curve and a few sweep steps is illustrated in Fig. 190. The laying-out of the face mold for the scroll wreath in this example demonstrates the adaptability of the principle involved in the development of a section, cut obliquely through a square block.

The most simple method to describe a scroll is shown in Fig. 191, viz., measure from *A* to *8* a distance equal to the width desired for the scroll; for example, *18* in. Divide this into eight equal parts, represented by numbers *1, 2, 3, 4,* etc. Find the

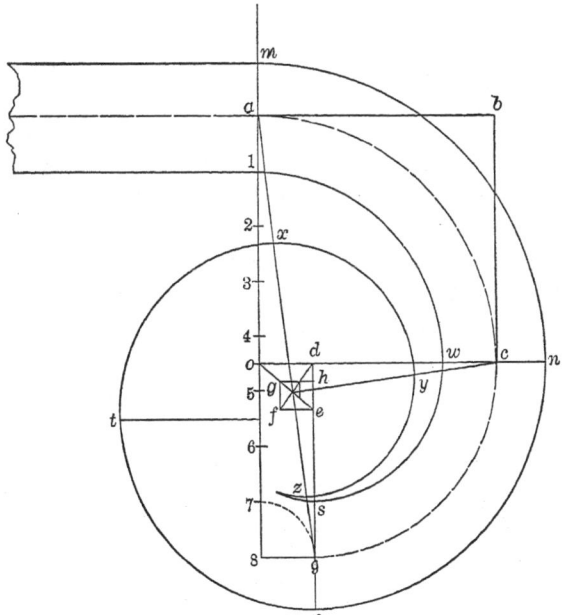

FIG. 191.—Diagram Showing How to Lay Out a Handrail Scroll.

center between the fourth and fifth divisions, indicated at *o*; from *o* draw a perpendicular line to *n*, and take *o* for a center, and with *o a* as radius describe the quadrant curve from *a* to *c*.

On each side of *a*, place half the width of the rail, indicated at *1* and *m*; from the same center *o* draw the quadrant curves shown from *m* to *n* and from *I* to *w*. Draw a line from *9* to *d*; also from *9* to *a*, and take *d* for the second center, and *d n* for the radius, and draw the quarter turn from n to r. Again take d as center, and with $d\ w$ as radius draw the quarter turn from w to s.

To find the third center, draw a line from c square with the line $9\ a$, and through the point of intersection draw a line from o to e; take e for a third center, and draw the quarter curve from r to t.

To find the fourth center, draw a line from d to f and from e to f, and take f for the fourth center, and draw the quarter turn from t to x.

Take g for the fifth center, and draw the quarter curve from x to y. Take h for the sixth center, and draw the quarter turn from y to z, thus completing the inside and outside curves of the scroll rail.

After drawing the scroll upon a thick piece of pasteboard or thin piece of wood, use it as a pattern or templet upon a drawing board, and trace the complete scroll to define the plan and center line of the scroll rail, indicated in Fig. 190. The center line in Fig. 191, from a through c to the point 9, indicates the center line of the stringer, as well as the center line of the rail, from 4 through c to the point 9 in Fig. 190. Upon this center line locate the risers, in Fig. 190, at 4, 3, and 2, and draw the sweep of each riser, shown by the curves of the steps. The curve of the scroll contains four risers; the fourth riser is placed in the springing of the scroll.

Erect a perpendicular line upon the springing point 4, Fig. 190, and measure upon it to $4'$, the height of the four risers contained in the scroll curve. Place the pitch board at $4'$, and draw the pitch of the straight steps through $4'$ to b'. From b' draw the level line to c', and make it equal in length to the line $b\ c$ of the plan. The line $4'\ b'$ is the elevation of the tangent 4 b, and the line $b'\ c'$ is the elevation of the tangent $b\ c$.

To lay out the face mold, in Fig. 192, make $a\ 4'\ b'$ equal to $a\ 4'\ b'$ of Fig. 190, and at right angles to it draw the line $b'\ c'$, equal in length to $b'\ c'$ of Fig. 190. Complete the square by drawing a line from c' to o and from o to 4. The line $4'\ b'$ in Fig. 192 represents on the face mold the raking tangent shown at $4'$ b' in Fig. 190, and the line $b'\ c'$ represents the level tangent $b'\ c'$ of Fig. 190.

The angle at b' is the angle required between the tangent upon the face mold, to give them the right direction to square the joints at each end.

The line c' o is the major axis, and the line o $4'$ is the minor axis. At $4'$ on the minor axis make the mold equal in width to that of the straight rail of the flight, and at the end c' make c' n and c' m equal to m n of diagram D, on the long edge of the bevel.

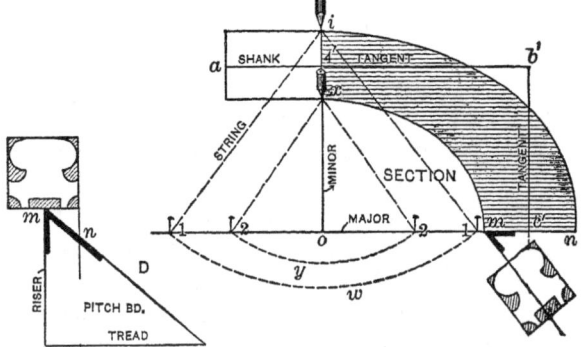

FIG. 192.—Face Mold for the Wreath Rail.

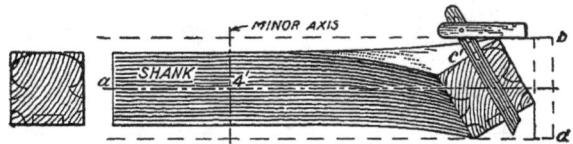

FIG. 193.—Showing How the Wreath is Squared.

To draw the curves of the face mold proceed as follows: place on the dividers the distance o n of the major axis, fix one leg of the dividers in i on the minor axis, and describe the arc w indicated by the dotted line, and cutting the major axis in the points 1 and 1. Place the pins and strings at 1 and 1, and extend strings to i, and from this point describe the outside curve from 3 to n. For the inside curve, place on the dividers the distance shown on the major axis from o to m; fix one leg of the dividers in the point x on the minor axis, and draw the arc y, cutting the major axis in the points 2 and 2. In these points place the pins with string attached, and extend to x on the minor axis, and describe the inside curve from x to m.

Measure from $4'$ to a distance equal to the shank $4'$ a of the elevation, Fig. 190. Make the joint at a square to the tangent $4'$ b', and at the end c' square to the tangent b' c', thus completing the laying-out of the face mold.

The bevel to square the wreath is shown in diagram D to be the upper angle of the pitch board, and it is applied to the end c', in Fig. 192.

In Fig. 193, the wreath is squared by applying the bevel to the end c' towards the inside of the wreath, and the distance from d to b in this figure indicates the thickness of plank required for the wreath. The square section of the rail at the end a, in addition to showing that a bevel is unnecessary at this point, also indicates that the wreath when squared should be kept in the center of the plank, from end to end.

The wreath extends above the curve in Fig. 190, from 4 to the joint at a; and as the bottom tangent b' c' is a level tangent, the wreath at the end c is level, after it is squared, and therefore butts square to the remaining level portion of the scroll and curve, and is an exact duplicate of the unshaded curve of the scroll in Fig. 190.

According to the construction in the elevation of Fig. 190, the scroll rail when in position stands above the top of the curtail steps, a distance equal to 2 risers, in addition to the length of the balusters of the straight flight. Assuming the length of the short balusters of the flight to be 2 ft. 4 in., then the balusters upon the curtail step, directly under the scroll curve, must be 2 ft. 4 in., plus the depth of two risers.

This treatment of a scroll rail may not be the best, but it is certainly the most simple. A great many stairbuilders and architects maintain that a scroll rail, to give the best effect when in position, should follow the nosing of the steps, so that the balusters all around the curve are the same length as those of the straight flight adjoining.

CHAPTER XIII

A SECOND METHOD TO CONSTRUCT A SCROLL WREATH

In Fig. 194 a second treatment of a scroll wreath is presented. In this the wreath part of the scroll is made to cover two quadrants of the curve instead of one.

By this method the balusters under and all around the scroll rail are the same length as those of the flight. The effect of this is to lower the scroll rail to the height of the balusters above the curtail step, instead of raising it two risers higher.

Fig. 194 shows only the center line of the scroll rail, all that is required to develop the face molds. The first quadrant is struck from *a* to *c*, with *o* as center; the second quadrant is struck from *c* to *e*, the point *2* as center. Both quadrants are inclosed by tangents—the first by tangents *a b* and *b c*, and the second by tangents *c d* and *d e*.

To find the pitch of these tangents, it is necessary to transfer them to the floor line, where *a b* is already in position. To transfer the other tangents make *b, c', d', e'* on the floor line, equal to *b, c, d, e* around the plan of the scroll, and erect indefinite perpendicular lines upon each point on the floor line. This operation is called the "unfolding" of the tangents. Measure from the springing point of the scroll, the height of the four risers, from *a* to *a'*. Place the pitch board of the flight at *a'*, and draw the pitch of the flight to *d''*. From *d''* draw a level line to *e''*. These last lines represent the pitch of the plan tangents. The bottom line from *d'* to *e''* is level and its position is at a height of half the thickness of the rail above the top of the curtail step. This indicates that the scroll rail when in position follows the nosing of the steps contained in the scroll curve, and that the level portion of the scroll rail is the height of the short balusters of the flight, from the top of the curtail step.

The wreath in this operation is made in two sections. The top section extends from a'' to the joint c'', and it has two equally inclined tangents. The bottom section extends from

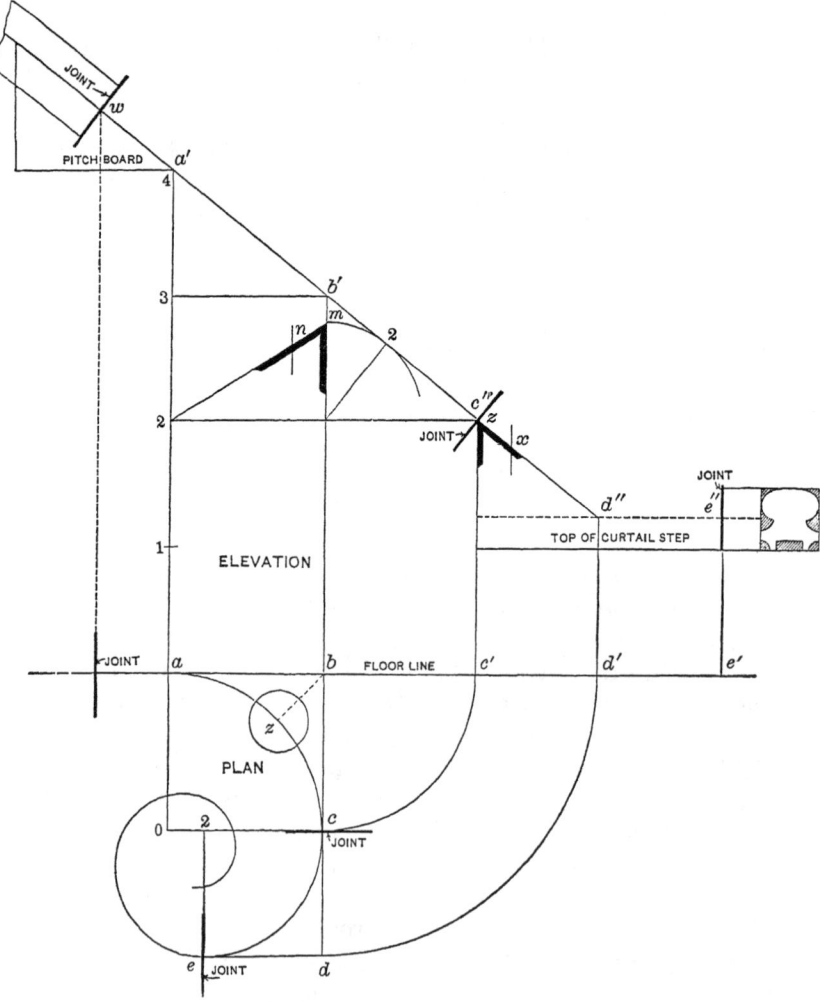

FIG. 194.—Plan and Elevation of Scroll Hand Rail Covering Two Quadrants.

the joint at c'' to the joint at e'', and has one tangent inclined uniformly with the two upper tangents, while the other tangent is level (as shown from d'' to e''), to butt plumb with the level portion of the scroll rail. To transfer these tangents to the face mold, and find the angle upon the face mold between them, is the main problem in the construction of wreathed hand rails.

Fig. 195 illustrates the method of finding the angle between the two inclined tangents a' b' and b' c'' of the upper wreath, shown in Fig. 194. In Fig. 195, draw the straight line X Y and transfer to it from the pitch line of the tangents in the previous figure, the point w, a', b', 2 and c''. From the point 2 drop a perpendicular line to c'' to connect b c'', thus forming the required angle between the tangents a b and b c'' upon the face mold, indicated at b, draw parallel lines to the tangents, from a to o and from o to c''.

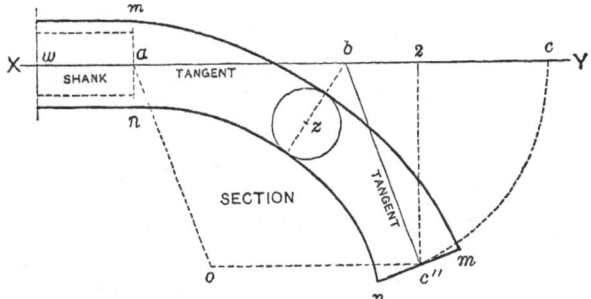

FIG. 195.—Face Mold Drawn by the Use of a Lath Bent to Touch Three Points Found to be Contained in the Curve.

To draw the curves of the face mold make b z of Fig. 195 equal to b z of Fig. 194. With z as a center, and a radius equal to half the width of the rail, describe the circle. The diameter of this circle determines the width of the mold at this point.

The width of the mold at each end is found from the bevel at m n of Fig. 194. Place the length of m n on each side of a and c'' in Fig. 195, as shown at n c'' m and at n a m. Take a flexible lath and bend it to touch the points m and m at each end, and the circumference of the circle Z, and run a pencil beside the bent lath for the outside curve. Again bend the lath to touch n and n, and the circumference of the same circle Z, and trace the curve for the inside.

At the end a a straight piece is shown added to the mold from a to w; this is called the shank, and the length is the distance from a' to w of Fig. 194. The joint at w is made square to the tangent $a\ b$, and at the end c'' to the tangent $b\ c''$, thus completing the face mold.

To construct the wreath the mold is placed on a piece of plank (of sufficient thickness for the purpose), and used as a templet to cut out of the plank the material for the wreath. It is cut square to the face of the plank all around, including sides and ends; then the bevels are applied to the ends or joints, at w and at c'', as shown in Fig. 196. The wreath is squared by cutting off the slab of wood from each end to the minor axis at $z;$ it is necessary during the operation to keep the wreath in the center of the plank.

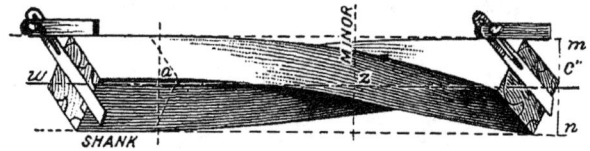

Fig 196.—The Wreath in Center Plank After it is Squared and Showing Application of the Bevels.

In Fig. 197 the face mold for the bottom wreath is laid out. This portion is indicated in Fig. 194, from the joint at c'' to the joint at e'', and the wreath has the upper tangent $c''\ d''$ inclined, and the bottom tangent $d''\ e''$ level.

The angle between the tangents, required upon the face mold for a wreath, when one tangent is inclined and the other level, is always a right angle. Referring again to Fig. 197, draw the square represented by the letters $c,\ d,\ e,\ o,$ in which $c\ d$ and $e\ o$ are made equal in length to the inclined tangent $c''\ d''$ of Fig. 194, and $d\ e$ and $o\ c$ are made equal in length to the level tangent $d''\ e''$ of Fig. 194. The angle at d in Fig. 197 is the required angle between the tangents of the face mold to square the joints at each end. The line $o\ c$ is the minor axis, and the line $o\ e$ the major axis.

To draw the curves of the mold in this figure, using string and pins, find the points on the major axis at which to place the pins. First make the width of the mold on the axis, at $1\ 2$, equal to the width of the straight rail, and the width at the end e'' equal to twice the length of $z\ x$, on the long side of the bottom bevel in Fig. 194.

To find the points on the major axis for placing the pins for the outside curve, take upon the dividers the length $o\ z$ on the major axis, Fig. 197. Fix the dividers in the point l on the minor axis, and draw the arc w indicated by the dotted line, cutting the major axis at the point a and a, the foci of the ellipse that constitute the curve of the face mold. From the pins in these points, extend the strings to l on the minor axis, and with a pencil at this point describe the outside curve from l to z.

To find the points upon the major axis at which to fix the pins for the inside curve, take in the dividers the length $o\ x$ from the major axis. Fix one leg in the point 2 on the minor axis, and draw the arc s indicated by the dotted line cutting the major axis in the points b and b; from the pins at these points, extend the strings to 2 on the minor axis; place the pencil at this point, and describe the inside curve from 2 to x.

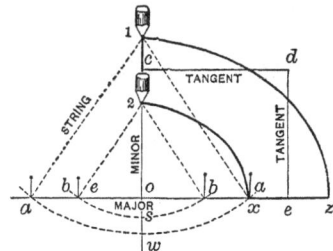

FIG. 197.—Face Mold Drawn by the Use of String and Pins.

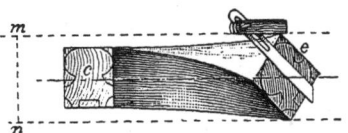

FIG. 198.—The Bottom Wreath After it is squared, Showing Bevel Applied to One End Only.

Because the tangent $c\ d$ on this face mold is inclined, and the tangent $d\ e$ is level, as shown in Fig. 194, it requires only one bevel to square the wreath; it is applied to the end e only, in Fig. 198, and toward the inside of the wreath. The other end c is vertical, owing to its position on the minor axis, and in consequence a bevel is unnecessary.

In Fig. 199 the method of drawing a face mold similar to the one indicated in the pervious figure by means of "ordinates" or level lines is shown. Draw the square $c\ d\ e\ o$ to equal the square $2\ c\ d\ e$ of the plan, Fig. 194, and draw the plan curve of the rail, from c to c. From d draw the pitch of the inclined tangent, $c''\ d''$ of Fig. 194.

Draw lines (any number) parallel to the level plan tangent $c\ d$ across the rail, at *3, 1, 2*, etc., and up to the pitch line $c''\ d$. From the points on the pitch line where these lines intersect

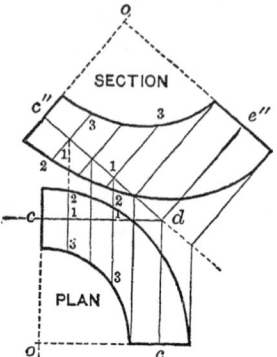

draw lines parallel to the level tangent $d\ e''$ of the face mold. Make each one equal in length to its correlative plan line, as *312* and *312*; and through the points *2 2* and *3 3*, etc., on the section, trace the inside and outside curves of the face mold.

Fig. 199.—Face Mold Drawn by Means of Level Lines or Ordinates.

The principle of operation involved in this construction may be applied to the laying-out of a face mold for all kinds of wreaths, by finding a level line on the plan and the corresponding level line on the section, and making the one on the section the same length as the one on the plan. The lines $m\ n$ in Figs. 196 and 198 indicate the thickness of the plank required for these wreaths.

CHAPTER XIV

A THIRD METHOD TO CONSTRUCT
A SCROLL WREATH

A third method of treatment for a scroll hand rail to stand over and above the four sweep steps contained in the scroll curve is illustrated in Fig. 200. The first method shows the construction of a wreath standing over and above one quarter turn only of the scroll curve, from c to 4 in Fig. 190; the second method illustrates the construction of a wreath in two sections standing over and above two quarter turns, shown in Fig. 194, from a to e.

A method to construct a wreath in one section, to stand over and above a part of the scroll curve, more than a quarter turn, and less than two quarter turns, is indicated in Fig. 200 from c to h, the curve of the center line of the wreath is drawn from the center o. The plan tangents are not at right angles to one another in this, as they are in the other operations.

From o draw a line to h, and at right angles to it draw the level tangent h g. The other tangent is the line from g to c, and the angle between them at g is an acute angle—that is, an angle less than a right angle. Draw a line from the center o to e, parallel to the level tangent h g. This last line is the plan of the minor axis, because it is a level line drawn parallel to the level tangent from the center o of the curve.

Erect perpendicular lines from c, e, and g; and upon the line drawn from c measure to the point 4, the height of the four risers contained in the curve of the scroll, in Fig. 190. From 4 draw with the pitch board the two steps marked 5 and 6, which are outside of the scroll curve. Draw a side view of the straight rail with its center line upon the nosing of the steps.

Determine the height for the eye of the scroll, above the top of the curtail step, shown from riser 1 to a, upon the line c c. From a draw a level line through g' to h', and the portion from g' to h' represents the elevation of the plan tangent g h. It is made the same length as the plan tangent $g\ h$ because it is level, and it is located at the height of 6 in. above the top of the curtail step.

To find the elevation of the other plan tangent $c\ g$, draw a

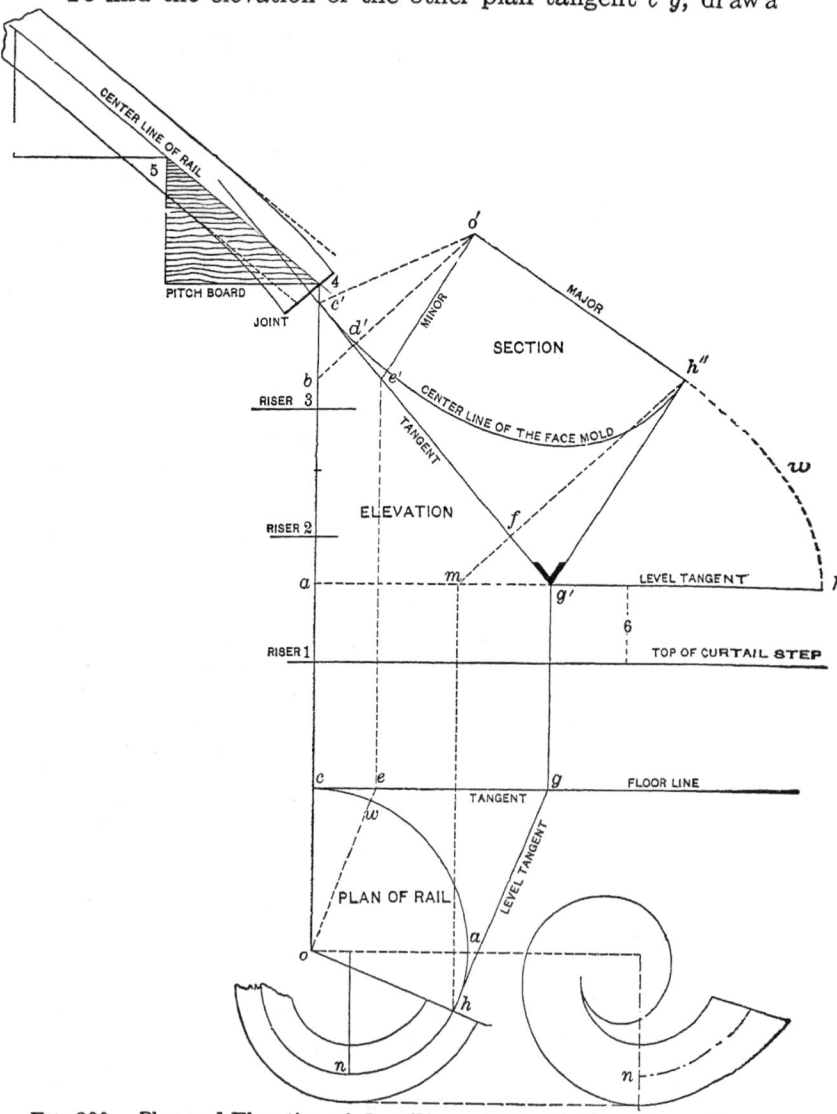

FIG. 200.—Plan and Elevation of One Piece of Wreath Covering a Curve Greater Than a Quadrant, the Curve Being a Part of a Scroll.

line from g' upon the level tangent to c' and beyond, to cut the center line of the straight rail of the flight. This line is the elevation and pitch of the plan tangent $c\ g$. Draw the easement upon the straight rail to align with the inclined tangent $c'\ g'$, and make the joint square to the line of the tangent.

The pitch and length of the tangents $c'\ g'$ and $g'\ h'$ represent the face mold tangents; the former inclined, and the latter level.

To draw the face mold, the lengths of these tangents are transferred to it, and the angle between the two, required upon the face mold to square the joints, is found as follows: From h in the plan, Fig. 200, draw the line $h\ m$ square to the floor line, and from m draw the line $m\ F\ h''$ square to the inclined tangent $g'\ c'$.

Place one leg of the compasses in g', extend the other to h' and turn over to h'', shown by the arc w; connect h'' and g'. This last line is the level tangent transferred to the face mold, while the other tangent of the face mold is the inclined tangent $g'\ c'$. The angle between the two, required upon the face mold to square the joints at each end, is at g'.

Draw a line from e' to o' parallel to the line from g' to h'', making it equal in length to the line $o\ e$ of the plan. The line $e'\ o'$ of the section is the minor axis of the face mold. Draw the major square to the minor from o' to h''. The center line of the face mold is drawn upon the section from c' through e' on the minor axis to h''. The method to draw the face mold complete is shown in Fig. 201.

Draw the straight line $X\ Y$ and transfer to it the points 4, c', d', e', f and g' from the inclined tangent, Fig. 200. From f draw the line $f\ h$ square to $X\ Y$. Draw $d\ o$ from d square to $X\ Y$. Connect o with e, making it equal in length to $o\ e$ of the plan, Fig. 200; also connect g with h, making it equal in length to the plan level tangent $h\ g$.

The line $o\ e$ is the minor axis, and by drawing a line from o to h square to the minor axis the major axis is shown from o to h. The angle between the tangents is at g, and the process to develop the section is similar, up to this point, to the process described in Fig. 200.

The joints of the face mold are made square to the tangents, at h to the tangent $g\ h$, and at c to the tangent $g\ c$.

The width upon the minor axis is the same as the width of
the rail, and it is necessary to know the width of the face mold
at each end.   To find the width at the end c, measure from c
to m and from c to n, the distance m n upon the long edge of the
bevel shown in Fig. 203.   To find the width of the end h, place
on each side of h, at h z and h x, a length equal to z z, on the
upper bevel in Fig. 203.

These two bevels are shown applied to the wreath after it
is cut square to the face of the plank at each end, in Fig. 202.

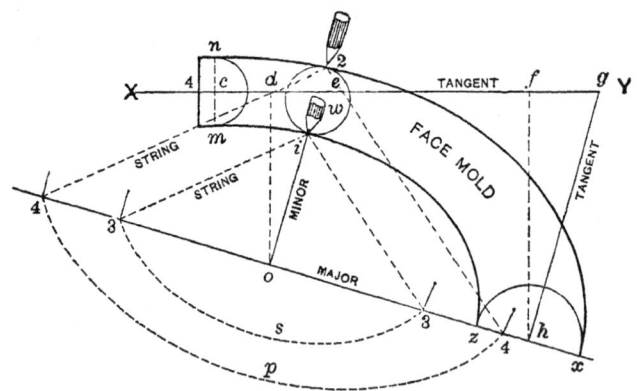

FIG. 201.—Face Mold for the Wreath Shown in Fig. 200.

To find the points at which to fix the pins on the major axis,
to draw the elliptical curves of the face mold, take the distance
o z of the major axis, Fig. 201, on the dividers, and with the
point i on the minor axis as a center describe the arc s, shown
by the dotted line, cutting the major axis in the points 3 and 3.
Place pins with strings attached in these points, and extend
the strings to the point i on the minor axis, and from this point
describe with a pencil the inside curve from m to z.

Take the distance o x of the major axis in the dividers, and
with point 2 on the minor axis as a center describe the arc p,
cutting the major axis in the points 4 and 4.   Place pins with
strings in these points and extend the strings to the point 2 on
the minor axis, and with a pencil describe the outside curve
from n to x.

The distance from c to 4 at the end c of the mold is made equal to c' 4 of Fig. 200, to join the easement of the straight rail of the flight.

The face mold is now complete, as shown in Fig. 201, and is ready to be used as a templet to cut out of the plank, square to its face, the material for the wreath.

Fig. 202 is a view of the wreath after it is squared, showing the bevels applied at each end.

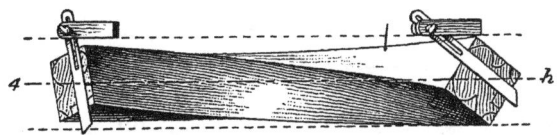

Fig. 202.—The Wreath After it is Squared, Showing Application of the Bevels, Also that the Wreath is Kept in the Center of the Plank.

Fig. 200 shows that the wreath is to cover the distance from c to h, and that the tangent h g is a level tangent. Owing to this condition, the wreath after it is squared is level at the point h, and therefore butts plumb and square to the remaining level portion of the scroll.

The wreath under consideration differs from all preceding examples. The pitch of the inclined tangent c' g', in the elevation of Fig. 200, is much steeper than the pitch of the straight rail of the flight; and the easement in the straight rail is constructed to align with the pitch of the tangent c' g'; this operation is necessary to guarantee a true square butt joint at c', or rather 4, between the rail of the flight and the wreath at the end c'.

Another difference between this wreath and those preceding is the length of its plan curve, shown in Fig. 200, from c to h, to be more than a quarter turn. This greater length of curve causes the tangents c g and g h to be at an acute angle to each other at g, instead of at a right angle, as in all the other examples.

To thoroughly understand the meaning of all the lines in Fig. 200, a view has been prepared, Fig. 204, representing an irregular shaped block cut obliquely to one side, indicated from c to g, and level to another side, from g to h.

Compare this figure with Fig. 200; trace upon it every point and line to correspond to those bearing the same reference letters in Fig. 204, and the past supposed mystery attending wreath construction becomes the very simple solution of developing an oblique section, cut through a solid block.

The bevels shown in Fig. 203, at z and m, and in Fig. 202, applied to the ends of the wreaths, are found as follows: Make the base line in Fig. 203 equal to o c, Fig. 200 (which is the radius of the plan curve); make c m equal to b d', Fig. 200, and c z equal to a b in the same figure. Connect z o and m o thus determining the bevels at z and m. The bevel m is applied to the end c' of the wreath, because its altitude is

DIAGRAM D
Fig. 203

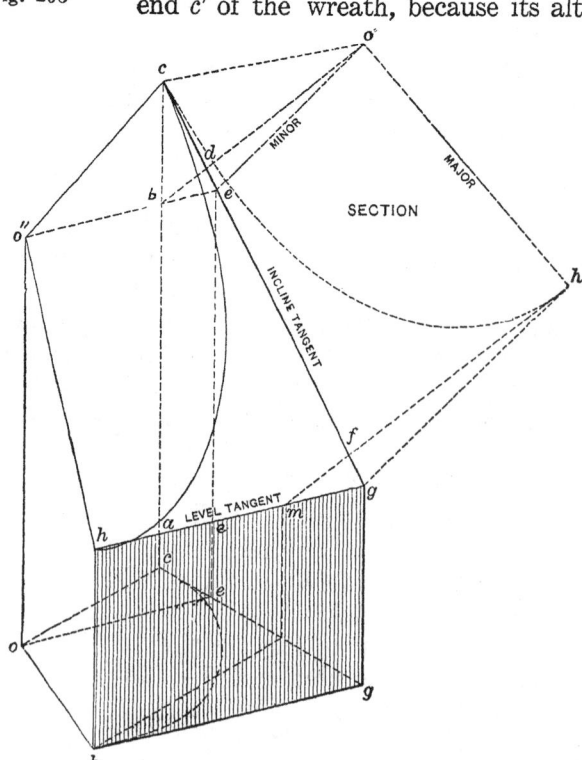

FIG. 204.—A View of Fig. 60 Folded in a Solid Block, Showing Graphically the Method of Developing a Section Cut Oblique to One Side and its Application to Handrailing.

measured from b to the tangent g' c', and because the altitude of bevel z is measured from b to a, a point continued upon the level tangent g' h'. It indicates that this bevel is applied to the end h of the wreath. The bevels in all cases are applied to the tangent from which their respective altitudes are measured.

CHAPTER XV

A WREATH RAIL OVER A 12-INCH CYLINDER CONTAINING EIGHT WINDERS

Fig. 205 represents the plan of a *12*-in. cylinder and a few adjacent steps; also the development of the tangents for one

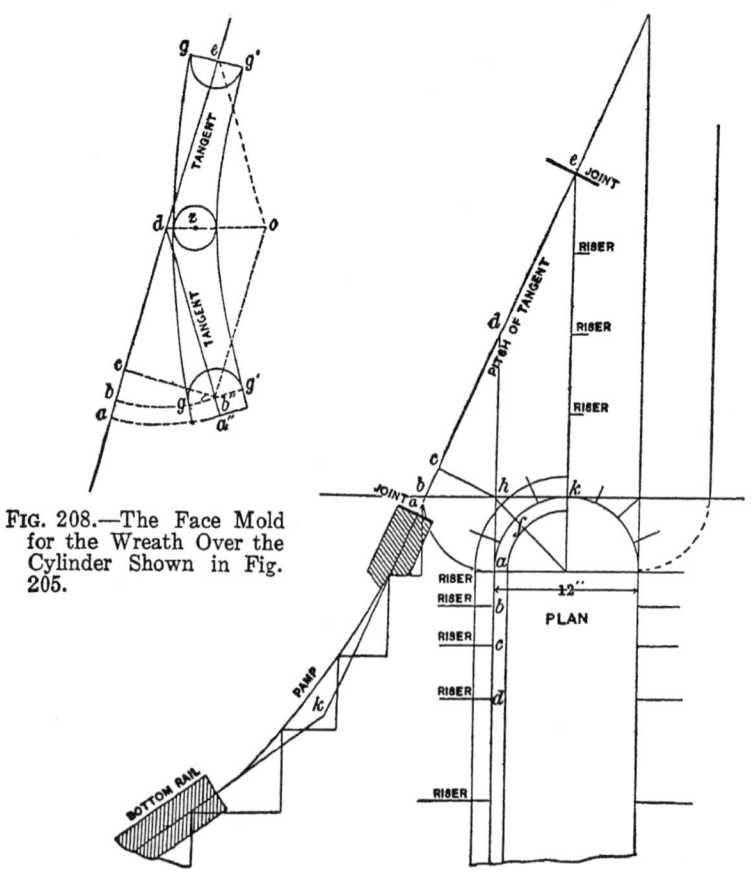

FIG. 208.—The Face Mold for the Wreath Over the Cylinder Shown in Fig. 205.

FIG. 205.—Plan of Stairway Having a 12-inch Cylinder Between Two Flights, the Cylinder Containing Eight Winders.—Showing the Method of Unfolding the Tangents and Obtaining the Pitch Over the Cylinder.

section of the wreath, for example, b to e. The adjacent steps are reduced to secure equal lengths for the balusters, and in order that the portion of the rail connecting with the wreaths may be gracefully curved to form a ramp between the center

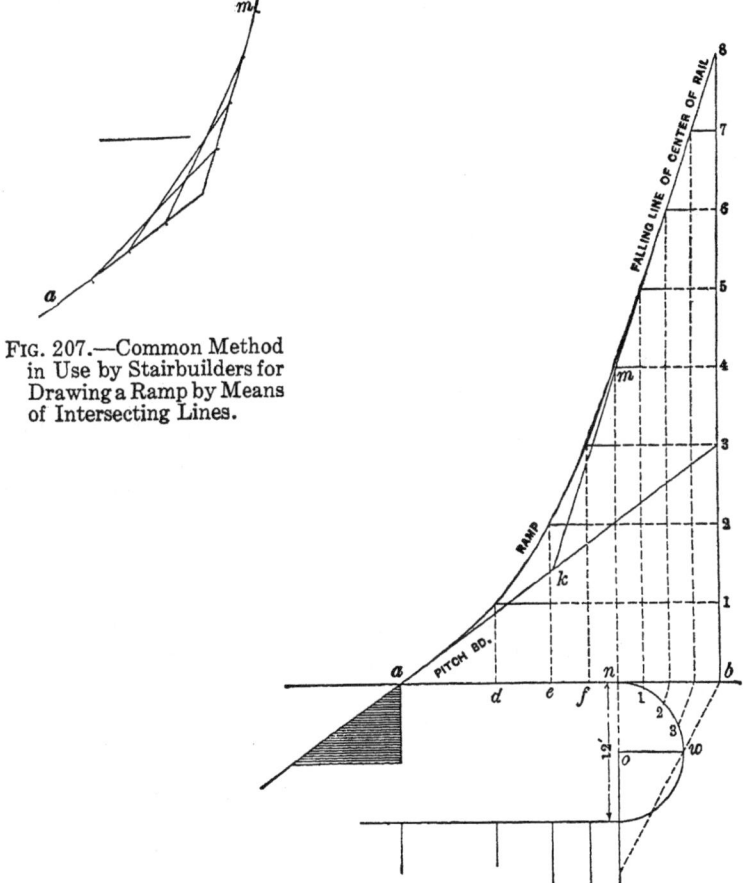

FIG. 207.—Common Method in Use by Stairbuilders for Drawing a Ramp by Means of Intersecting Lines.

FIG. 206.—Diagram Showing How to Reduce Steps Adjoining a Cylinder so as to Secure a Pleasing Appearance to the Finished Rail.

line of the straight rail and the pitch line of the developed tangents, prolonged from a to k, where the intersection occurs.

A very simple method is shown in Fig. 206 for reducing steps adjacent to cylinders. Draw the line *a b* from *o* as center, describe the center line of the wreath with a *6*-in. radius; make *n b* equal to the stretchout of the quadrant *n w*. Upon *b* erect the ine *b 8*, equal in length to eight risers; at *a* place the pitch board and continue its pitch to *3*. Now bisect *a 3* in *k*, and draw a line from *8* to *k*, and the curve from *m* to *a*. The curve is described by intersecting lines, in Fig. 207, or by drawing a line at right angles to *a k* from *a*, and another at right angles to the line *m 8* from *m*. Where these lines intersect is a center that may be used to describe the curve from *a* to *m*. In Fig. 206 draw a level line from *1 2 3 4*, etc., to intersect the curve and the straight line from *m* to *8*. From each intersection drop a line to the line *a b*, and the dimensions of the reduced steps adjacent to the cylinder, as at *d e f*, etc., are found.

Return to Fig. 205 and place the distance *d e f* along the plan line of the stringer, and draw the elevation as follows: The height from *k* to *e* is made equal to the height of four risers; that is one-half the number contained in the cylinder. The side plan tangent, *h a*, is revolved to *b*. Then the line *b d e* is drawn, which represents the pitch line of the two tangents *b d* and *d e*, respectively. From *h* the line *h c* is drawn square to the pitch line of the tangents.

To lay out the face mold, transfer the points, *a, b, c, d, e* from the pitch line of the tangents in Fig. 205 to Fig. 208 and from *c* in this figure drop a line to *b''*. Place one point of the compasses in *d*, extend the other to *b*, and turn over to *b''*; connect *b''* with *d*. Draw *b'' o* parallel to *c d*, and *e o* parallel to *e d*; then connect *d* with *o*; make *d z* equal to *h z* in Fig. 205, and on *z* as center draw a circle having a radius equal to one-half the width of the plan rail, and on each side of *b''* as *b'' g* and *b'' g'* place the distance *c d* taken from the bevel in Fig. 209, and the same on each side of *e*, at *e g* and *e g'*. Bend a lath to touch the points *g* and *g*; also the circumference of the circle, for the outside of the mold, and the points *g'* and *g'* for the inside curve of the mold. The joint at *e* is made square to the tangent *d b''*. The distance from *b''* to *a* indicates a piece of straight rail added to the mold to extend the joints outside the cylinder shown in Fig. 205 from b'' to a.

The bevel in Fig. 209 is found as follows: Make $n\,h$ equal the radius of the cylinder, and $h\,c$ equal $h\,c$ in Fig. 205; connect $c\,n$. The bevel c is applied to each end of the mold at

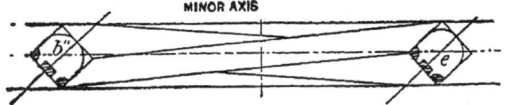

FIG. 210.—View of the Wreath After it is Squared, Showing How it is Done by Applying the Bevels to the Ends; in This Case Reversely.

FIG. 200.—Bevel for the Wreath Shown in Fig. 208.

the end b'' in the direction of the inside, and at the end e in the direction of the outside, all clearly indicated in Fig. 210, where a view of the wreath after it is squared is given. In this figure the center of the wreath coincides with the center of the plank—a condition that must be kept in mind when squaring the wreath.

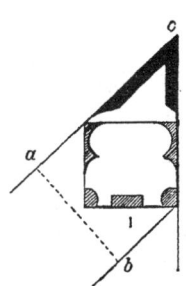

FIG. 211. — Diagram Illustrating a Method to Ascertain the Thickness of Plank Required for a Wreath.

Fig. 211 shows a method for finding the thickness of the plank required for the wreath. The bevel at c is the one shown in Fig. 209. A square section of the rail is drawn, one side parallel with the blade of the bevel. The distance from a to b indicates the thickness of the plank. Fig. 212 is the plan and elevation of the cylinder and a number of the reduced steps adjacent to it on both sides, also the face molds laid out upon the pitch line of the tangents over and above the plan cylinder. It is presented here as an object lesson of the complete construction.

Fig. 213 is a plan of a drum, and Fig. 214 is the elevation. Around this drum the stringer for the cylinder is bent. There are various methods in use for bending these stringers; the one exhibited here is simple and easily executed. A piece of board, Fig. 215, is prepared by taking sufficient material from its back to leave a veneer thin enough to bend around the drum. The veneer is shown shaded in Fig. 213; blocks known as keys are glued upon it, and carefully joined to one another, until the entire space from *a* to *b*, Fig. 213, is

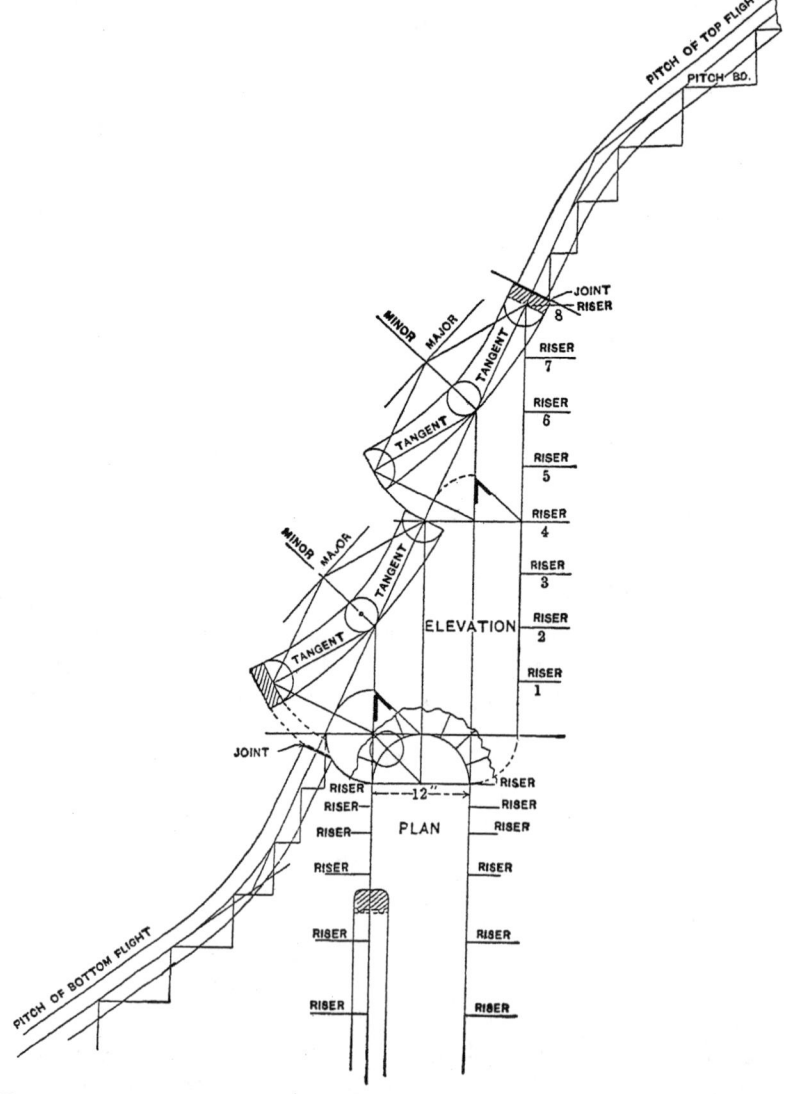

FIG. 212.—Diagram Illustrating the Complete Development of the Cylinder; Steps Adjoining; Tangets; Face Molds, and Bevels.

tightly filled. A few of these keys (indicated at a in Fig. 214) are made longer than the width of the stringer; through the overlapping ends of the keys, nails or screws may be driven.

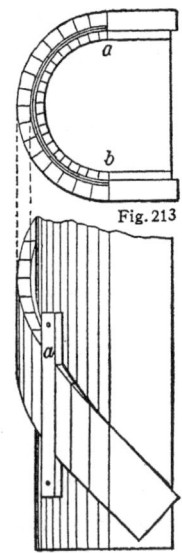

Fig. 213

FIGS. 213 and 214.—Plan and Elevation of the Drum to Bend the Stringer Around the Cylinder.

FIG. 215.—Showing the Veneer Prepared for Bending as Shown Around the Drum in Fig. 213.

securing in this manner the stringer to the drum until the glue is set.

CHAPTER XVI

SHOWING HOW TO CONSTRUCT A WREATH OVER A CYLINDER ADJOINING A LEVEL LANDING

Fig. 216 is a partial plan of very common stairway construction, including a cylinder on the bottom landing; the wreath winds around the cylinder, from a level landing rail, up to the rail of the flight adjoining.

In this construction it is important to place the risers in and around the cylinder to the best advantage, to facilitate the making of the wreath and to secure symmetry.

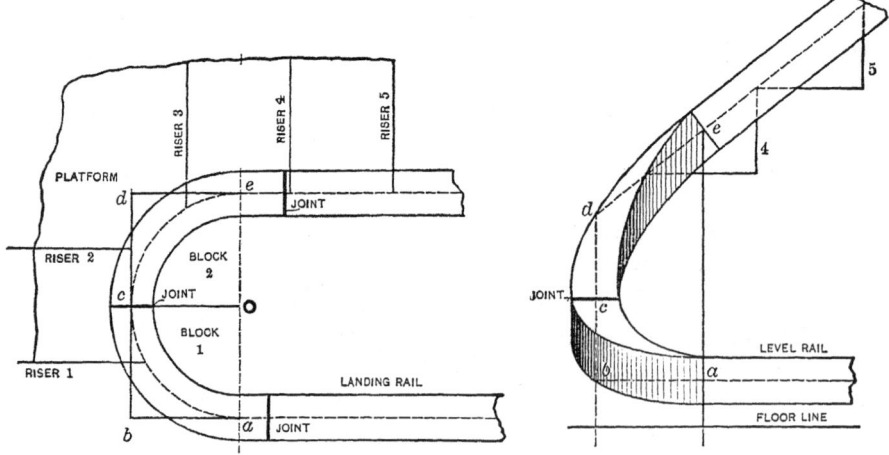

FIG. 216.—Plan of Cylinder and Steps Adjoining. FIG. 217.—Vertical Projection of the Wreaths.

By placing risers *2* and *3* at a distance from *d* equal to one-half the width of the tread, the best possible arrangement of the risers is obtained. The curve of the rail in Fig. 216 is drawn from the center *O*, and the center joint of the wreath is at *c*.

The tangents are at *a b, b c, c d* and *d e*, forming two squares; and the projection of the wreath is shown in Fig. 217,

140

the top angle of the pitch board and is to be applied to the end a' only. Only one bevel is required for the upper wreath also, but in this case it is to be applied to both ends because the two tangents are equally inclined. This bevel is found in Diagram D, by making o m equal to the length of any of the stretchout of the plan tangents, also the points *1, 2* and *3* to represent the risers within the cylinder, and from *3* in Fig. 218 measure to *6*, the height of three risers, and at *6* place the pitch board. Draw the pitch down over the steps to b', and from b' draw the level line to beyond a', to represent the center

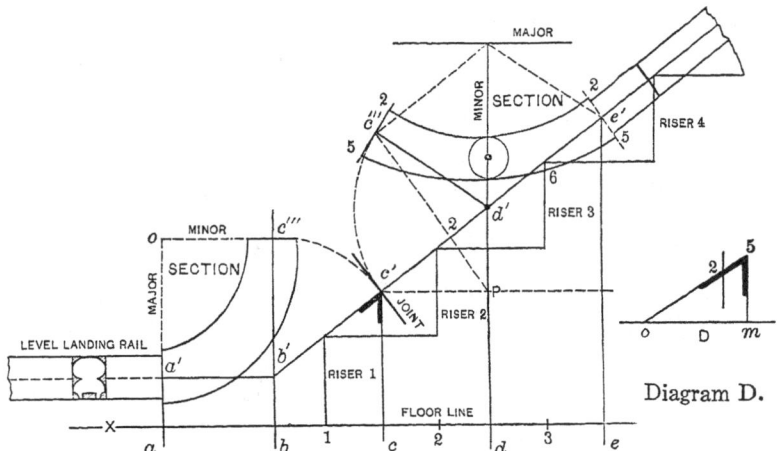

FIG. 218.—Showing Elevation of Steps, Pitch Line of Tangents and Face Molds.

line of the level landing rail. In this manner the length and pitch of each tangent required for the two face molds is obtained.

For the bottom wreath the two tangents thus found are at a' b' and b' c'. The tangent a' b' is level, and the tangent b' c' is inclined.

For the top wreath the tangents at c' d' and d' e' are inclined equally, and are of the same inclination as the tangent b' c' of the bottom wreath—a condition due to the necessity of joining the two wreaths at the point c'.

Only one bevel is required to square the bottom wreath,

because only one tangent is inclined. It is shown at c' to equal winding around the cylinder from the level landing up to the inclined rail of the adjoining flight.

Fig. 218 is the elevation of the steps and tangents. Referring to the diagram, let X Y represent the floor line. Transfer to it from Fig. 216 the distance a, b, c, d, e, to represent the plan tangents, or the radius of the cylinder; and m 5, equal to the length of the dotted line drawn square to the inclined tangent c'-d' from 2 to p, in the elevation of Fig. 218. Connecting 5 with o, the angle at 5, defines the required bevel.

The face molds for the two wreaths in Fig. 218 are constructed upon the pitch line of the tangents. To lay out the bottom face mold, place one leg of the compasses in the point b', and extend the other to c'. Revolve the point c' to c''' and connect c''' with b'. The line c''' b' is the inclined tangent as required upon the face mold. The level tangent of the face mold is the level line a' b', and the angle required upon the mold between the two to square the joint is the right angle at b'.

Draw a line from c'' to o and from o to a', forming the square of the section. The line c'' o is the minor axis, and o a' is the major axis.

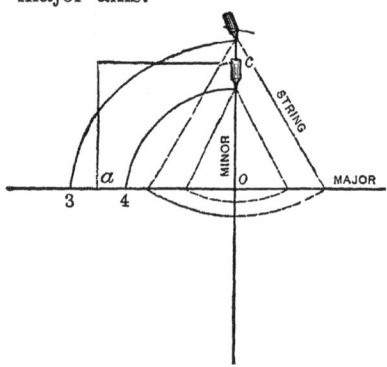

The curves of the molds are shown drawn with the strings and pins in Fig. 219.

The face mold for the top wreath is laid out in Fig. 218, by drawing a line from P to 2 and extending it to c'', square to the pitch line of the tangents. Now by placing one leg of the compasses in the point d' and extending the other to c', revolving the point c' to c'', and connecting c''' with d',

FIG. 219.—Face Mold for Bottom Wreath, the Curves Being Drawn by Means of Pins and String.

the tangent c' d' is transferred into the face mold. The other tangent of the mold is the line d' e'.

Square the joints with the tangents at each end, and deter-

mine the width by placing on each side of c''' and e the distance
2 5 shown on the bevel in diagram D.

The width of the mold upon the minor axis equals that of
the plain rail. Draw the curves with a lath or with string
and pins.

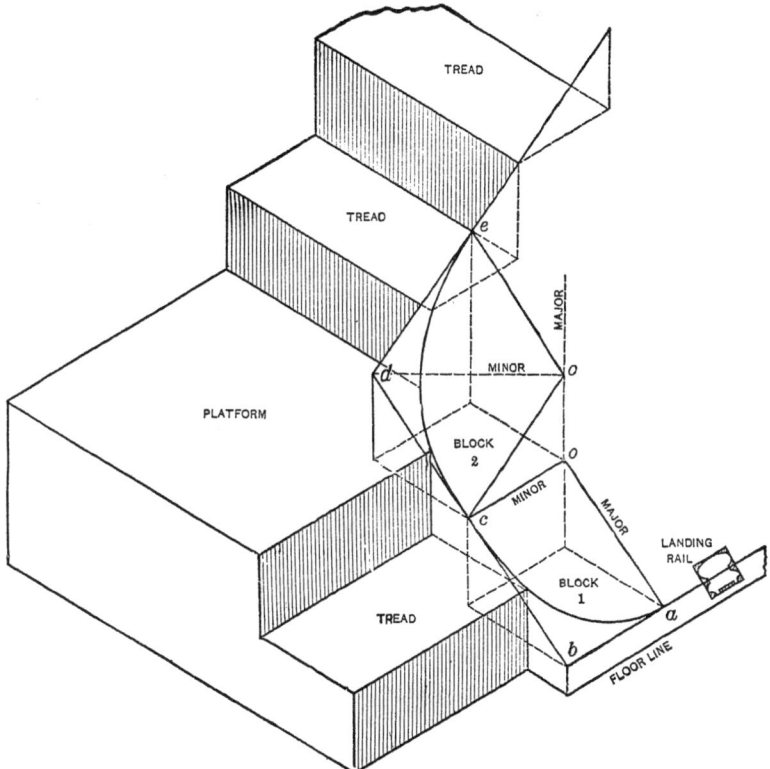

FIG. 220.—Isometric View of a Few Steps Within and Adjoining the Cylinder; the Sections Cut Through the Two Square Blocks; the Center Line
of Wreath Lying on the Inclined Plane of Sections, Illustrating the Adaptability of the Operations to the Construction of Wreathed Handrails.

In Fig. 220 the steps contained in the cylinder are shown,
also the square blocks *1* and *2*, as well as the sectional cuts
made through them to the pitch of the tangents in Fig. 218,
and the minor and major axes of each block, and the center
line of the two sections of the wreaths lying on the surface
of the sectional cuts from a through c to e.   The forms of these

sections in Fig. 218 appear upon the face molds bearing the same reference letters as in Fig. 220.

The same method as applied here for laying out a face mold for a bottom landing cylinder is equally effective when the cylinder is placed at the top landing, and the wreath winds around the cylinder from a level landing rail down to the flight adjoining.

CHAPTER XVII

WREATH FOR A STAIRWAY CONTAINING A CURVE MORE THAN A QUADRANT AT THE STARTING; AND A QUADRANT CURVE AT THE INTERSECTION OF TWO FLIGHTS

The plan is shown in Fig. 221, and the plan and developments of the stretchout curve at the bottom, in Fig. 222.

This curve contains *8* risers as shown in the plan, Fig. 221, from the newel to *c*. Their total height is shown in Fig. 222 from *c* to *c'*.

From the point *c'* draw a few of the straight steps with the pitch board, indicated by the shaded portions above the point *c'*. Prolong the pitch of these steps to *b'*, or to any point desired for the height of the wreath at the newel.

From *b'* draw the short line *b' b*, and from this point draw a line to the newel at *a*. This last line is the bottom level tangent, and because it is drawn from *b'* and evel it is the same height from *b* to *a*, a trifle higher than the third riser. This means that the wreath according to this arrangement is the distance from *b* to *b'*, higher above the nosing at the newel than at the end *c'*, where it is shown upon the nosing of the ninth step.

If the wreath is to follow the nosing line of the step, around the curve from *c* to *a*, then the pitch line *c' b'* must be continued beyond the point *b'* to *d*, and the level tangent drawn from *d* to *a*, indicated by the dotted line *d a*. By this process the height of the wreath at the newel *a* may be determined at will.

To lay out the face mold the bottom level tangent *b a* must be transferred to it from *b'* to *a'*, and it is accomplished by drawing a plumb line from *a* at the newel to *w*, and from *w* a line through *m* square to the pitched tangent *c' b'* to *a'*. Make *b' a'* equal in length to the plan tangent *b a*. The angle at *b'* between this line and the pitched tangent *b' c'* is the one required

145

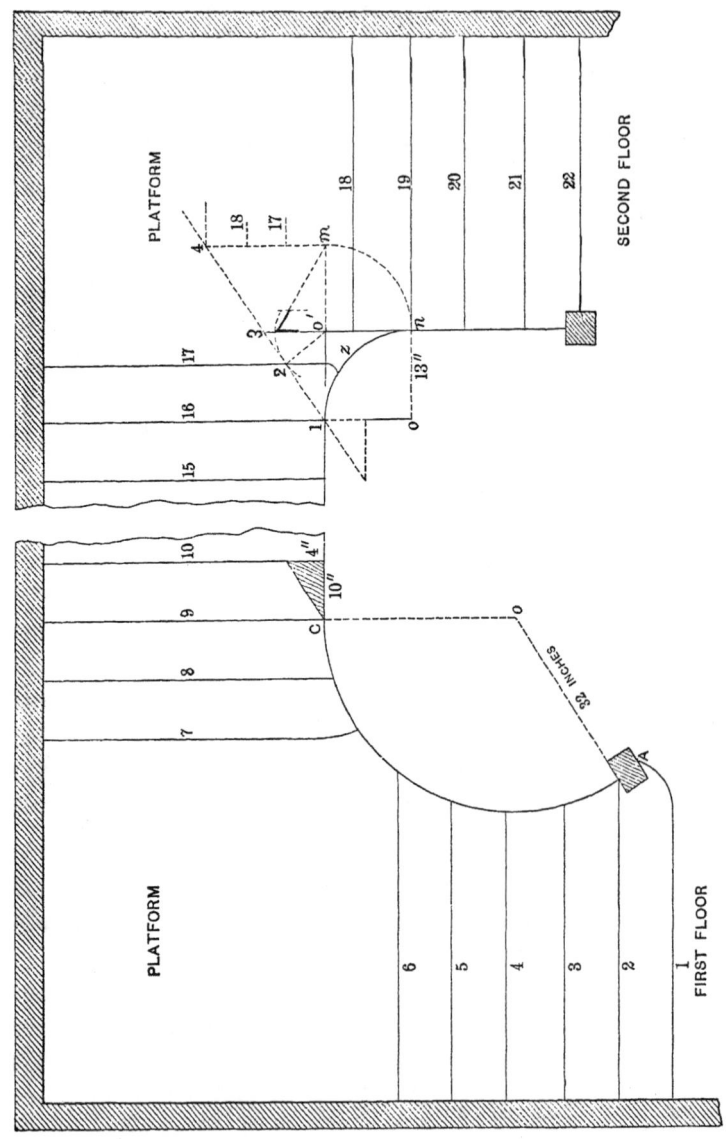

Fig. 221.—Plan of a Cylinder Stairway Containing Stretchout Curve More Than a Quadrant at the Starting, a Quarter Turn at the Intersection of the Two Flights and a Goose Neck Curve on the Rail Connecting the Newel of the Second Story Landing.

between the tangents of the face mold to square the joints at each end.

To find the major and minor axes, draw a line from the plan center O, parallel to the plan level tangent $a\ b$, shown by the

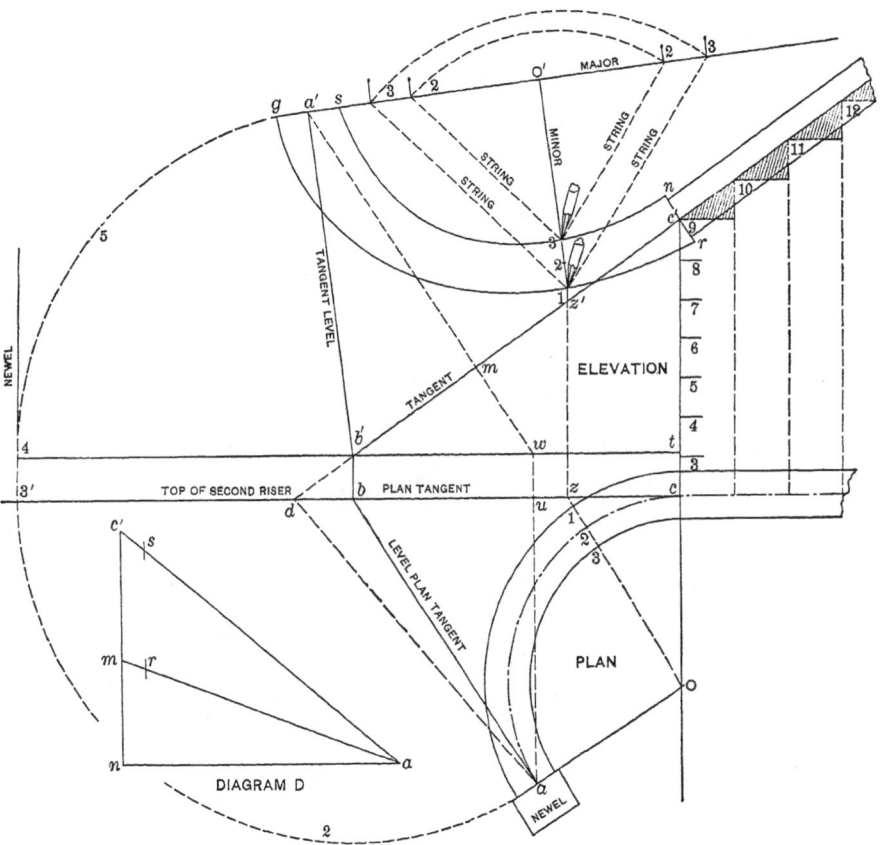

FIG. 222.—Plan, Elevation and Face Mold of the Stretchout Rail at the Starting of the Stairway Shown in the Previous Figure.

dotted line $O\ z$. This line is the plan of the minor axis. Draw from z the plumb line $z\ z'$, and draw $z'\ o'$ parallel to the level tangent $b'\ a'$ of the face mold, and make $z'\ o'$ equal in length to $z\ O$ of the plan. The line $z'\ o'$ is the minor axis, and a line from o' to a' gives the major axis.

Upon the minor axis mark the points *1, 2, 3*, at the same distance from *o'*, as the same figures are shown to be from the plan center *O* across the plan rail. Place the length *o' s* of the major axis in the dividers, and with *3* on the minor axis as center draw the arc cutting the major axis in the points *2* and *2*. Again place in the dividers the length of *o' g* on the major axis, and with *1* on the minor axis as center strike the arc cutting the major axis in the points *3* and *3*. The points *2-2* and *3-3* upon the margin indicate the location where the pins are to be fixed

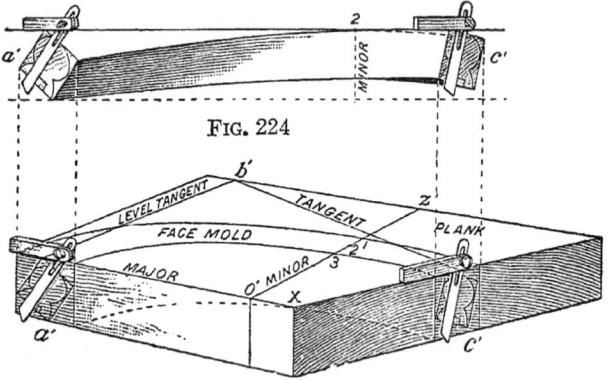

FIG. 223.—View of the Plank from Which the Wreath is Cut Square to its Surface and the Bevels Applied at Each End, Showing How the Wreath is Twisted.

FIG. 224.—View of Wreath After it is Twisted and the Bevels Applied.

to draw the curves of the face mold. Fasten the string to the pins, and with the pencil on the minor axis draw the curves from the end *a'* of the mold to the end *c'*. Make the joints at each end square to the tangents, thus completing the form of the face mold.

The width of the mold at each end is taken from the bevels shown in diagram *D*. In order to find the bevels, make *a n* of the diagram the same length as *a u* of the plan, Fig. 222. Make *n m* the same length as the line *w m* in the elevation; connect *m* with *a*, and the angle at *m* is the bevel to apply to the end *c'* of the mold.

Make *n c'* of diagram *D* equal in length to the line *c' t* of the elevation, and connect *c'* with *a*. Then the angle at *c'* is the bevel to apply to the end a' of the face mold, where the wreath connects with the newel.

The face mold is applied to the plank in Fig. 223, indicating the method of cutting out the material for the wreath. The material is cut out square to the face of the plank, and the bevels are applied to both ends; at the end a' towards the inside, and at the end c' towards the outside of the wreath. Fig. 224 shows the wreath after it is twisted and the bevels applied.

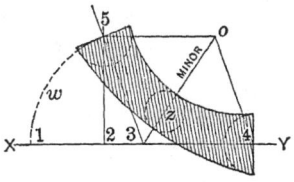

FIG. 225.—Face Mold Curves Described by Means of a Flexible Lath Bent to Touch Points Contained in the Curve.

To lay out the face mold for the quarter turn placed between the second and third flights of stairs in Fig. 221 proceed as shown in that figure by placing one point of the compasses in the point o' as center, and extending the other to n; turn over to m and then make m 4 equal in height to the three risers which are contained in the quarter turn, namely, the *17th*, *18th* and *19th*. From 4 draw the pitch of the flight above to *1*, Fig. 221, and square to this line draw a line from o' to *2*.

Draw the straight line $X Y$, Fig. 225, and transfer to it the points *1, 2, 3, 4* from the pitch line in Fig. 221, and from *2* in Fig. 225 draw

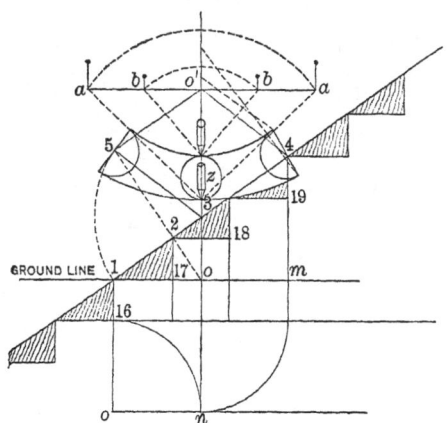

FIG. 226.—Diagram Showing How to Draw the Face Mold with String and Pins.

a perpendicular line to the point 5. Place one leg of the compasses in the point *3*, extend the other to *1*, and turn over to *5*, connect *5* with *3*; this gives one tangent of the face mold; the other is from *3* to *4*. Make the joints at *4* and *5* square to the tangents, and place on the minor axis the point z at a distance from *3* equal to $O z$ of the plan, Fig. 221. Make

the width of the mold at this point equal to that of the rail, and
at each end ½ in. wider, and draw the curves by bending a
thin lath to touch the points thus found.

Fig. 226 shows the manner of laying out the mold by
means of a string and pins. Draw the plan and elevation;
from *o* draw a line square to the pitch through *2* to *5*, and
connect *5-3* which is the bottom tangent as required upon
the face mold; the line 3-4 being the top tangent, and the
angle at *3* the one required to direct the face mold tangents
to square the joints. Draw a line from *5* parallel to the top
tangent *3, 4,* and a line from *4* parallel to the bottom tangent
5-3 meeting in *0*.

Now connect *0' 3* which
will be the minor axis; the
major axis is drawn through
o' and square to the minor.

Find the points upon the
major to fix the pins shown
at *b, b* and *a, a* and sweep the
curves as shown.

In Fig. 227 a method of
drawing the gooseneck curve
connecting the rail to the top
landing newel is shown.
Commence by continuing the
bottom of the landing rail
through *b* to *o*. Drop from
b to *a*, and make the line *a c*

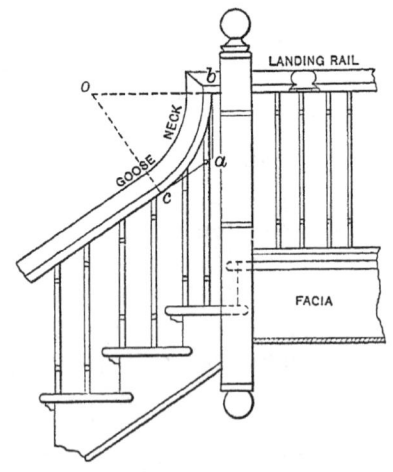

FIG. 227.—Partial Elevation of the
Landing Newel, Landing Rail and
Goose Neck on the Pitch Rail.

equal to *a b*. Draw a line from *c* to *o* square to the pitch
line of the flight rail, and with *o* as center draw the curves
from *c* to *b*.

CHAPTER XVIII

SHOWING HOW TO CONSTRUCT A WREATH IN ONE, AND IN TWO SECTIONS OVER A 13½-INCH QUADRANT

The plan, Fig. 228, represents a design prepared by an architect who obviously did not consider, as he should have done, the necessity of arranging the risers in and around the cylinder in order to obtain the best results for the finished rail.   With such a plan as this it is an impossibility to make a presentable job on the rail and to follow the nosing line of the steps.

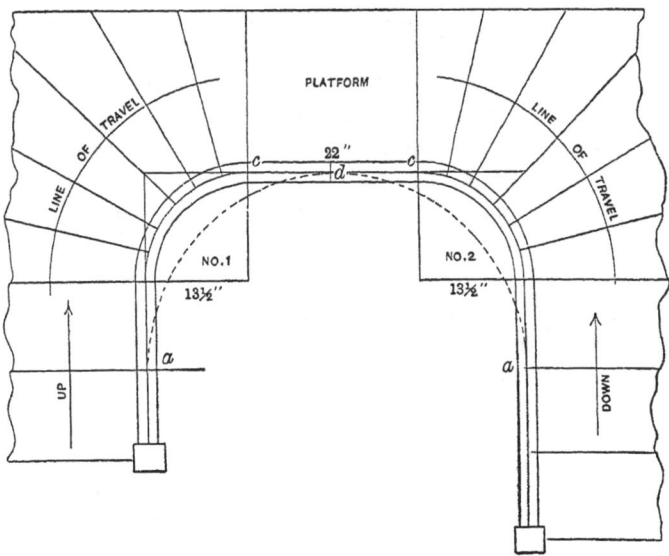

FIG. 228.—Plan of Stairs.

In this plan there are two straight steps, *10 1/2* in. wide from the starting newel to the springing of a quadrant *13 1/2*-in. radius; into this six winders are crowded; then there is a level landing *22* in. in width, connecting with another quadrant containing the same number of winders, and adjoining a few straight steps leading to the newel on the second floor.   The falling line of a rail for such an arrangement is a zigzag line of varying pitch from newel to newel, causing the finished rail to present a most unsightly appearance. Another very undesirable result of such a plan is the change in the stepping facilities. There are a few straight steps connecting the newels; then the *12* narrow winders, each about *4* inches in width, and a *22*-inch platform, necessitating the greatest vigilance in ascending and descending to avoid a false step, and making the construction unpractical in its present location (a public building), where crowds are important factors in connection with stair transit.

A plan which eliminates all these undesirable features is outlined in the dotted semicircle from *a* to *a* of Fig. 228. Distributing the risers at an equal distance along a semicircular line, as from *a* to *a*, gives a straight falling line, equal winders, and a graceful curve for the finished rail, and combines safety and beauty. In addition to these advantages there is also a great saving of labor in the manipulation of the wreaths; in this instance there are only two pieces—of the simplest kind—one from *a* to *d*, and the other from *d* to *a*, that is, wreaths of equally inclined tangents requiring only one bevel for the four joints—namely, the two ends of both wreaths to which the bevel is applied for the purpose of their squaring or twisting.

According to the original plan in Fig. 228, the wreaths must be laid out to stand over and above the two quadrants. Fig. 229 shows how this is done in two sections over the first quadrant, designated as No. 1. The first process is to lay out the elevation and pitch lines of the tangents. From *Y* on *X Y* measure the height of six risers to the point *4*. Draw a level line to represent the platform floor; above this line draw another parallel to it at a distance, say of *6* inches, more or less, to represent the central line of the platform rail. In the plan, draw the diagonal line *o b'* and tangent to the central curve of the plan rail draw the lines *b* and *c*. The plan as it now appears indicates four tangents—namely, *a*, *b*, *c* and *d*, two for each piece of wreath. Transfer these to *X Y*, at *a'*, *b'*, *c'*; the tangent *d* is already in position.

Place the pitch board at *a'* and draw the pitch of the two straight steps shown in Fig. 228, from the newel to the quadrant; and from *4*, the highest point in the elevation, draw a straight line to m, to represent the pitch lines of the four tangents. At m, where this line intersects with the pitch line of the two straight steps, a graceful ramp is formed, to align with the pitch line of the tangents. Another ramp from 4 must be formed to connect the platform landing rail with the pitch of the tangents. The joints are fixed at 4, 1, and S.

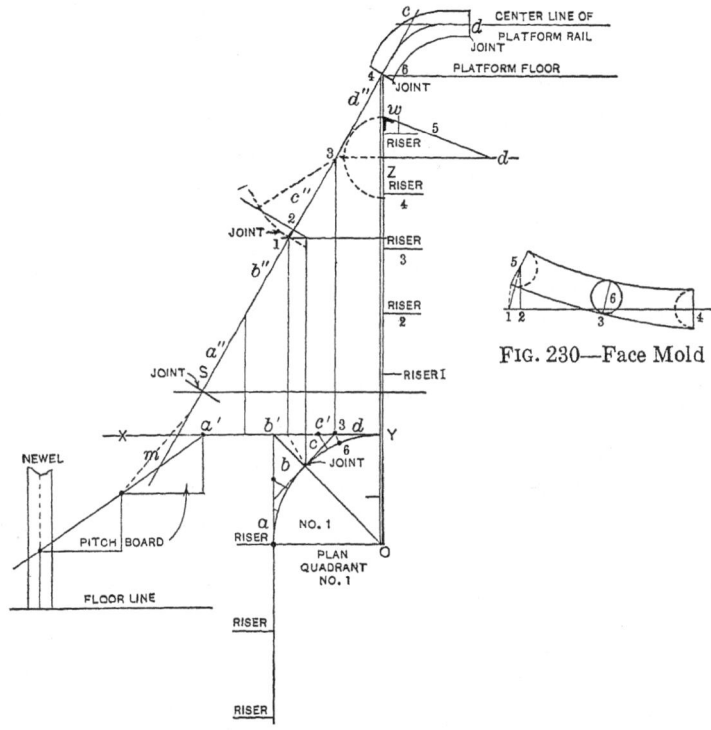

FIG. 230—Face Mold

FIG. 229.—Laying Out Wreath to Stand Over First Quadrant.
FIG. 230.—Drawing the Face Mold.

To find the bevel place one leg of the compasses in Z, extend the other to touch the pitch line of the tangents and turn over to w. The distance between w and Z will be the height of the bevel, the base Z-d equals the radius of the plan curve. The bevel is shown at w and it constitutes the only bevel required for the two wreaths, which in all cases where tangents are equally inclined is applied to each end, and in this case is used for the two sections because the two coincide.

Fig. 230 shows the simplest method in practice of drawing the face mold. Let *1, 2, 3, 4* in this diagram equal *1, 2, 3, 4* of Fig. 229. In Fig. 229 *1-3* stands for the bottom tangent of the upper section of the wreath, and *3 4* for the top tangent. The same numbers represent the tangent in Fig. 230. To find the angle required on the face mold between the two, erect from *2* a perpendicular line indefinitely, and place one leg of the dividers at *3*, and extend the other to *1*; turn over to cut the line drawn from *2* in *5*, and connect this point with *3*, giving the bottom tangent required on the face mold as a directing line to square the joint at the end *5*. The upper tangent *3 4* is already in its correct position in relation to the bottom one, and the joint at *4* is made square to *3 4*.

From *1* draw a line to *5*, and from *3* draw a line parallel to it, making *3 6* equal *3 6* in the plan, Fig. 229, and draw the circle with a radius equal to half the width of the straight rail. The circumference of this circle indicates the width of the face mold at this point, because it is on the minor axis.

The width at the ends *4* and *5* is taken from the bevel in Fig. 229, and the curves are drawn by bending a lath to touch the points thus found for both the inside and outside curve. This mold fills the conditions for the bottom wreath also, both sections containing similar plan and pitch lines.

Quadrant No. 2, in Fig. 228, is at the junction of the platform and the upper flight landing to the second story. Fig. 231 is the plan development and pitch of the tangents, and in this case is in one piece from springing to springing. Draw a line to represent the floor line of the platform. From *c″* erect the line *c″ 5′*, equal in height to the combined depth of the seven risers shown in the quadrant. Draw a line *X Y*, and the pitch line of tangents from *5′* to *2*. Above the platform floor draw the platform rail to correspond to the height from the platform floor to the center of the platform rail in 229; also draw the ramp to align with the pitch line of the tangents. This ramp is a duplicate of the one shown from *4* to the center of the platform rail in Fig. 229.

From *b″* on *X Y* draw the line *b″ 3*, square to the pitch of the tangents. By revolving the point *3* to *Z*, the only bevel required is found; this, because the tangents are equally inclined, must be applied to each end of the wreath.

For the face mold, in Fig. 232, draw a straight line, and upon it transfer the points *1, 2, 3, 4, 5,* from the pitch line of the tangents in Fig. 231. From *3* draw a perpendicular line indefinitely. Place one leg of the compasses in *4;* extend the other to

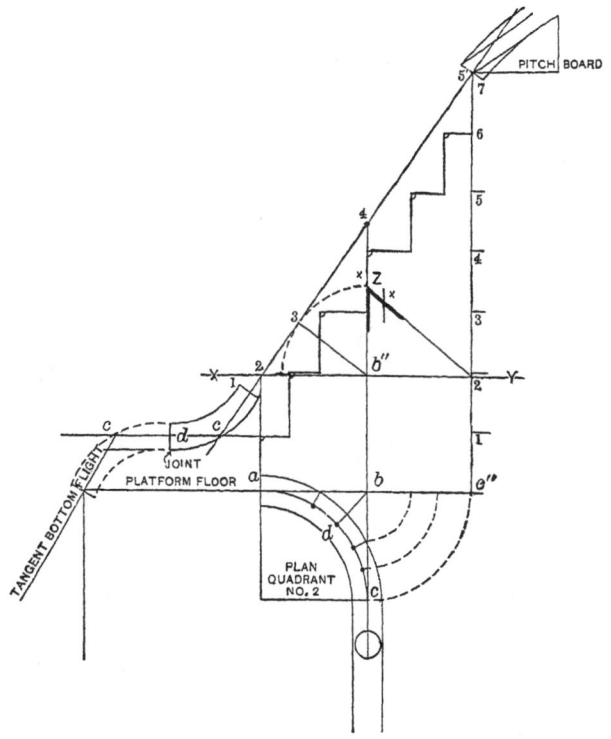

FIG. 231.—Plan Development and Pitch of Tangents.

2; turn over to cut the line drawn from *3* in *6* and connect *6* with *4*. The lines *6 4* and *4 5* are the tangents on the face mold; the joint at *5* is made square to the tangent *4 5*, and at *6* to the tangent *6 4*. A short straight piece is added to the end *6*, from *6* to *7*, corresponding in length to *1 2*, shown in Fig. 231.

To draw the curves, first find a point on the minor axis at *d'*. In this case it is found by making *4 d* equal to *b d* on the plan in Fig. 231. The circle around *d* represents the width of the

straight rail. The radius of the semicircle at *5* equals *XX*
(shown on the bevel in Fig. 231) and determines the width of the
mold at this end, and also at *6*, because tangents are equally inclined. Draw the inside and outside curves by bending a lath
to touch the circumference of the circles and semicircles.

In Fig. 231 at *d* above the platform
floor, is a joint between two ramps,
which connects the two quadrants.
The dotted ramp from *4* to *d*, Fig. 231,
belongs to the bottom flight and quadrant. It is placed here to show its relation with the other ramp, as both
ramps must meet at the distance *d*
from the platform. The tangents of
the bottom quadrant, both in this and
in Fig. 229, intersect the central line
of the platform rail at *c*, and the tangents of the upper quadrant also inter-

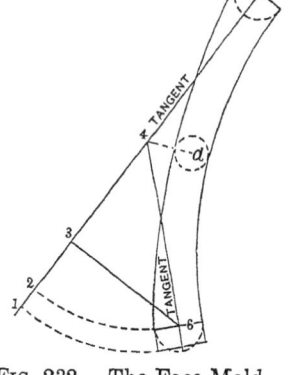

FIG. 232.—The Face Mold.

sect at *c* of the central line of the platform rail. Thus, point *d*
on the same line stands relatively to both quadrants at the
same distance from the platform floor.

CHAPTER XIX

HOW TO CONSTRUCT A WREATH OVER A CYLIN-DER AT THE TOP OF A STAIRWAY

Figs. 233 and 234 illustrate the construction of a wreath to wind around a small cylinder at the top of a stairway, the wreath to connect with a level landing rail.

Fig. 233 is a partial plan indicat ng a 4-in. cylinder and the upper step of the adjoining flight.

The pitch board in this figure is made up of a 9-in. tread and an 8-in. riser.

Fig. 234 shows the elevation of the last step and the development of the cylinder tangents. The center line of the flight

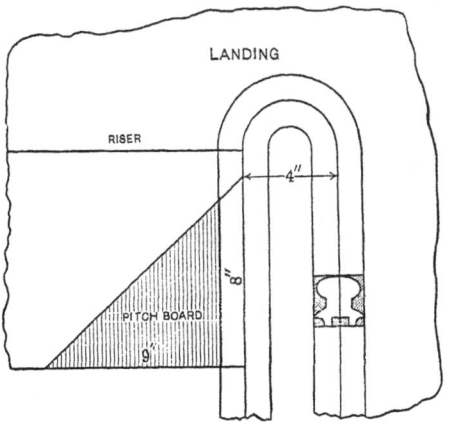

Fig. 233.—Plan of Stairs.

rail extended cuts the side tangent $a\ b$ in b'. A line drawn from b' to w would indicate the height of the center line of the landing rail above the floor line if the operation was to follow the method usually employed in connection with cylinders of 8 in. and over in diameter, but in this case the level landing rail would be too low, barely 2 in. above the floor line, whereas it should be at least the height of half a riser.

The height of a level landing rail when in position ought to be at least *2* ft. *10* in. from the floor line to the center of the rail; if the space allows the use of a cylinder *9* in. in diameter, the prescribed height is obtained for the landing at the point *b′* of Fig. 234. The same point *b′* is shown in Fig. 235 at the height of half a riser above the floor line.

Whenever space allows, it should be utilized to determine the size of the cylinder (relative to the pitch of the adjoining flight) that will produce the necessary height for a level landing rail, similar to the example shown in Fig. 235. The wreath required

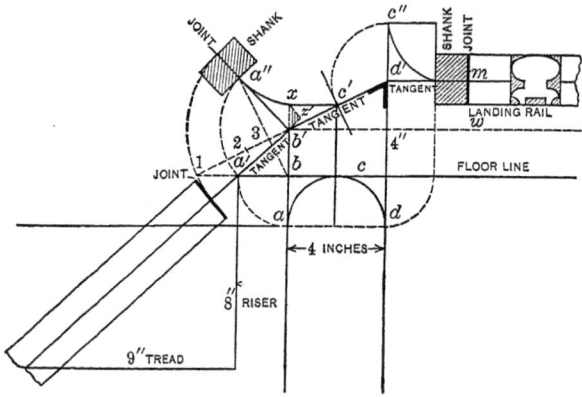

FIG. 234.—Plan of Center Line of Rail with Elevation and Pitch Line of Tangent for a 4-in. Cylinder at the Top of a Flight.

for this example is one to cover only the first quarter of the semicircular cylinder, and the method to lay out the face mold and find the bevel is the simplest in the construction of wreath hand rails. The rail for the other quarter turn (shown shaded in the diagram) is not a wreath, but merely the form of the plan rail, and does not require bevel, twist, or face mold.

The operation shown in Figs. 233 and 234 is intended to explain the construction of a wreath rail over and above a small cylinder. The line *b′ w* of Fig. 234 indicates the height above the floor line at which the pitch rail of the flight will strike the side of the cylinder. In this case the line is only *2* in. above the floor line, while in Fig. 235 the same line is *4* in. above it, the height required for the level landing rail. The problem in Fig. 234 is to raise the rail from *w* to *m*, so that the landing rail is

4 in. above the floor line instead of *2*.   Proceed in Fig. 234 by drawing the center line *d' m* of the level rail *4* in. above the floor line, and from *d'* draw a line to *b'*.   In this manner the pitch line of the tangents for the two wreath pieces that will cover the distance all around the curve of the cylinder is obtained.

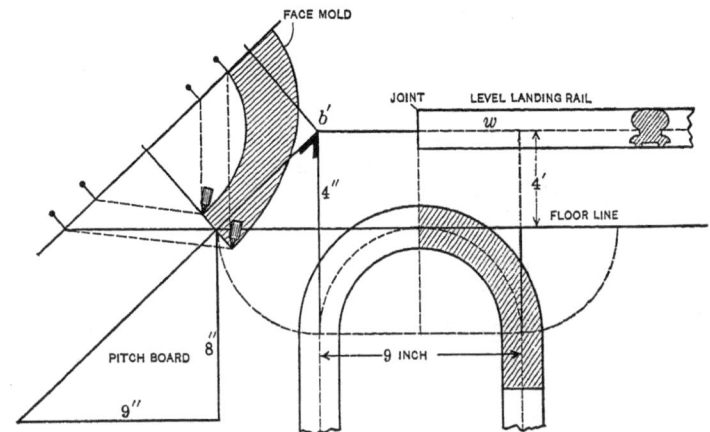

FIG. 235.—Method of Constructing a Wreath Over a 9-in. Cylinder at the Top of a Flight Upon a Landing.

The first two tangents are inclined as shown at *a' b'* and *b' c'*, *a' b'* inclining the same as the flight and *b' c'* not quite so steep.

Draw a line from *b* square to the tangents *b' c' d'*, and revolve tangent *a'* to cut the line in *a''*.   By connecting the point *a''* and the point *b'*, the angle at *b'* indicates the angle between the two tangents required upon the face mold to square the joints of the wreath.

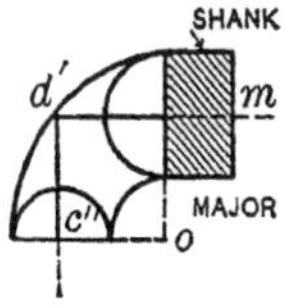

The curve of the center line of the wreath extends from *a''* to the joint at *c'*, and the bottom pitched tangent of the upper piece of wreath extends from the same joint *c'* up to *d'*, and is the same pitch as tangent *b'* of the bottom piece of wreath; this is necessary, because the joint at *c'* is made square to both tangents.

FIG. 236.—Top Face Mold for Wreath Shown in Fig. 234.

The top tangent *d'* is level, also necessary, because the joint at *m* is made square to the level landing rail.

The angle between the two top tangents required upon the face mold is a right angle, at d'. It is found by simply revolving tangent c' to its right angle position at d' c''. The center line of the wreath is shown merely to illustrate the nature of the construction.

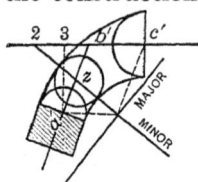

FIG. 237.—Bottom Face Mold for Wreath Shown in Fig. 234.

The face mold complete for this wreath is in Fig. 236, and the tangents c'' d and d' m are equal to the same tangents bearing similar reference letters in Fig. 234.

Fig. 237 shows the face mold complete for the bottom piece of the wreath, and the operation of laying it out may be readily seen by comparing it with the operation in connection with the tangents a' and b' in Fig. 234, and in both cases the same reference letters are used. One bevel only is required for the top wreath in Fig. 234.

Because the two tangents are inclined, two bevels are required for the bottom wreath, and they are shown in Fig. 238. Here the base line m is equal to the radius of the plan of the center line of the rail, while the height c is equal to the line b 3 of Figs. 234 and 239. By joining the point c with the base the bevel is

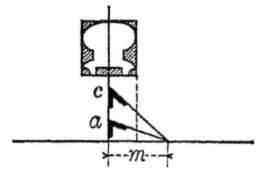

FIG. 238. — Bevels for Bottom Wreath.

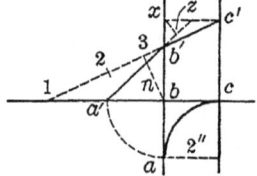

FIG. 239.—Elevation of Tangents a' b' and b' c' Preparatory to the Laying Out of the Face Mold.

found at c. The bevel is applied to the end c' of the wreath shown in Figs. 234 and 237. The bevel at a, Fig. 238, is found by having the base length the radius of the plan curve, while the height from m to a is made equal to the length of the line x z in Figs. 234 and 239. Joining a to the base m the bevel is found at a, and is applied to the end a in both figures.

The bevel c is applied to the wreath toward the outside, and the bevel a toward the inside, holding the stock of the bevel square to the respective tangents in each case. The bevel shown at d' in Fig. 234 is applied to the end m of the upper wreath. One tangent is level, and in consequence the other end of the wreath does not require a bevel.

Stairbuilders usually draw a diagram similar to the one in Fig. 239, preparatory to the laying-out of the face mold. This figure represents the plan and elevation of the first quadrant of the cylinder, and also contains the plan tangents with their respective pitches; all this is a duplication of the first quadrant and tangents in Fig. 234, bearing the same reference letters. The numbers 2 3 b' c' in Figs. 237 and 239 are transferred to the line 2 3 b' c' of Fig. 237, and the face mold is completed as partially shown and explained in Fig. 234.

CHAPTER XX

SHOWING HOW TO LAY OUT A WREATH OVER A 4-INCH CYLINDER ADJOINING A TOP LANDING

Commence as shown in Fig. 240, by locating the center of the level landing rail 4 inches above the floor line; and continue the pitch of the stairway to cut this line in the point c.

Drop a line from c to b in the plan; and from b draw a line to d, tangent to the plan curve; and make the joint at d square to this tangent.

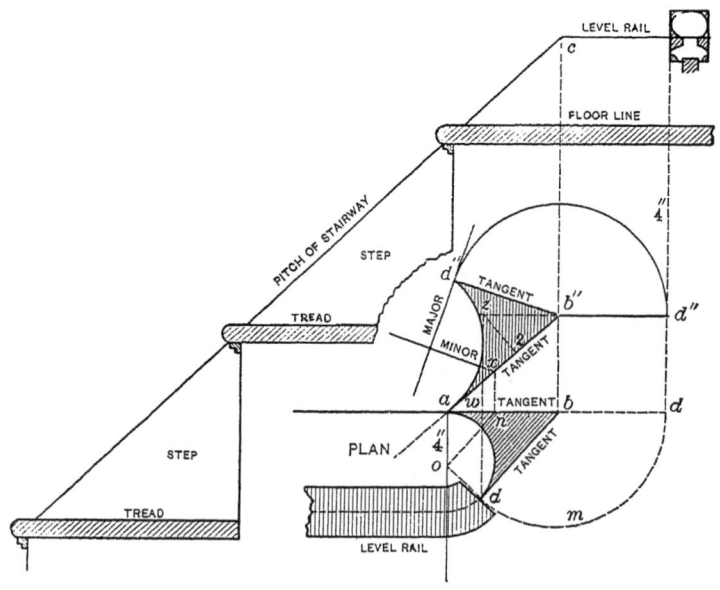

Fig. 240.—Showing Method by Which to Raise the Landing Rail Above the Floor Line to the Height of Half a Riser, the Wreath Being Made in One Piece, Extending Over More than Half the Cylinder.

In this manner the length of the plan curve from a to d is determined; also the length of the two plan tangents a, b and b, d. To develop these tangents and curve, for the face mold, draw a line from a to b'' the same pitch as the flight

162

steps, and from d draw the perpendicular line to z and through z draw a line to d'' square to the pitch line a, b''.

Now connect d'', b'', which will be one of the face mold tangents; the other will be the line a, b''.

To find the minor and major axis, draw a line from the plan center o parallel to the plan tangent d, b and from n draw the line n, x.

Draw the minor axis from x parallel to the developed tangent d'', b'' and the major at right angles to the minor.

The developed center line of the wreath is shown from a to d''.

Fig. 241 illustrates the method to complete the laying out of the face mold. Draw a straight line x, y and to it transfer the points a, x, 2, b'' from the pitch line a, b'', Fig. 240.

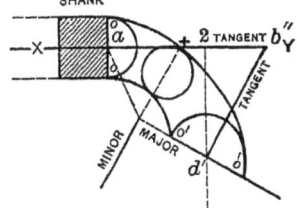

FIG. 241.—Face Mold for the Acute Plan of Wreath in One Piece Shown in Fig. 240.

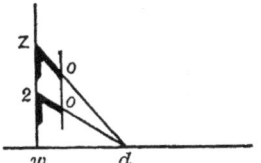

FIG. 242.—Bevels for the Obtuse Angle Plan Tangents Shown in Fig. 240.

From 2 draw an indefinite perpendicular line as shown through d; from b'' draw a line to d equal in length to the plan tangent d, b, Fig. 240; the line d, b'' will be the level tangent upon the face mold; the pitched tangent will be the line b'', a; and the angle at b'' will be the one required between the face mold tangents.

The major axis is drawn square to the level tangent d, b'' and the minor parallel to the same tangent from x intersecting the major as shown.

To draw the curves, make the width upon the minor the same as that of the plain rail; the width at each end is determined by the bevels as shown at z, o and 2-o in Fig. 242.

To find the bevels, make the line d, w, Fig. 242, equal d, w, Fig. 240; make w, 2 equal z, s, Fig. 240; and w, z equal w, z in the same figure.

By connecting *z*, *d* and *2-d*, the bevels are found at *z* and *2*, and by placing the line *o, o* at a distance from the line *w, 2, z* equal half the width of the plain rail, the long edges of the bevels will indicate half the widths of the face mold at the ends *d* and *a* Fig. 241.

CHAPTER XXI

THE RIGHT AND WRONG WAY OF ERECTING A QUADRANT BETWEEN TWO FLIGHTS

Fig. 243 is a partial plan of two intersecting flights, with a quadrant cylinder of 7-inch radius in the intersection. The last riser of the bottom, and the first of the upper flight, are

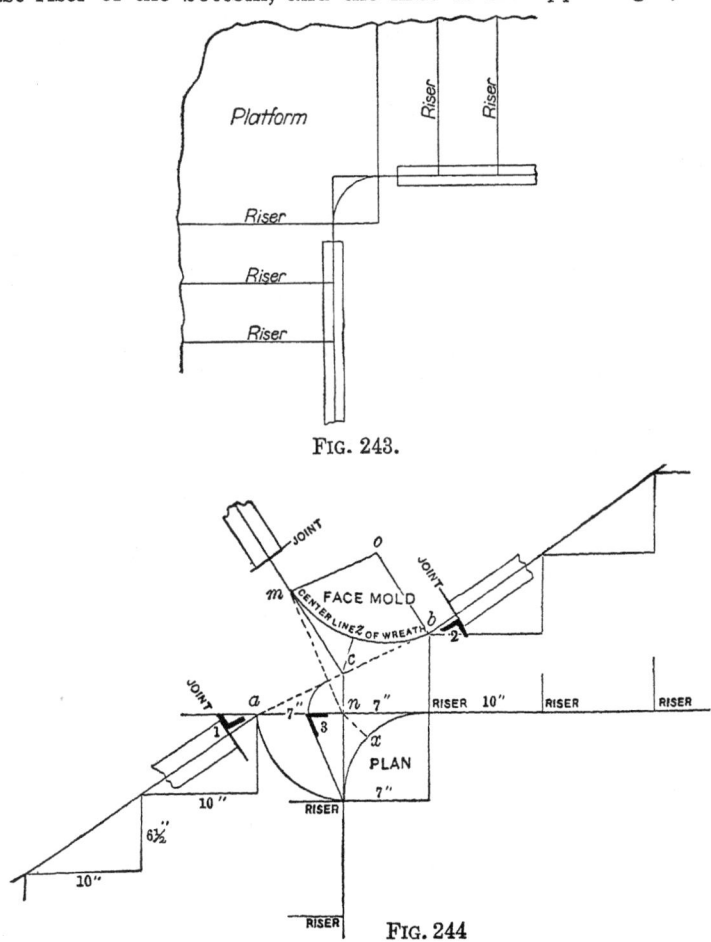

Fig. 243.

Fig. 244

placed in the springing of the quadrant. The steps of the two flights are made up of *10*-in. treads and *6½*-in. risers.

The result of this plan arrangement is shown in the elevation, Fig. 244; the pitch over the cylinder is different to the pitch over the two flights, necessitating the ramping of the wreath and the extra thickness of plank and of two extra bevels shown in Fig. 244 at *1* and *2*.

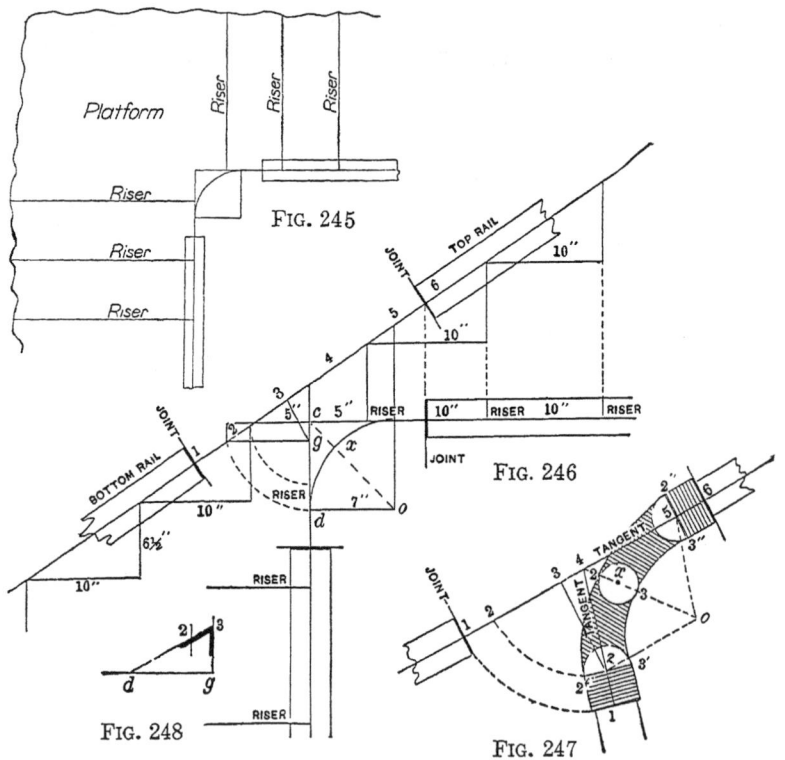

Fig. 245

Fig. 246

Fig. 248

Fig. 247

The center line of the wreath is developed in Fig. 244, as follows: from *n* draw a line square to the pitch line of the tangents *a c b*; make *c m* equal to *c a*; draw *m o* parellel to *c b*; make *c z* equal to *x n* of the plan. Bend a lath to touch the points *m z b*, and sweep the curve of the center line of the wreath

The bevel *3* is to square the wreath, and is applied to both ends, while the two extra bevels *1* and *2* are applied to the sides after the wreath is squared, in order to produce a square butt joint with the adjoining rails of the flights.

Fig. 245 shows the correct method of treatment for this kind of a stairway, where the two risers nearest the corner *c* are placed at a distance from *c* equal to one-half the width of the treads of the adjoining flights. The treads are *10* in. wide; therefore the first riser from *c* in the upper flight, and the first riser from *c* in the bottom flight, are placed *5* inches from *c*. The elevation of treads and risers, and the development of the tangents, a uniform pitch over the flights and quadrant, shown by the line *1 2 3 4 5 6*, which rests on the nosing of the steps. This result simplifies the wreath construction also.

Fig. 247 represents the face mold, and is developed as follows: draw a straight line; transfer upon it points *1 2 3 4*, etc., from Fig. 246; from point *3* draw the line *3 z*; make *z 4* equal the length of *4 2*, which represents the bottom tangent; draw *z o* parallel to *3 5*, and *5 o* parallel to *3 z*; make *4 x* equal to *c x* of Fig. 246.

In this manner three points which are contained in the curve of the center line of the wreath of the face mold are found, namely, *z x 5*, and it is necessary to find the width of the mold at each point. At *x* the circle represents the width of the straight rail of flights; *x* is a point on the minor axis where the wreath in all cases is equal in width to the width of the straight rail. The width at *z* and *5* is taken from the bevel in Fig. 248. Make *z 2* and *z 3* each equal to *2 3* of Fig. 248; also make *5 2* and *5 3* each equal to *2 3* of Fig. 248. The outside and inside curve of the mold may be described by bending a lath to touch the points *2' 2 2'* for the outside curve, and the points *3' 3 3''* for the inside curve. To complete the mold add the shanks *z 1* and *5 6*, respectively; both additions drawn in alignment with the connecting tangents. The mold is applied to the plank, and the wreath material is cut out square to the face of the plank; then the bevel in Fig. 248 is applied to each end to square the wreath.

The bevel in Fig. 248 is found as follows: make *d g* equal to *o d*, the radius of the plan quadrant in Fig. 244, and *g 3* equal to the line *g 3* of Fig. 246; connect *3* with *d* in Fig. 248, and the bevel is found at *3*.

CHAPTER XXII

EXAMPLES OF CURVES INTERSECTING FLIGHTS AND LANDINGS

Fig. 249 is a plan of a stairway consisting of two intersecting flights placed at right angles to each other. There is a platform in place of winders at the intersection, thus eliminating the objections often urged against continuous rails, which hitherto have been considered necessary adjuncts of stairways containing winders. The last riser in the bottom flight, and the first riser in the upper flight, are placed at a distance from the corner c equal to one-half the width of the tread, similar to the examples shown in Figs. 245 and 246 in the last chapter. This arrangement causes the pitch of the two tangents to align with the pitch of the two flights illustrated in Fig. 250. The alignment thus secured reduces the amount of labor entailed in the manipulation of the wreath.

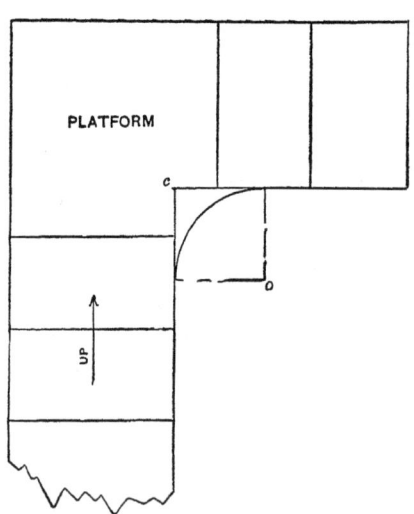

FIG. 249.—Plan of Stairway Having a Quadrant Turn Between Two Flights Placed at Right Angles to Each Other.

The elevation and development of the tangents is represented in Fig. 250, of the drawings; the tangents are shown from 1 to 4 on the nosing line to conform with the pitch of the two flights adjoining. The line from 2 to n is drawn square to the pitch line, and its length represents the height of the bevel, from a to 2 in Fig. 251, and the base o a of the bevel is made equal to the radius of the plan curve.

Fig. 252 shows the method of drawing the face mold for the wreath. From the pitch line in Fig. 250 transfer to any line, as a b, the figures 1 2 3 4. From 2 drop a line 2 n. Place one leg of the dividers in 3, and extend the other to 1, then swing around, describing the arc 1 n; connect n with 3. By this process the angle n 3 4 between the tangents n 3 and 3 4 and re-

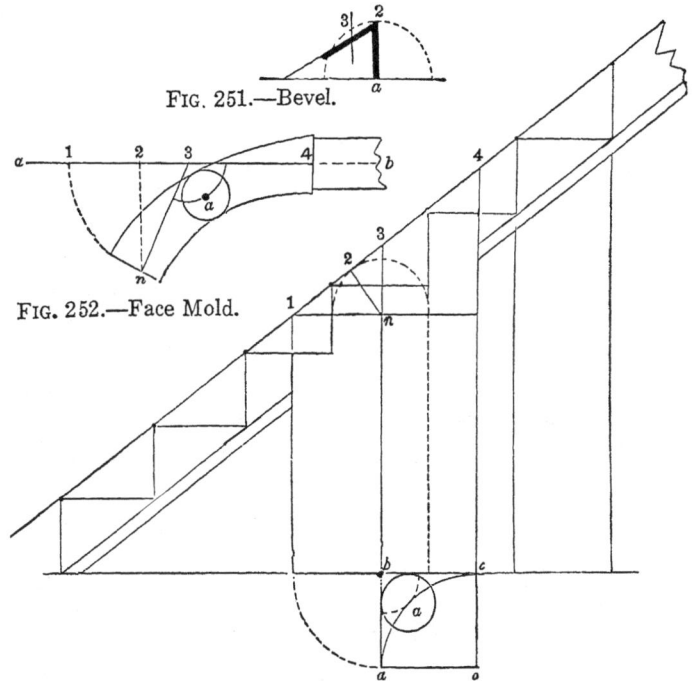

FIG. 251.—Bevel.

FIG. 252.—Face Mold.

FIG. 250.—Elevation.

quired upon the face mold is found. The joint at n is made square to the tangent n 3, and the one at 4 square to the tangent 3 4. Place on each side of the points 4 and n, respectively, the distance 2 3 of Fig. 251; this determines the width of the mold at each end. Make 3 a equal to b a of Fig. 250. With a as center, and a radius equal to one-half the width of the straight rail, describe the circle shown. Bend a lath to touch the points thus determined, and the form of the mold is described.

The plan of another stairway for a curve between two flights is represented in Fig. 253. In this case the curve is less than a quadrant, and the flights are fixed at an obtuse angle. By placing the last riser in the bottom flight, and the first in the upper flight, at a distance from the corner c equal to one-half the width of a tread, as in Fig. 250, the same results are obtained in respect to the tangents. They have the same pitch as the flights, as shown in Fig. 254, from *1* to *4*, where the line of nosing is a continuous straight line over flights and tangents. The line $m\,n$ in Fig. 254 is made square to the line of the nosing, and its length represents the height of the bevel, at $a\,m$ in Fig. 255. The base of the bevel is equal to the plan radius of the central line of the curve, from o to c, or from o to a in Fig. 254. This is the only bevel required for the wreath, but as the two tangents are inclined it is applied to both ends. Fig. 256 represents the face mold for this wreath. To the line $a\,b$ transfer from Fig. 254 the reference figures *1 2 3 4*, and the mold is formed precisely the same as in Fig. 252.

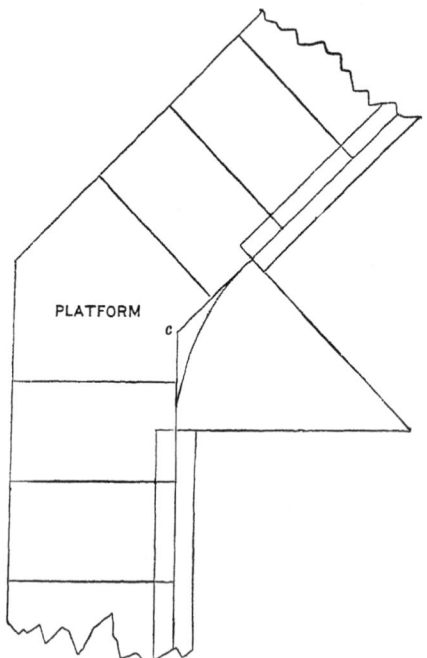

FIG. 253.—Plan of a Stairway Having a Curve Less Than a Quadrant Between Two Flights Placed at an Obtuse Angle to Each Other.

Another example of a stairway having a curve less than a quadrant is exhibited in Fig. 257, of the drawings. In this case, however, it is placed at the upper end of the flight, adjacent to a landing where the wreath is made to ramp with the landing rail. This example of a wreath therefore is one with the bottom tangent inclined and the upper tangents level, in order to align with the level landing rail. The last riser in the flight in this example is also placed at a distance from the corner c equal to one-half the width of a tread, and shown at g.

The plan is reproduced in Fig. 258, and the tangents are developed, showing the bottom one 3 x inclining and conforming with the inclination of the flight, while the upper one, 3 4, is level, to align with the level landing rail.

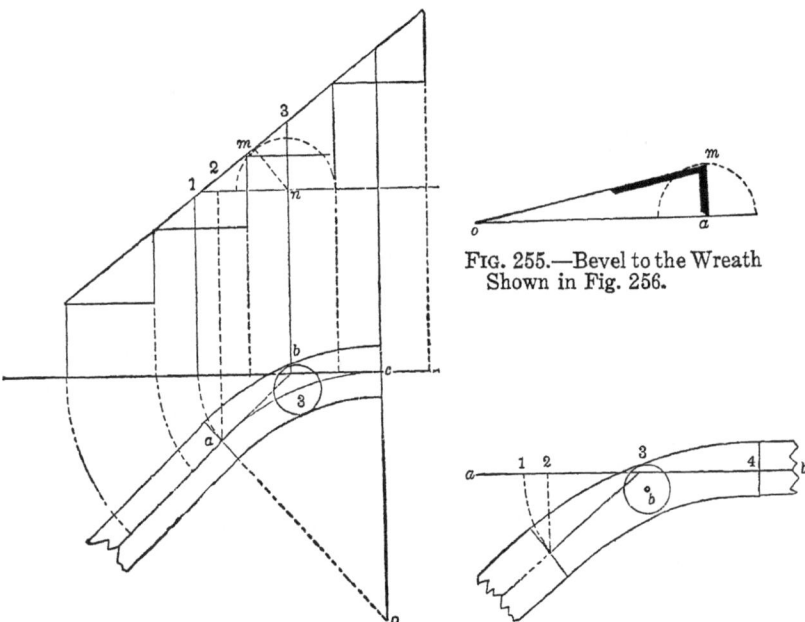

FIG. 255.—Bevel to the Wreath Shown in Fig. 256.

FIG. 254.—Elevation and Development of Tangents of the Plan Shown in Fig. 253.

FIG. 256.-Face Mold for the Wreath Shown in Figs. 253 and 254.

In order to draw the face mold, extend indefinitely a line from g of the plan through 2 to 5, and then with one leg of the dividers fixed in 3 extend the other to x, describing the arc x 5, cutting the line g, 2, 5 in 5. By connecting 5 with 3 the angle between the tangents of the face mold is determined at 5 3 4.

To find the bevels required to square this wreath, draw a line from o of the plan, parallel with the plan tangent c d, shown by o z'; transfer the point z' to w on the ground line, indicated by the arc z' w; from w drop a line to intersect the pitch line at m; draw also a line square to the pitch line from w to z.

To determine the bevels in Fig. 259, make the base o g equal to the radius of the plan central line of the rail; make o w equal to w z, shown in Fig. 258. The bevel at w is applied to the end 5 of the wreath. Again, make o n equal to m n of Fig. 258; the bevel at n is applied to the end 4 of the wreath, and both held parallel, with the joints directed towards the outside of the wreath. The bevels are applied reversely in the other two ex-

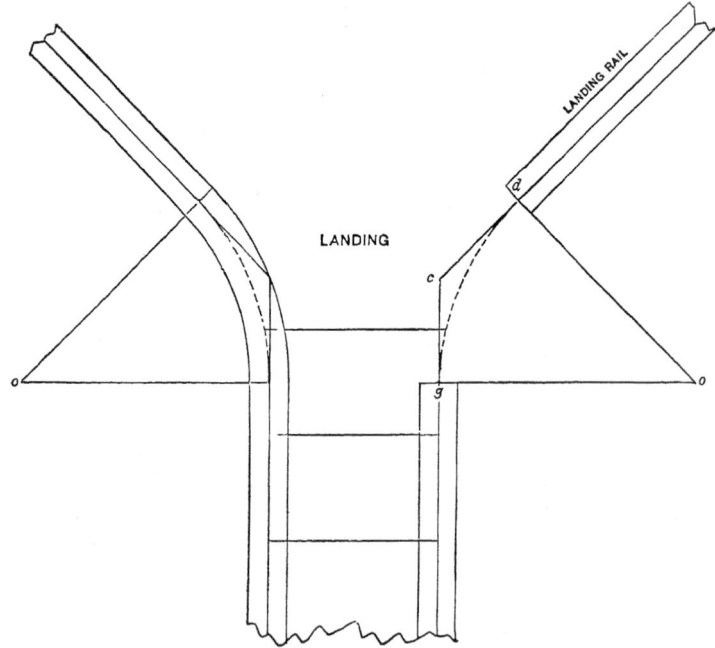

FIG. 257.—Plan of Stairway Containing a Curve Less Than a Quadrant at the Top Landing.

amples in Figs. 252 and 256; that is, the stock of the bevel is applied parallel to the joint, and the bevel directed at one end toward the outside of the wreath, and the other end toward the inside.

A very simple method of drawing the face mold for the wreath shown in Fig. 258 is indicated in Fig. 260. To the line a b transfer from Fig. 258 the reference figures 1 2 3 4. Drop a line from *2* to *5*; make *3 5* equal to the bottom tangent *3 x* of Fig. 258, thus determining the angle *5 3 4*, between the tangents required in the face mold.

To draw the curve the "ordinate method" is used. It consists in drawing the ordinates or level lines on the plan, in Fig. 258, at *a c b* and *a b c*. Transfer them to the face mold,

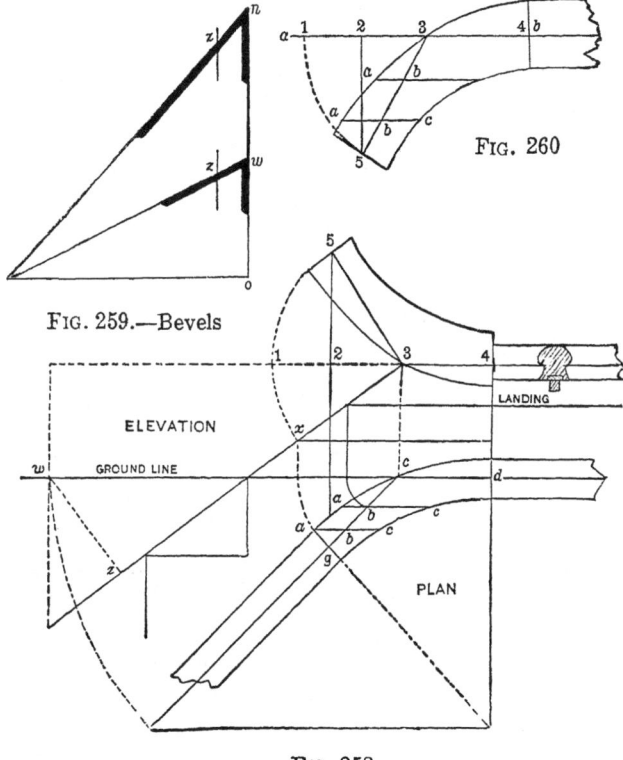

FIG. 260

FIG. 259.—Bevels

FIG. 258

FIG. 258.—Elevation of Steps and Development of Tangents of the Plan Fig. 257.

FIG. 259.—Bevels of the Wreath Shown in Fig. 260.

FIG. 260.—Face Mold for the Landing Wreath as Shown in Figs. 257 and 258.

shown by the same reference letters in Fig. 260. The method here illustrated is to trisect the plan tangent *g c,* indicated at *b* and *b,* and through these points to draw the level lines, in order to cut the outside and inside line of the plan rail, at *a a* and *c c,* respectively. Trisect the tangent *5 3* on the face mold, indicated in the figure at *b* and *b*. Through these points draw the level lines *a b c* and *a b c*. These on the face mold are made equal in length to those on the plan, Fig. 258. The points *a a* and *c c*, thus defined, are contained in the contour of the mold.

Place on each side of the end *4*, in Fig. 260, the distance *n z* of Fig. 259, and on each side of the end *5* the distance *w z* of 259; bend a lath to touch the points thus found for both sides of the wreath. The joint at *4* is made square to the tangent *3 4*, and at *5* to the tangent *3 5*, thus completing the mold.

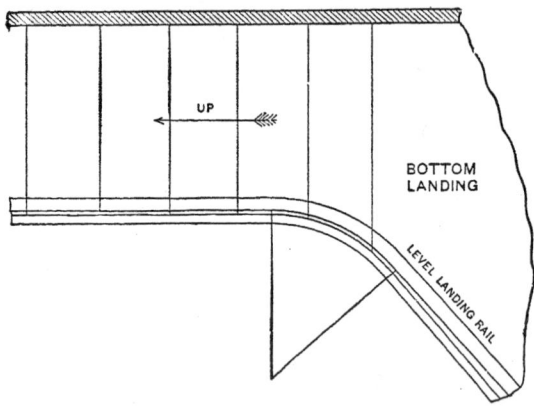

Fig. 261.—Plan of Stairway Having a Curve Less Than a Quadrant at the Bottom, the Wreath Connecting Both the Level Rail and the Rail of the Flight Adjoining.

The plan of the stairway having a curve less than a quadrant at the bottom of a flight, the wreath connecting the inclined rail of the flight and the level rail of the landing, is presented in Fig. 261 of the drawings. In this example the bottom tangent of the wreath is level, aligning with the landing of the level rail, and the upper tangent is inclined, conforming to the inclination of the flight rail. The elevation of the tangents is shown in Fig. 262, at *2 3* and *3 5*, respectively. In order to find the angle required between the two on the face mold, a line is drawn from *b* of the plan to *6* on the line *X Y*, and another line is drawn square to the pitch line of the rail through *6*, from *4 6* to *s*. The point *s* is determined in revolving the point *5* on *X Y* to *s*, by placing one leg of the dividers in *3*, and extending the other to *5*. Connecting *s* with *3* gives the line which represents the bottom tangent required on the face mold correlative to the upper tangent *2 3*. The two thus established give the correct direction to square the joints of the face mold.

The development of the central line of the wreath is shown from *2* to *s*, and is a portion of a semi-ellipse having for its axes the line *o w* (minor) and the line *o s* (major).

These axes are determined as follows: from *o* of the plan, the

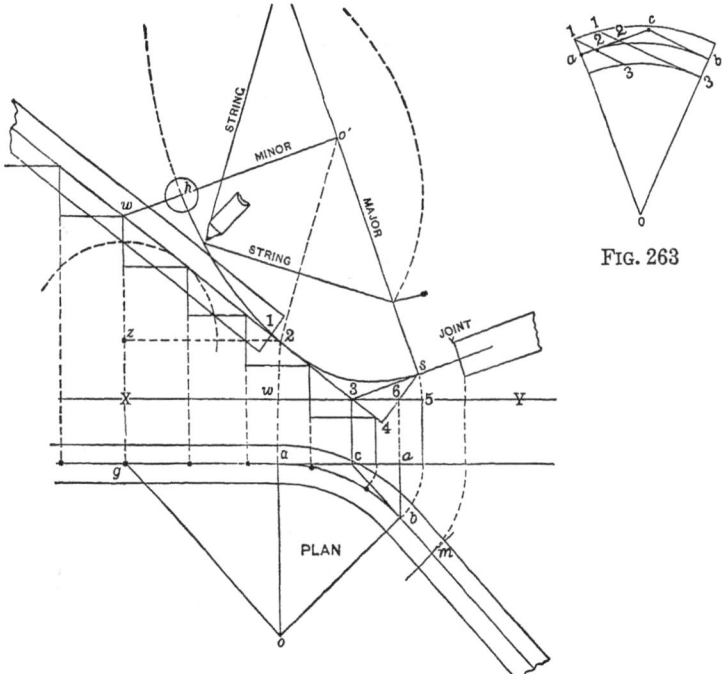

Fig. 263

FIG. 262.—Elevation of Steps, Pitch Line of Tangents and Development of Central Line of Plan Rail.

center from where the plan curve of the rail is described, draw the line *o g* parallel to the level tangent *b c*. As the line *o g* s drawn parallel, it makes it a level line; and as it is drawn from *o*, the center of the plan curve, it is the plan line of the minor axis. Upon *g* erect a line to cut the pitch line of the rail at *w*, and from this point draw a line parallel to the developed level tangent *3 s* to *o'*, making it equal in length to the line *o g* of the plan. The minor axis therefore is the line *w o'*, and the major axis is the line drawn square to it from *o'* to *s*.

Measure from *o'*, along the minor axis to the center of the small circle *h*, a distance equal to the plan radius of the central line of the rail. This radius is shown in the plan at *o a* and also at *o b*. Place the length of the semi-major axis *o' s* in the dividers; fix one leg in the center of the circle on the minor axis at *h*; describe the dotted arc cutting the major axis at the point where the pins are shown inserted, and fasten the string to each pin, and stretch it out to touch the center of the circle of the minor axis. Place a pencil there and sweep the curve through *1* and *2* to *s*. The portion of the curve *2* to *s* represents the central line of the wreath.

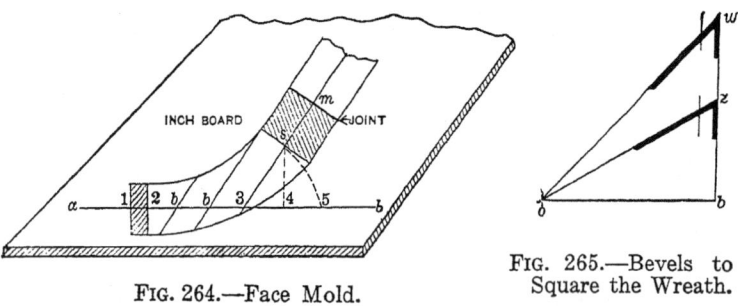

FIG. 264.—Face Mold.

FIG. 265.—Bevels to Square the Wreath.

Fig. 263 is a reproduction of the plan curve shown in Fig. 262 with the addition of *2* level lines for the purpose of showing how to draw the face mold by level lines as shown in Fig. 264.

Fig. 264 shows how the face mold is drawn by having corresponding level lines in the development. Upon a line, as *a b* for example, place the distance *1 2 3 4* taken from the pitch line, Fig. 262. Upon *4* erect *4 s*, and make *3 s* equal to the length of the bottom level tangent in Fig. 262 at *3 s* and in Fig. 263 at *c b*. Trisect the space from *2* to *3* in Fig. 264, at *b b*, and through these points draw level lines parallel to the level tangent *3 s*. Make these lines on each side of the line *2 3* equal in length to the lines *1 2 3* of Fig. 263, and through the points thus determined draw the curve of the mold. The shaded portions represent the piece of shank added to each end, for the purpose of having the joints clear of the curve.

In Fig. 265 the two bevels required to square the wreath are shown. The line o b is made equal to the radius of the plan central line of the rail. The distance from b to w is made equal to the distance from X to w of Fig. 262, and the distance from b to z is made equal to the distance in Fig. 262, from z to the pitch line, indicated by the dotted arc. The bevel at w is applied to the end s, and the one at z to the end 2, of the wreath.

CHAPTER XXIII

WREATHS FOR A THUMB ELLIPSE PLAN CURVE

Fig. 266 is a plan of a stairway of *3* flights, intersected by a platform; the rail on both sides is continued from the bottom newel to the level landing rail on the second story.

The plan curve of the rail is struck from *3* different centers, *o, o, o*, shown on right side of the figure.

The plan tangents are in position at *a, b, c, d, e, f, g, h*. The risers along the center line of the plan rail are placed at

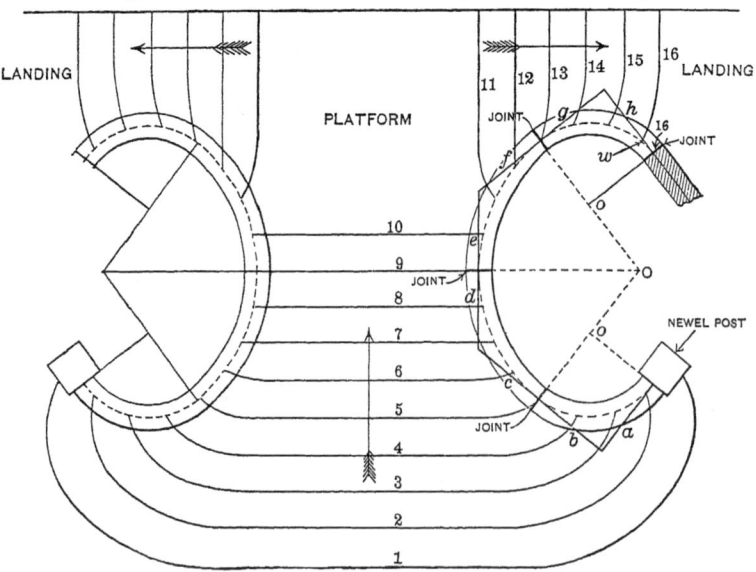

Fig. 266.—Plan of Stairway Showing Rail and Rail Tangents.

equal distances, so that the falling line of the rail is a straight line, coinciding with the nosing steps, and thus determining equal lengths for the balusters, all the way from the newel post to the level landing rail.

In Fig. 267 the manner of developing the plan tangents is illustrated. Draw a line to represent the floor, and to this line transfer from Fig. 266 the length of each tangent at a, b, c, d, e, f, g, h, in Fig. 267. Erect the perpendicular lines on each point on the floor line.

Upon tangent h measure the height of *16* risers, the total number of risers contained in the stairway in the plan, Fig. 266. Measure from *16* to w, a distance equal to the distance from riser *16* to the joint shown on plan, Fig. 266. Place the first riser in the center of the newel post.

Draw a line to connect the first and last riser; this represents

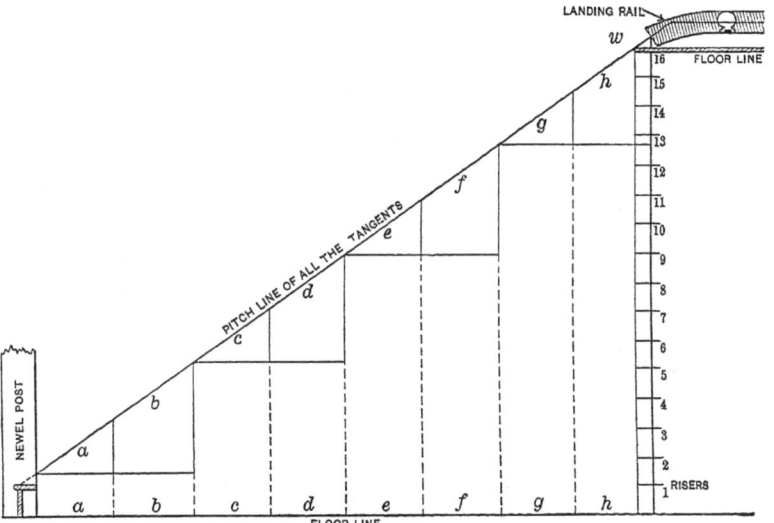

FIG. 267.—Showing How to Draw the Elevation and Find the Pitch of the Tangents.

the pitch of all the tangents. Draw the level landing rail at any distance desired above the landing floor, and draw the ramp shown by the shaded portion above the floor line.

Fig. 268 shows the development of the face molds upon the pitch line of the tangents shown in Fig. 267.

In order to meet the newel post at right angles (indicated at a in the elevation, Fig. 268) it is not necessary to incline the bottom tangent a. By this arrangement the rail has an easement at the starting.

To draw the face mold for this section of the rail, proceed as in Fig. 268. Draw the minor axis at right angles to the pitch of tangent b, and the line to m, parallel to the minor axis. Connect *m* with *o*; this is the major axis. Find the points to place the pins on the major axis, and describe the inside and outside curves of the face mold.

To lay out the face mold shown in Fig. 269, over the same plan tangents *a-b*, when it is not desired to have an easement in the rail, draw the dotted line *n, m*, square to the pitch line of the tangents *a, b, c, d*, and make *z m* equal in length to the

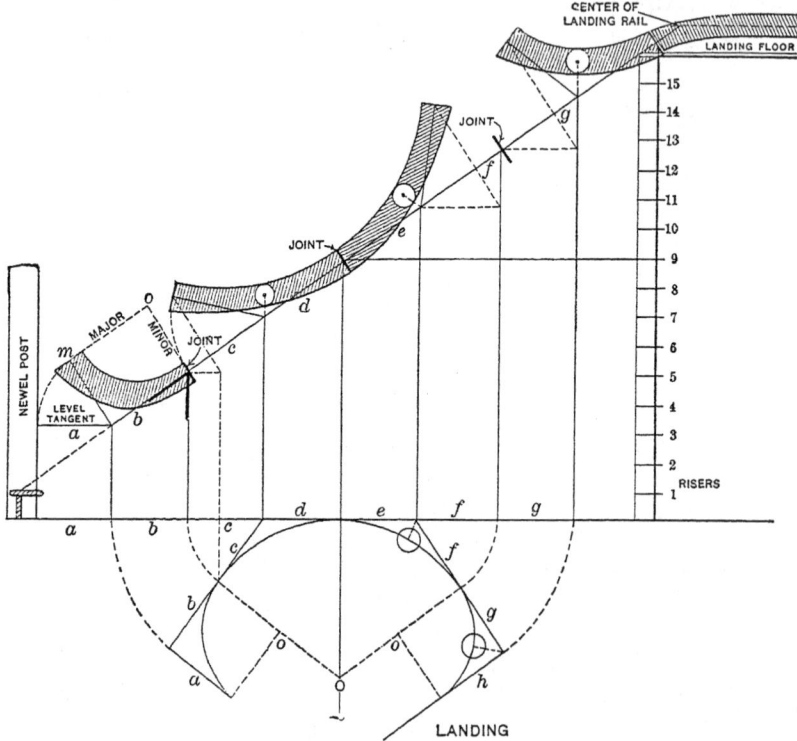

Fig. 268.—Showing the Development of the Face Mold Upon the Pitch Line of the Tangents.

tangent *z x*. The angle at *z*, shown between the tangent *b* at the line *z-m*, is the angle required between the tangents upon the face mold to square the joints at each end.

To find the bevel to square the wreath, place the compasses in *n*, and extend to touch the pitch line of the tangent *a*. Turn over as shown by the arc. Connect the point where the arc cuts the perpendicular from *n* with *z*, thus obtaining the bevel. This is the only bevel required to square this portion of the rail, and it is applied to both ends of the wreath. To draw the curved form of the face mold, make *z-2* equal in length to *1-2* in the plan. Take *2* as center and draw the circle equal in diameter to the width of the finished rail. This is the width of the face mold at this point.

Make the width at each end about ¼ in. wider, and bend a lath to touch the points found for both inside and outside curve, thus completing the form of the face mold for the piece of the

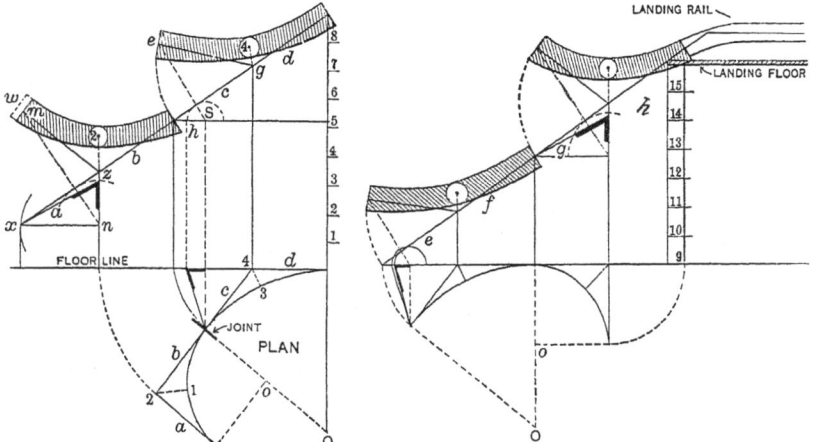

FIG. 269.—Diagram Showing How to Lay Out the Face Molds for the Two Bottom Sections of the Rail.

FIG. 270.—Diagram Showing How to Lay Out the Face Molds for the Two Top Sections of the Rail.

rail that stands over and above the tangents *a* and *b*. This face mold, unlike the one illustrated in Fig. 268, is for a rail that does not have an easement at the starting.

The face mold over the tangents *c* and *d* in Fig. 269 is laid out as follows: draw the perpendicular line from the joint on the plan up to *S*, and from *S* draw the dotted line, *S-e*, square to the pitch line of the tangents *c* and *d*. Make *e-g* equal in length to the tangent *c*; *g* is the angle between the tangents *c* and *d*, required upon the face mold to square the joints.

Make *g-4* equal in length to *3-4* of the plan, and draw the circle equal to the finished width of the rail. Make the width at each end ¼ in. wider, and bend a lath to touch the points on the inside and outside curve.

To find the bevel for this wreath, place the compasses in *S* and extend to touch the pitch line of tangent *c*.   Turn over to *h*, describing the arc indicated by the dotted line.   Drop a line from *h* to the floor line and connect with the joint.

The face molds for the two top sections of the rail, in Fig. 270, are laid out by a similar method and do not require further explanation.

CHAPTER XXIV

WREATH OVER AN ELLIPTICAL PLAN STAIRWAY

A plan representing the center line of the rail, and rail tangents for an elliptical stairway, when the rail is to be made in *3* sections, is illustrated in Fig. 271. It starts from a newel post, and winds around up to a level landing rail, shown shaded in Fig. 271.

The risers are placed at equal distances along the center line in plan, Fig. 272, from riser *1* to r ser *23*.

Fig. 272 is presented to show the elevation of the steps, stringers, and the falling line of the rail which follows the nosing of the steps, and determines equal lengths of balusters along the stairway.

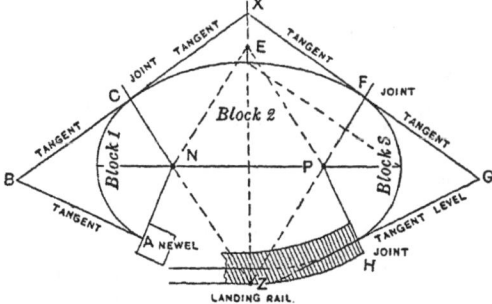

Fig. 271.—Plan of Center Rail and Tangents for an Elliptical Rail Construction in Three Sections of Wreath.

Fig. 273 is another plan of the center of rail, showing in addition the plan tangents arranged for a continuous rail constructed in *3* sections.

This figure shows also the pitch of all the tangents from the newel to the level landing rail, where the bottom and top tangents are level and all the others equally inclined.

By this arrangement of a level bottom tangent, an easement is formed in the bottom section of the rail to butt at right angles to the newel; and by having the top tangent level an easement is formed in the top section to align with the level landing rail.

183

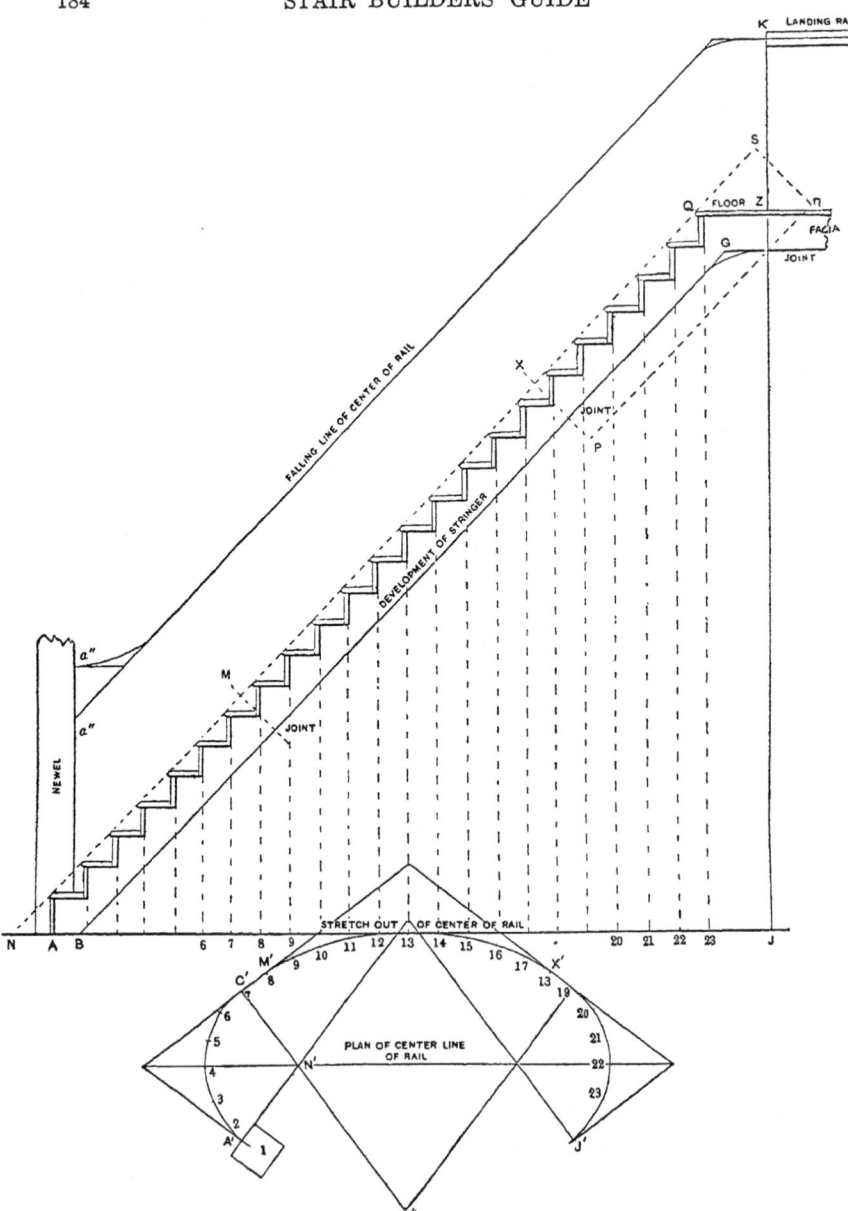

FIG. 272.—Plan of Center Rail Also Elevation Showing Development of
the Stringer and How Soffit is Ramped to Intersect Level Line of the
Landing Fascia.

Fig. 274 is another plan and elevation and pitch of tangents indicating the method for laying out the wreath, if it is to be made in *4* sections instead of *3*.

The only difference in the two methods is that the middle section marked "block *2*" in Fig. 273 is cut into two sections in Fig. 274.

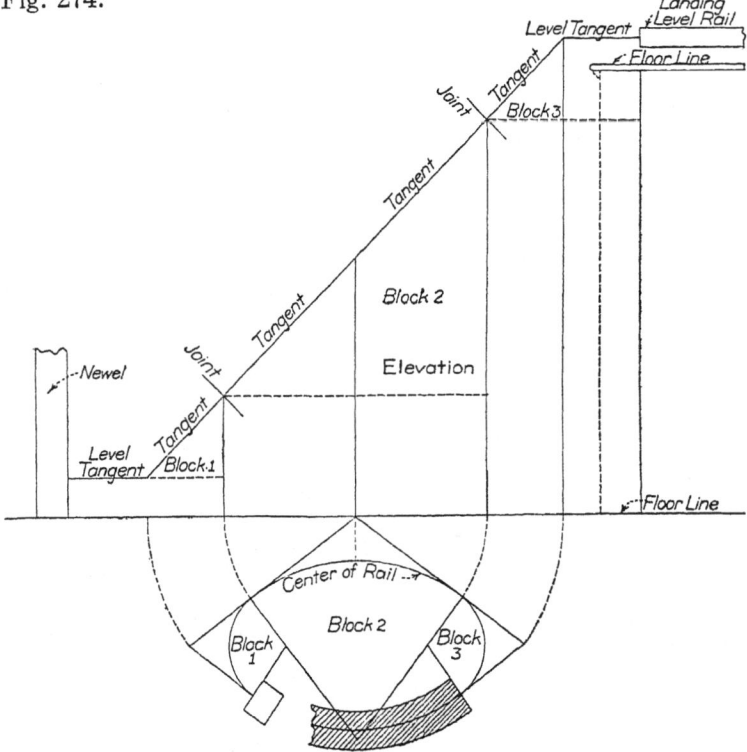

FIG. 273.—Elevation of Tangent for the Plan Shown in Fig. 271.

The elevation of the tangents in both figures is the same, except the additional joint at *E*, in the plan and elevation of Fig. 274.

The plan of the same center line of rail is again shown in Fig. 275, but in this figure the plan and elevations of the tangents are arranged for a continuous elliptical rail made in *6* sections.

Figs. 274 and 275 are presented as illustrations of the various methods that may be used in the construction of a continuous

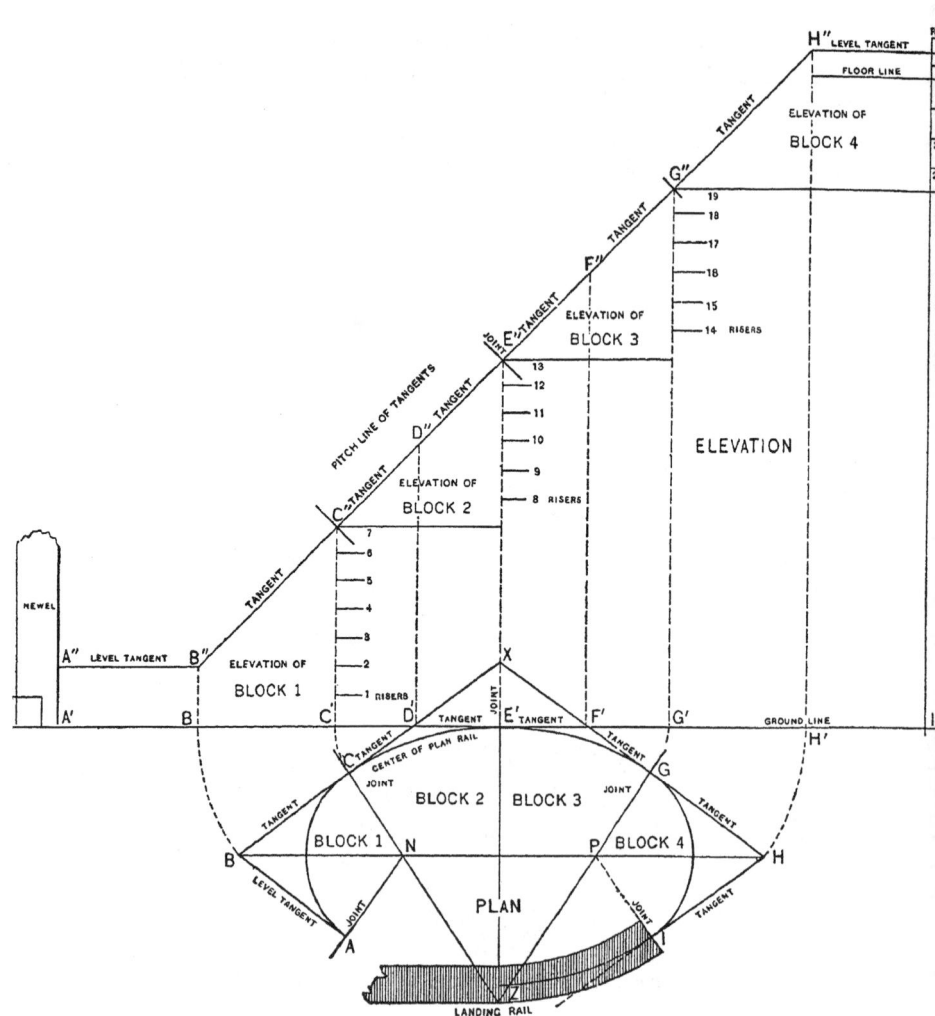

FIG. 274.—Plan and Elevation of an Elliptical Stairway, the Plan Indicating the Method of Treating the Tangents When the Rail is to be Constructed in Four Sections.

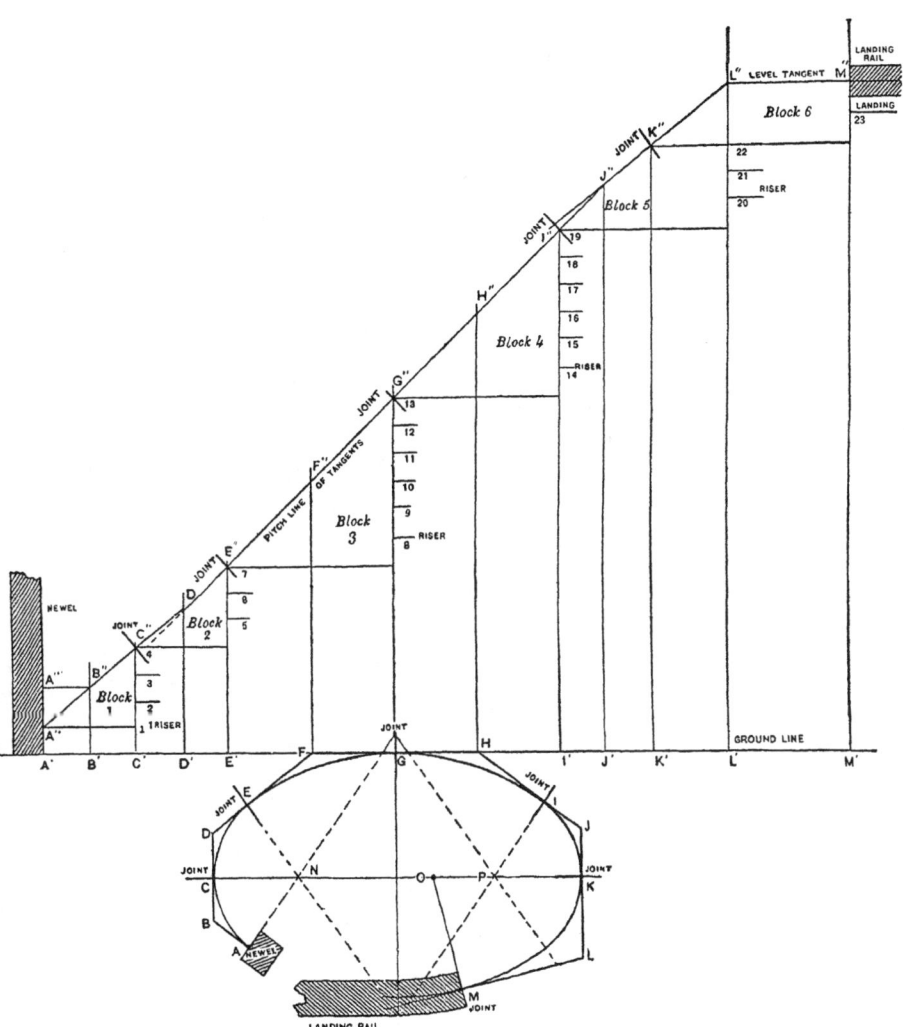

FIG. 275.—Plan, Elevation and Inclination of Tangents for a Rail of an Elliptical Stairway Made in Six Sections.

rail over an elliptical curved plan; in these figures all the different methods depend fundamentally upon the principles involved in manipulating plan and elevation tangents.

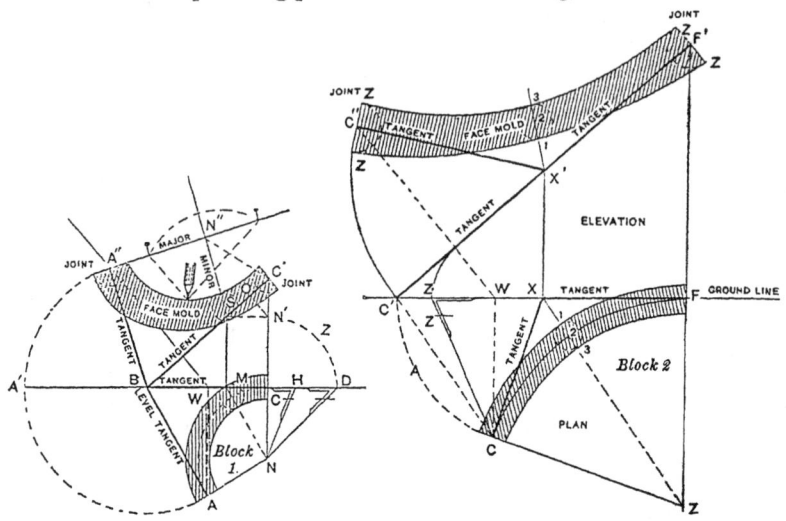

FIG. 276.—Diagram Showing Development of Block 1, Fig. 273. FIG. 277.—Face Mold for Block 2, as Shown in Fig. 275.

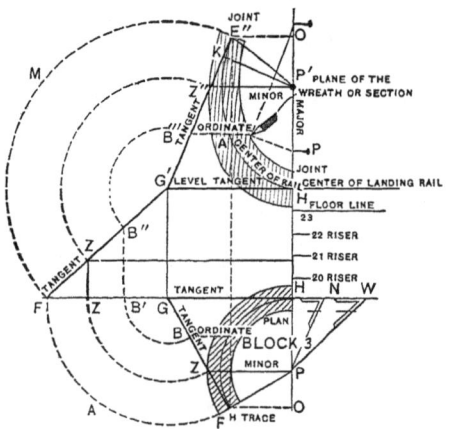

FIG. 278.—Face Mold for Block 3, Fig. 273.

Referring again to Fig. 273, where the method of constructing the rail in *3* sections is illustrated, the pitch of the tangents represents the exact length of each tangent required upon the face molds for the *3* sections.

Figs. 276, 277 and 278 illustrate the operation by which the face mold is laid out for each section, and the method to find the correct bevels to twist the wreaths.

The operation to develop the face molds in these figures is the same as in all the other figures preceding. The same is also true of the method to find the bevels to twist the different sections of rail illustrated in the figures.

CHAPTER XXV

LAYING OUT RAILS FOR A STAIRWAY CONTAIN- ING COMPLICATED PLAN CURVES

This example, Fig. 279, contains *3* different curves; the first is the ordinary turnout at the starting; the second a quarter turn at the top adjoining the newel on the second floor, and the third a segmental curve from another newel on the second floor to the wall of a platform gallery.

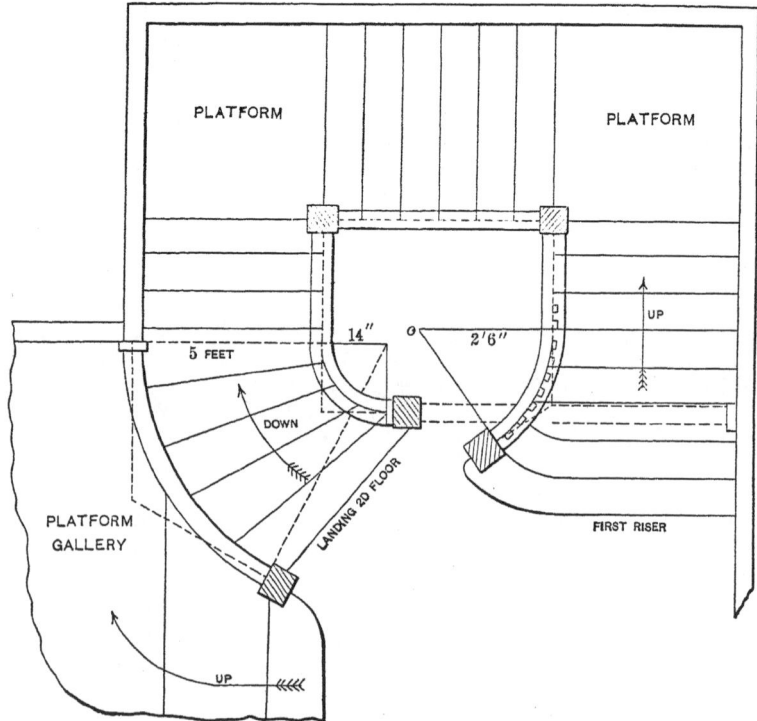

FIG. 279.—Plan of the Stairway in Question.

The turnout in Fig. 279 contains *4* risers, and in the elevation, Fig. 280, the wreath contains an easement in order to butt at right angles to the newel post. Fig. 280 also shows how to lay out the gooseneck easement, and how to find the lengths of the first two newel posts, etc.

To lay out the wreath shown in Fig. 281, draw a few lines full size, to represent the center line of the plan rail, the plan tangents and the elevation of the plan tangents. In Fig. 281 *a-b* represents the center line, *a-c* and *c-b* the plan tangents. To find the elevation of the plan tangents, measure from *b* to *b'* the height of *4* risers. Draw the pitch of the steps from *b'* to *c'*, and draw the level tangent from *c'* to *a'*.

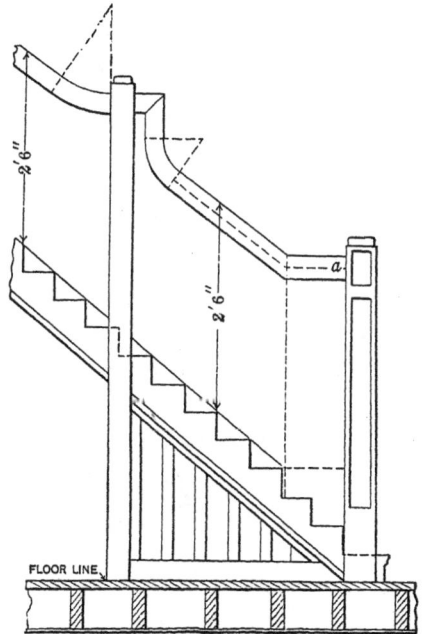

FIG. 280.—Elevation of the Bottom Flight Rail and Newels.

The last lines are the elevation of the plan tangents, showing the elevation of the plan tangent *c, b* inclining, and the plan tangent *a, c* level.

In Fig. 282 it is shown how to lay out the face mold. Draw the plan of the turnout rail, then a line from *a* to *w*; from *w* draw a line at right angles to the inclined tangent *c, b* to *a'*; connect *c, a'*.

Now draw the lines *o, o*, etc., parallel to the line *c, a'* and make them equal to their correlative lines *o, o* shown upon the plan curve. The curves of the face mold are drawn by bending a lath to touch each point o, o, etc., on both the inside and outside of the tangents. The two bevels required to twist the wreath are shown in Fig. 283. The base, a-n, is made equal to the line a-n in Fig. 281 while the height of bevel b is made equal to w, x,

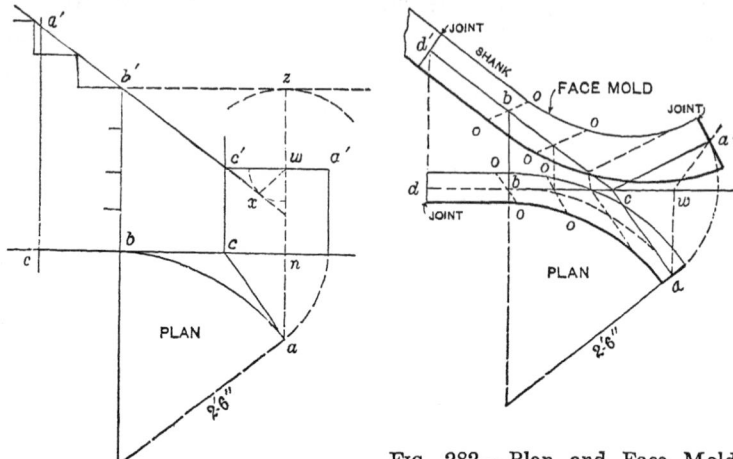

FIG. 281.—Plan and Elevation of the Turnout Tangents.

FIG. 282.—Plan and Face Mold for the Turnout at the Starting of the Stairway.

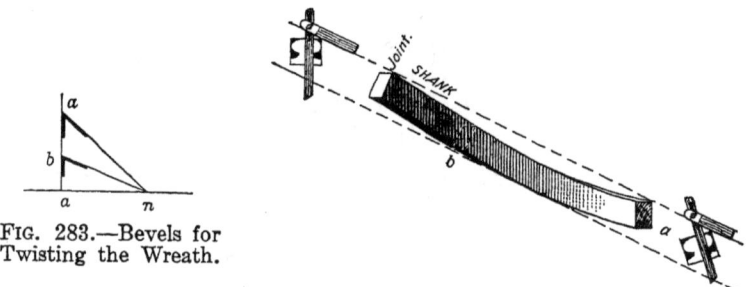

FIG. 283.—Bevels for Twisting the Wreath.

FIG. 284.—Showing Application of the Bevels to the Wreath Material.

and the height of bevel a made equal to w, z, shown in Fig. 281.

The bevels are shown in Fig. 284 applied to the wreath material. They are held parallel to the joints at each end, and directed towards the inside of the wreath.

Fig. 285 shows how to lay out the face mold for the curve indicated in the plan, Fig. 279, upon the platform gallery.

Draw the plan of the rail and plan tangents a and b; turn tangent a around to x and from x draw the pitch.

This pitch line, a', b', indicates the pitch of the plan tangents a and b.

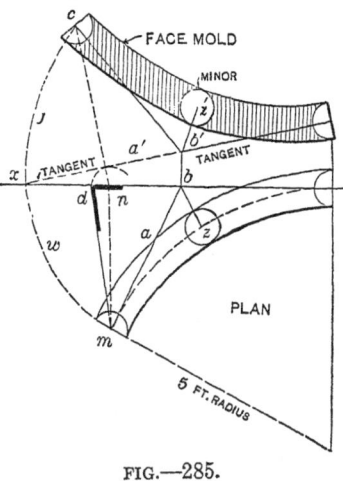

Now draw a line from m to n and from n to c; connect c, b'; make b', z' equal b, z on plan; draw the circle upon z to equal the width of the plain rail; make the width at each end ¼ inch wider, and trace the curves, thus completing the face mold.

The bevel to twist this wreath is shown at d.

In Fig. 286 the bevel is shown applied and the wreath twisted.

FIG.—285.

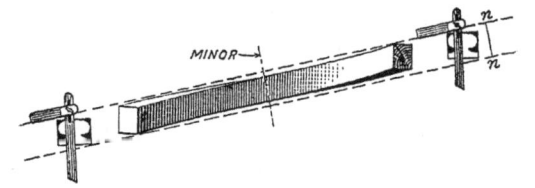

FIG. 286.—The Twisted Wreath Over the Gallery, 5-ft. Curve.

Fig. 287 illustrates the elevation of the steps the rail is to wind around.

Fig. 288 illustrates a plan, elevation and pitch of the tangents for the 14″ quarter turn at the top of the stairway and Fig. 289 the elevation of the steps, rail, newels and landing adjoining.

Fig. 290 shows how to lay out the face mold. Draw the line x, y, transfer to it from the pitch line of the tangent, c', b', Fig. 288, the points c, w, n, — 4, b', 2. Draw a line from 2 to a and a line from a to b'; draw a line from n to o parallel to a, b' and from o to a parallel to n, 4, b'.

Now connect 4 with o. This is the minor axis; draw the major through o at right angles to the minor.

Mark the point z on the minor axis, at a distance from o, equal to the plan radius of the curve, which is 14 in., and upon z as the

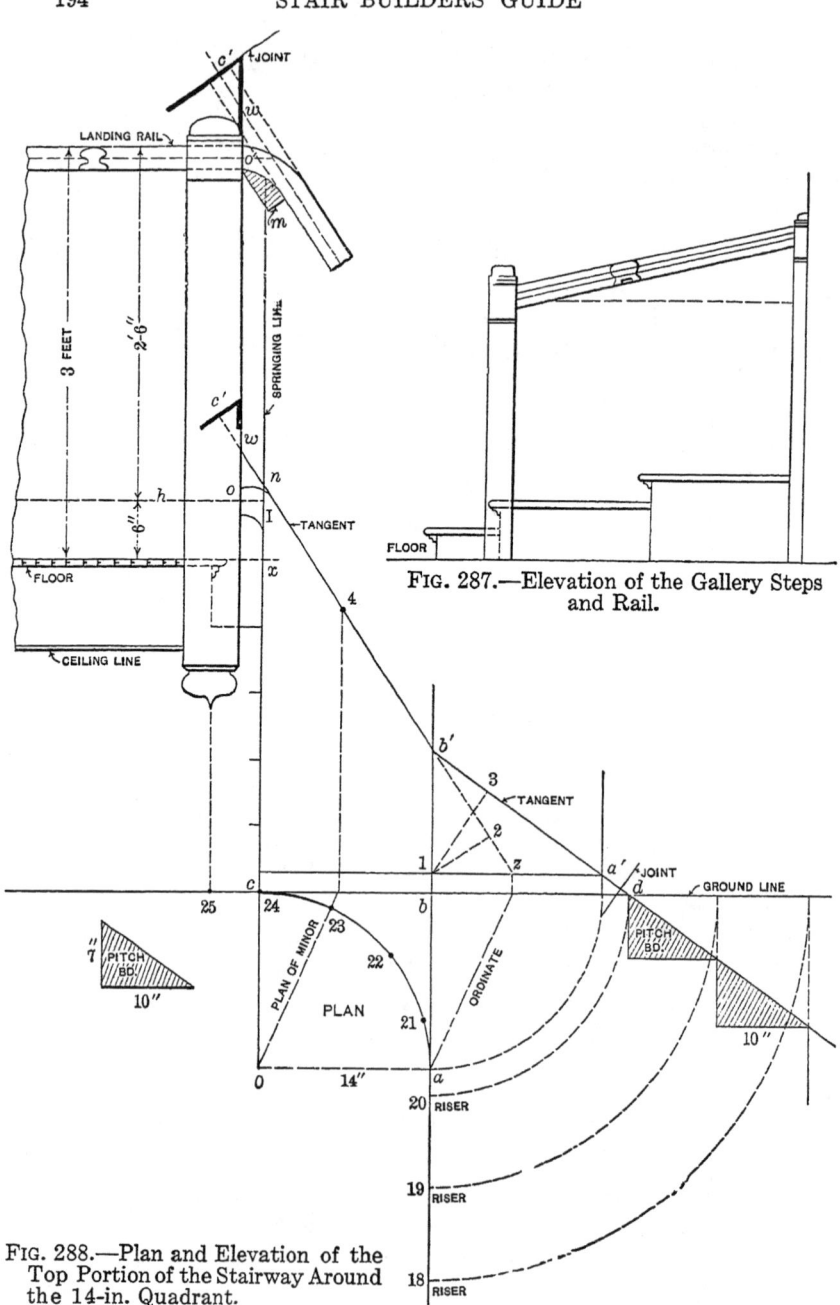

FIG. 287.—Elevation of the Gallery Steps and Rail.

FIG. 288.—Plan and Elevation of the Top Portion of the Stairway Around the 14-in. Quadrant.

center describe a circle of the same diameter as the width of the plain rail.

The mold at each end is wider, and the width must be found from the bevels shown at z-z and x-x in Fig. 291. The length z-z is placed at the end c of the mold, and the length x-x at the

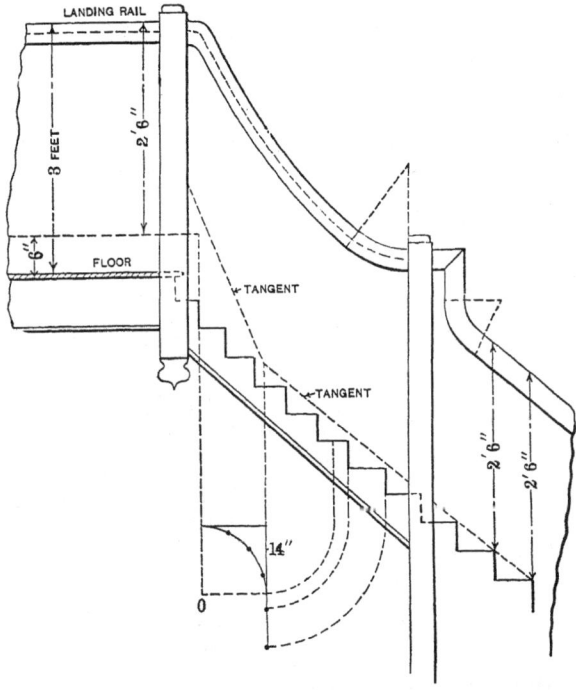

FIG. 289.—Elevation of the Top Flight and Landing Rail, Showing Goosenecks and Length of Newels.

end a, indicated in Fig. 290. The curves may be drawn by bending a lath to touch the three points—x, the circle, and z—for both the inside and outside curves.

The method of finding the bevels is illustrated in Fig. 291 The base 1-O of bevel c is made equal to the radius of the plan curve, and the height 1-2 equal to 1-2 shown in Fig. 288 to be a square line to the upper tangent b'-c' drawn from 1. The bevel is found in the angle c, and because its height is taken from the upper tangent it is applied to the end c of the wreath.

The base *1-m* of bevel *a* of Fig. 291 is made equal to *1-z* of Fig. 288, and the height *1-3* is made equal to *1-3*, a square line to the bottom tangent *a′ b′*, drawn from point *1* in Fig. 288.

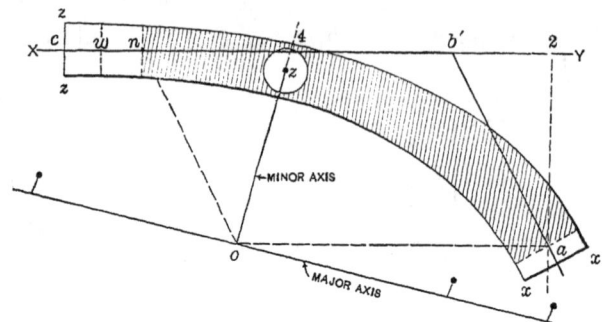

FIG. 290.—Face Mold for the 14-in. Top Curve.

In Fig. 292 these bevels are applied to the wreath for the purpose of giving it the required twist. The bevel *a′* is held toward the inside of the wreath, and bevel *c* toward the outside. At *4* the position of the minor axis is indicated, where the wreath appears to be level and therefore does not need a bevel. In squaring or twisting the wreath it is only necessary to mark a section of the rail at the ends *a′* and *c′* parallel with the bevels, and to see that the center of the wreath coincides with the center of the plank, always keeping in mind the fact that at point *4*—the minor

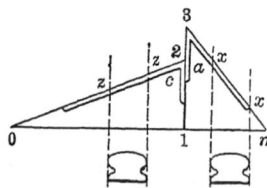

FIG. 291.—Bevels to Twist the Wreath Shown in Fig. 14.

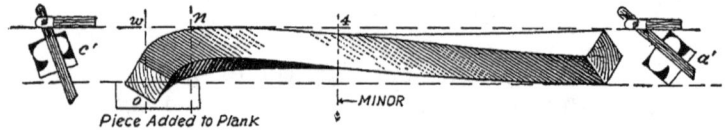

Piece Added to Plank

FIG. 292.—Showing How the Wreath is Twisted by the Application of the Bevels.

axis—the wreath does not have a twist. Therefore in squaring the wreath, work the twist from each end gradually until it attains a level position at the minor axis.

The wreath thus constructed covers the distance shown in Fig. 288 from the bottom joint *d* to a point *c′*, almost in the center of the newel post, while it is only necessary for it to reach to the side of the newel at w. As the joints of the wreath are made square to the face of the plank and also the tangents—the manner in which joints are invariably made in ordinary construction—the joint at the end c' does not fit against the newel because, as indicated in Fig. 288, it is made square to the tangent line c-w-n-b'. To make it fit and butt at right angles, as shown at the top of the newel post, it is necessary to use on the end c' of the wreath the bevel at c'. This bevel is applied in the manner indicated at the top of the newel post. The dotted lines here present the side of the wreath. The stock of the bevel is held against the square end of the wreath, and the blade parallel to the side of the newel at w, the point where the wreath is cut. The point w in Fig. 288 is much too high to meet the landing rail at o'; but it is necessary for the rail to reach it owing to the easement shown at o.

Fig. 292 shows how the easement is worked and that the length of the wreath after it is finished in this manner covers the distance, in Fig. 288, from the bottom joint at d to the side of the newel post at o.

When the stair rail including the wreath is raised 2 ft. 6 in. above the nosing of the steps, the point o' of the wreath aligns with the landing rail at the top of the newel post in Fig. 288.

CHAPTER XXVI

WREATH RAIL OVER A "THUMB ELLIPSE" CURVE AND A QUADRANT INTERSECTING TWO FLIGHTS

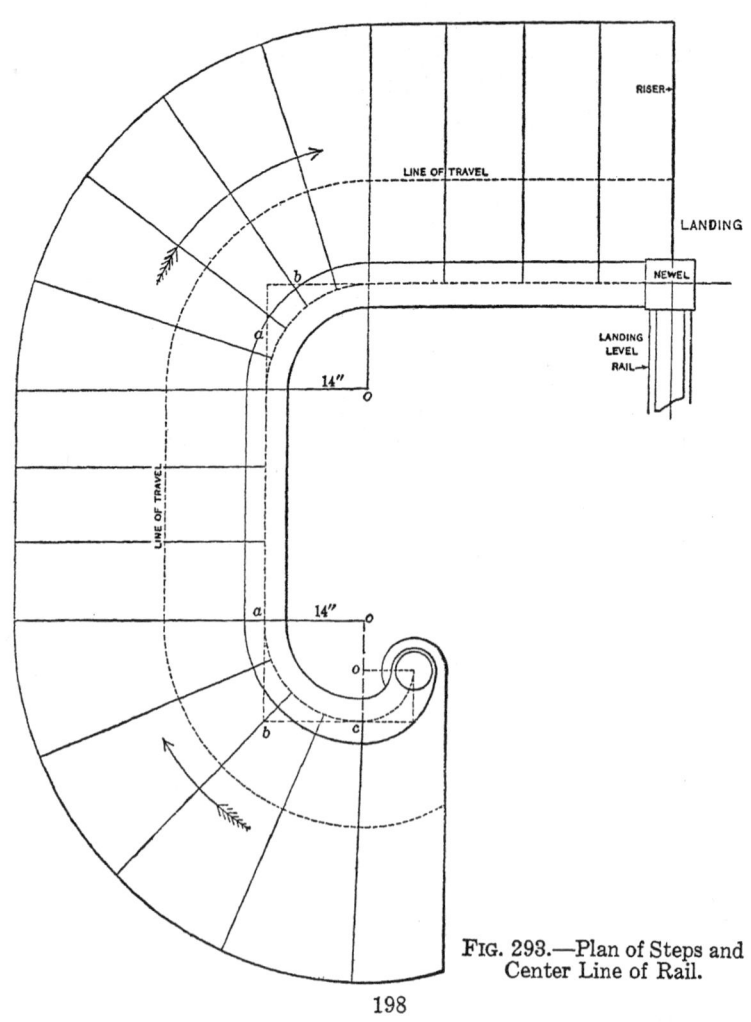

FIG. 293.—Plan of Steps and Center Line of Rail.

The plan of the thumb ellipse rail where the curve is composed of two unequal quadrants, struck respectively from the centers o and o', is shown in Fig. 294. In a curve of this description the rail should be as low as possible at the newel post, because it gives a better appearance to the work when finished, and shows the curve of the rail to better advantage.

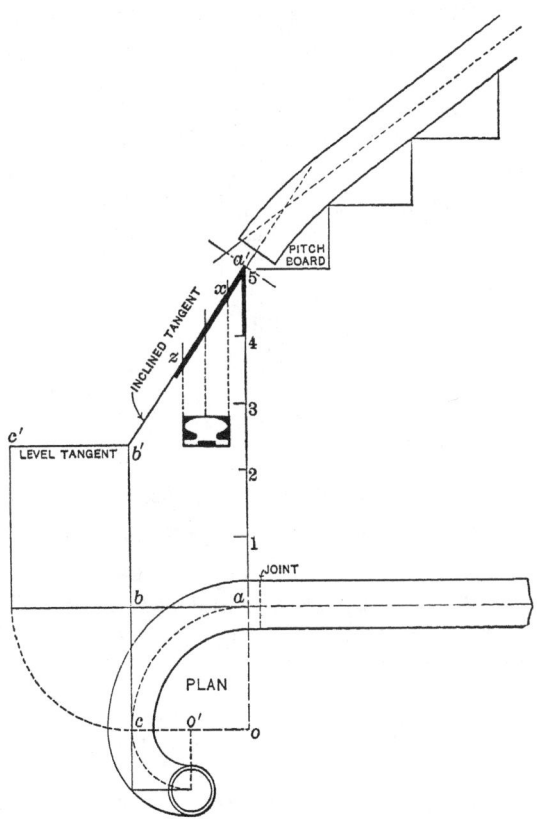

FIG. 294.—Plan and Elevation of the Wreath.

The first process in the operation of laying out the wreath is to find the pitch over and above the plan tangents c-b and b-a. From the point a, Fig. 294, mark the height of five risers; these risers are contained within the curve of the quadrant, Fig. 293. From the point 5 of Fig. 294 commence laying out the straight steps of the adjoining flight, and upon the nosing of these steps draw lines to represent the side of the straight rail. Draw a line from 5 to b' at any pitch desired, and from b' draw a level line to c'.

These last lines are the elevation of the tangents c-b and b-a of the plan curve, and represent the exact length of the tangents required upon the face mold, to square the joints of the wreath; the one that stands over and above the plan tangent b-a is inclined, while the one that stands over and above the plan tangents c-b is level.

In Fig. 295 the tangents are shown in position upon the face mold; the angle between the two at b' is a right angle. The joint at the end a' is made square to the tangent b'-a', which represents the inclined tangent in Fig. 294, and the joint at the end c' is made square to the level tangent c'-b'.

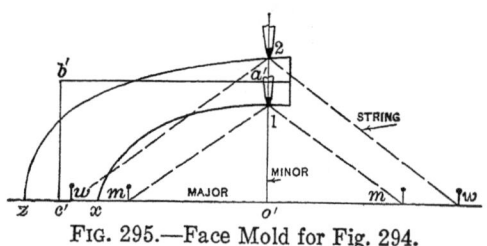

FIG. 295.—Face Mold for Fig. 294.

The width of the mold at the end a' is the same width as the plain rail of the flight, because it is upon the minor axis. This line is the minor axis because it is parallel to the level tangent c'-b', and drawn from the center o'. The major is a line drawn through the center o', at right angles to the minor axis in Fig. 295.

A bevel is not required at the end a' because it is on the minor axis. The bevel for the end c is shown in Fig. 294 at 5 to be the intersecting angle between the inclined tangent b'-a' and the perpendicular line a'-a. The width of the mold at the end c' is ascertained by crossing this bevel by lines representing the width of the plain rail shown in Fig. 294 upon the bevel at z and x. Place the width z-x on the end c' of the mold in Fig. 295. The distances from o' to x, and also to z, represent the lengths of the major axes for both the inside and outside curves, while the distances from o' to 1 and to 2 represent the lengths of the minor axes.

Place in the compasses the length of the major axis o'-x, fixing one leg in 1 on the minor axis, and turn around to cut the major axis in m and m; these are the points at which to place the pins for the inside curve.   The points for the outside curve are found by a similar process, manipulating in this case the points 2 and z upon the axes to find the points w and w for the pins.   Fasten the string to these points, extend to the minor axis and sweep

the curves from 2 to z for the outside, and from 1 to x for the inside curve, thus completing the
laying-out of the face mold.

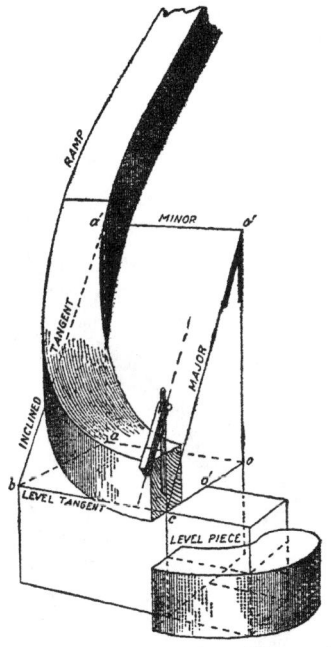

The mold is first used as a
templet to cut the material for
the wreath; this is cut from the
plank square to its face, and the
ends or joints cut out square to
the tangents.

Apply the bevel to the end c',
by holding the stock parallel
with the joint and the blade
toward the inside of the wreath,
illustrated in the perspective
view of the preceding figures in
Fig. 296.

The wreath is shown here in
position over and above its plan
curve, and twisted in a manner
to give it a level position at the
end c, indicating that the remainder of the curve to butt
square at c must be level.   This

FIG. 296.—Perspective View of Preceding Diagrams Clearly Showing the Operations Up to this Point.

piece is shown at the bottom of the figure as a curved piece cut square from the face of the plank.

The first method to lay out and construct the wreath over and above the 14-in. quarter turn is shown in Fig. 297, where, owing to the difference in pitch over the connecting flights and the pitch over the quarter turn, the necessary ramps are made in the straight rails of the adjoining flights.

To find the pitch line of the tangents, measure from the

ground line, the height of the five risers contained in the curve. Place the pitch board at the point *5*, for the pitch of the top flight, and upon the pitch draw the rail.

To draw the ramp of the bottom flight, unfold the plan tangent *a*, shown by the dotted arc *k*, and place the pitch board at *c* for the pitch of the bottom flight. Upon the pitch draw the bottom rail, and connect the top and bottom rail from *5* to *m*.

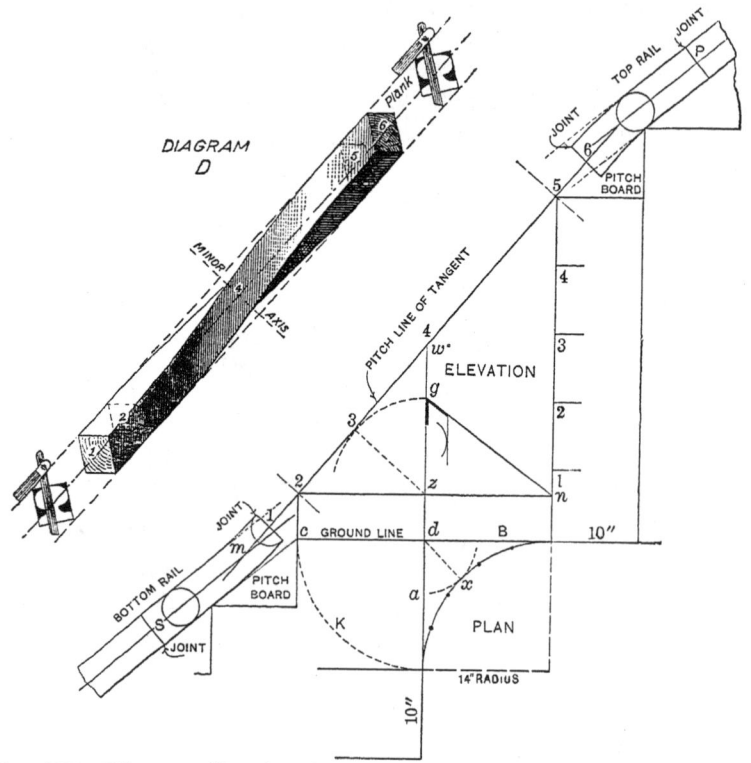

FIG. 297.—Diagrams Showing the Method of Constructing a Wreath Over a Quadrant Curve Containing Five Winders with Ramps in the Bottom and Top. Straight Rails of the Connecting Flights.

This line is the pitch of the tangents over the quarter turn, and deviates from the pitch of the flights, therefore making the ramps necessary, indicated at both the top and bottom rails.

The laying-out of the face mold is illustrated in Fig. 298 of the diagrams. The line *1-2-3-4-5-6* in this diagram is a reproduction of the pitch line of the tangent in Fig. 297. From point *3* upon the line in Fig. 298 draw a perpendicular line indefinitely. In the point 4 place one leg of the dividers, open the other out to 2' and turn around to cut the perpendicular line in the point 2', and draw a line from 2' to 4, the angle between tangents required on the face mold to square the joints.

Bisect this angle and make 4-x equal in length to d-x of the plan, Fig. 297, and draw the circle to equal the width of the plain rail, which also represents the width of the face mold at this point.

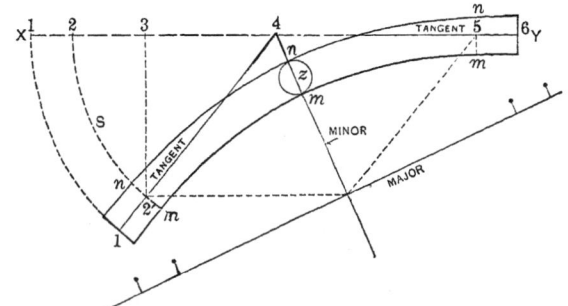

FIG. 298.—Face Mold for the Construction Shown in Fig. 297.

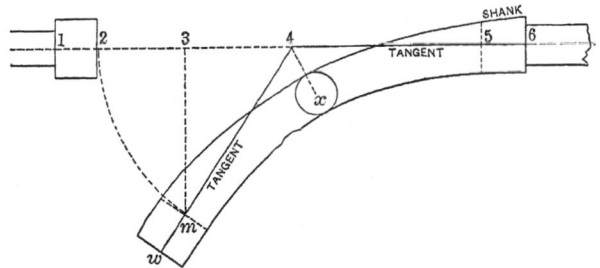

FIG. 300.—Face Mold for Fig. 299.

Make the width at the ends 5 and 2' about 3-16 of an in. wider than at z, and trace the curve by bending a lath to touch the points upon the inside and outside of the mold, and draw the shank at each end at 5-6 and w-n. This completes the laying-out of the face mold.

The bevel to twist the wreath is found, in Fig. 297, by placing one leg of the compasses in z, and extending the other to 3 on the pitch lines of the tangents; turn over to g, and draw a line from g to n.

The two tangents of the wreath are equal in length and pitch, and in consequence only one bevel is required.　This, because the tangents are inclined, must be applied to both ends, as shown in Diagram D, Fig. 297.

The method illustrated in these figures is said by the stair-builders to be the most simple known; the only objection to it is that, because the ramps are made in the straight rails, it is necessary to have two extra joints to connect the ramp pieces

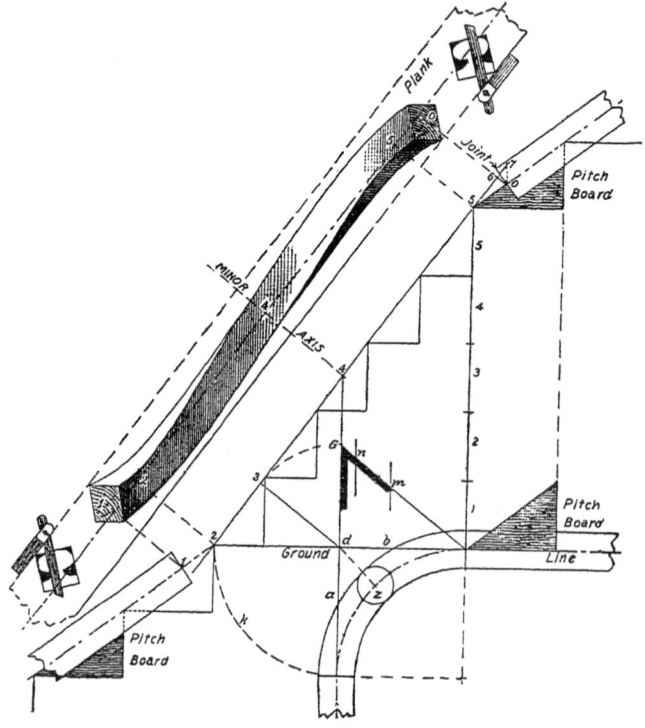

Fig. 299.—Diagrams Showing How to Lay Out a Wreath Ramped at Both Ends.　This Figure Shows a Ramped Wreath After it Has Been Squared and Twisted.

to the straight rails, shown in Fig. 297 at S on the bottom straight rail and at P on the top straight rail.

Fig. 299 shows the plan and elevation of a wreath that does not require the ramping of the straight rails, thereby eliminating the necessity of the extra joints.　According to the operation indicated in this figure the ramps are worked in the wreath itself.

The face mold Fig. 300 is developed by the same operation as the one in Fig. 299. In Fig. 300 the bevel is shown applied to the plank, and the wreath as it appears after it is squared or twisted. In this case the center of the wreath deviates slightly from the center of the plank, from *2* to *1* at the bottom end, and from *5* to *o* at the top end. This creates the necessity of having a thicker plank for this wreath. The difference in thickness is found from *o* to *7* at the top joint in Fig. 299.

To square this wreath two "sides molds" known as "falling molds" are required—one for the inside, and the other for the outside. They are shown in Figs. 302 and 303.

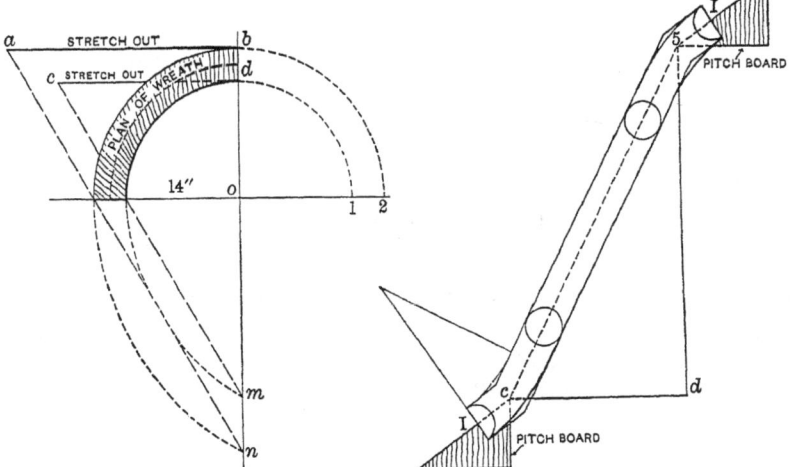

FIG. 301.—Diagrams Showing How to Find the Stretchout Length of Curves.

FIG. 302.—Falling Mold for Inside of Rail.

To lay them out draw the plan of the wreath in Fig. 301; *c-d* is the stretchout length of the inside, and *a-b* of the outside curve. Take the length *c-d* for the base, and the height of *5* risers for the altitude of the triangle, in Fig. 302. Connect 5 and *c* for the pitch. At *c* and 5 place the pitch board, and draw the pitch of the flights and form the ramps at *c* and *5*. The width of the mold is equal to the thickness of the plain rail.

Fig. 303 shows that the mold for the outside curve is laid out by a similar operation; the only difference is in the length of the base line *a-b* and *c-d*.

Fig. 302 is the side of the mold to apply to the inside, and Fig. 303 to the outside of the wreath.

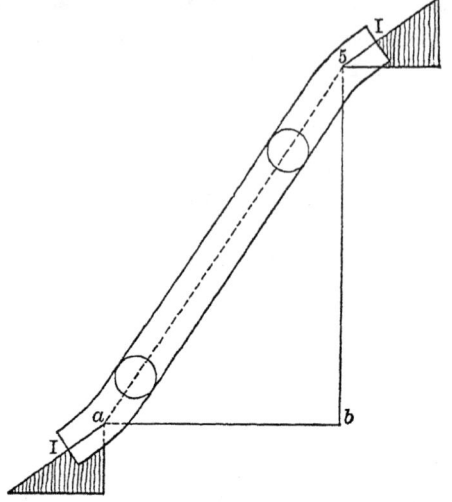

FIG. 303.—Falling Mold for Outside of
Rail.

These molds are made out of pasteboard or tin, and are applied to the side of the wreath after the sides have been worked plumb. Their use greatly facilitates the manipulation of squaring the wreath, especially when the work is done by unskilled workmen.

CHAPTER XXVII

LAYING OUT PANEL SOFFIT FOR A CIRCULAR STAIRWAY

Soffits of geometrical stairways are generally finished with plaster or ceiling board, but occasionally the stairbuilder is

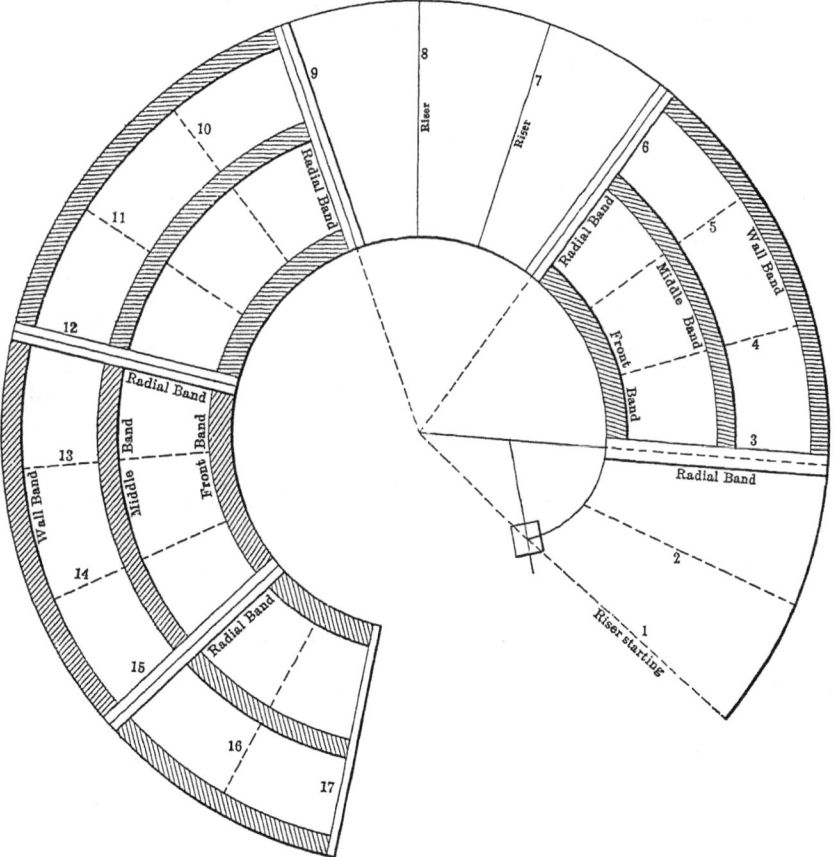

FIG. 304.—Plan of a Framed Soffit for a Circular Stairway.

called upon to frame a panel soffit elaborate in design, and containing many molded members; each member assumes a twisted form owing to the winding of the stairway, and a knowledge of a method for developing each member geometrically becomes a necessity.

Fig. 304 is a compound diagram containing the plan of stringers, steps and panel work of soffit, for a stairway circular in plan. The method explained here is adapted to soffits that wind around the different varieties of cylinders.

The stairway Fig. 304 contains *17* risers starting from a newel post. Each one radiates to the center of the curves of the inside and outside of the stringers, and they are placed along the stringer at equal distances apart.

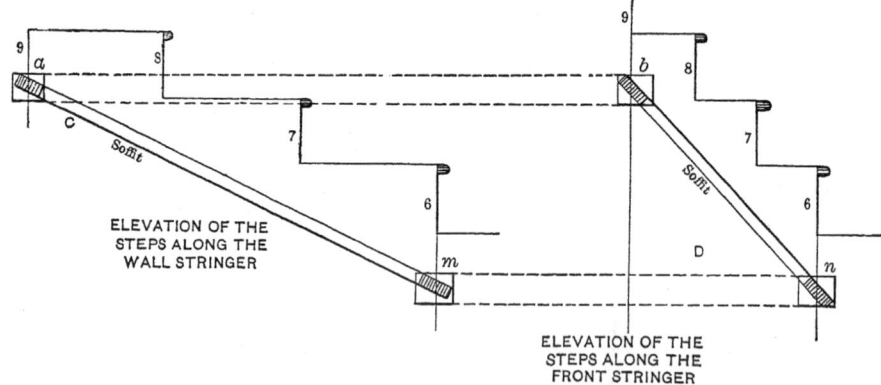

FIG. 305.—Diagram Showing How the Bevels to Twist the Radial Bands Are Found.

The soffit framed panel extends from the third to the *17*th riser, while from the sixth to the ninth riser there is a space, covering three steps, omitted from the panel framing; this is the portion of the framed panel under consideration. The framed panel complete is made in five sections, from the third to the sixth riser; from..the sixth to the ninth; from the ninth to the twelfth; from the twelfth to the fifteenth, and the last portion covering only two steps, *16* and *17*.

Radial bands extend across the stairs between each section from the front stringer to the wall stringer, forming the stiles to the circular rails of the framed panels. The rails are shaded in the diagram, and are designated as "front," "middle" and "wall" bands.

Fig. 305 shows the method of laying out the radial bands. On the right hand of the diagram is the elevation for the steps *6*, *7*, and *8* along the front stringer, and on the left hand side the elevation of the same steps along the wall stringer. The parallel lines marked "soffit" are drawn parallel to the pitch of the steps on each side and at a distance equal to what the soffit will actually be in the finished construction. The heavy shaded portion of the parallel soffit lines at *a b* and *m n* represents the thickness and width of the bands, while the square surrounding them represents the size of material required in the rough for the twisting necessitated by the winding plan of the framework.

Fig. 306 shows how the band under the ninth riser in Fig. 304 is twisted. Make the distance between *a* and *b* equal to the distance between the front and wall stringer, through the center of

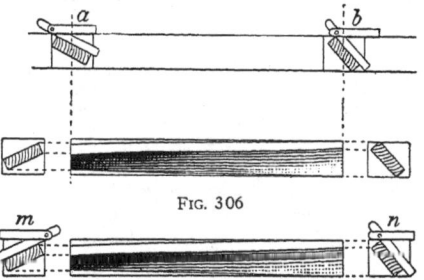

Fig. 306

Figs. 306 and 307.—Showing How the Radial Bands Under the 9th and 6th Risers Are Twisted and their Appearance After the Operation.

the ninth riser. At the end *a* draw the shaded section of the band at an angle to the line *a b*, equal to the pitch of the soffit *C*, Fig. 305, at *a*, and at the end *b* equal to the pitch of the soffit *D*, Fig. 305, at *b*. These two pitches are actually the pitches of the respective steps of the front and wall stringers, and the bevel to twist the radial band may be taken directly from the steps and applied to the material at *a* and *b* in Fig. 306.

The lower portion of Fig. 306 illustrates the appearance of the band after the twisting by means of the bevels, while Fig. 307 represents the radial band under the sixth riser.

All the radial bands of the complete soffit are of the same length and form, because each band extends in length from the front stringer to the wall stringer along the center line of the risers, above the relative position of the bands in the soffit.

Fig. 304 shows five of the radial bands under the *3d, 6th, 9th, 12th, 15th,* and *17th* risers, all the same length. When finished they have the same twist, which is the one in Fig. 306, procured by the use of bevels equal, respectively, to the relative pitches of the front and wall stringers.

The manner of laying out the circular front, middle and wall bands is shown in the remaining diagrams. Fig. 308 represents the portion of the soffit omitted in Fig. 304, between the *6th* and *9th* risers, while the shaded portions represent the bands to be laid out.

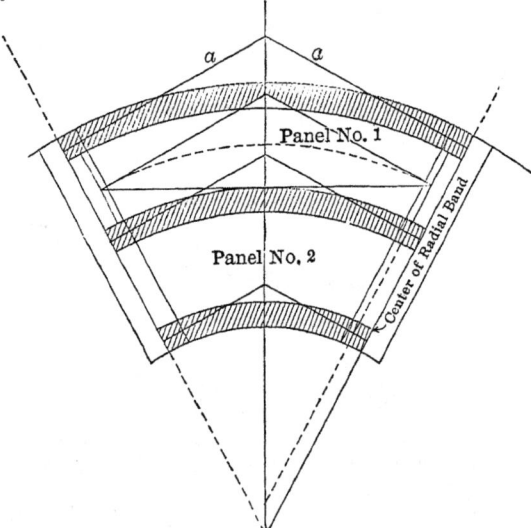

Fig. 308.—Plan of a Section of the Framed Soffit From the 6th to the 9th Riser.

The wall band, which in the diagram is the longest of the three, is the one in the soffit that follows the wall stringer. From the center of the band draw the tangents *a a* square to the radial bands. The band and tangents presented assume the appearance of a plan and plan tangents of a hand rail, and as it is a plan of a member which is to follow the winding steps of the stairway (similar to a hand rail) it is evident that the method used to develop a hand rail also applies to the development of this member.

Fig. 309 shows how this is done. Draw the plan of the band; at the end *c* erect the line *c 1 2 3* to represent the height of the three risers, which is the height the band risers, from riser *6* to riser *9*. From *3* draw the pitch of the wall stringer steps to *m*, bisect this line in *h*, and drop a line to *b*. From *d* in the plan draw a line square to *b m*, and from where it cuts *b m* draw an indefinite line square to the pitch line *h m*. Fix one leg of the compasses in *h*, and extend the other to *m*; turn over to *w* and

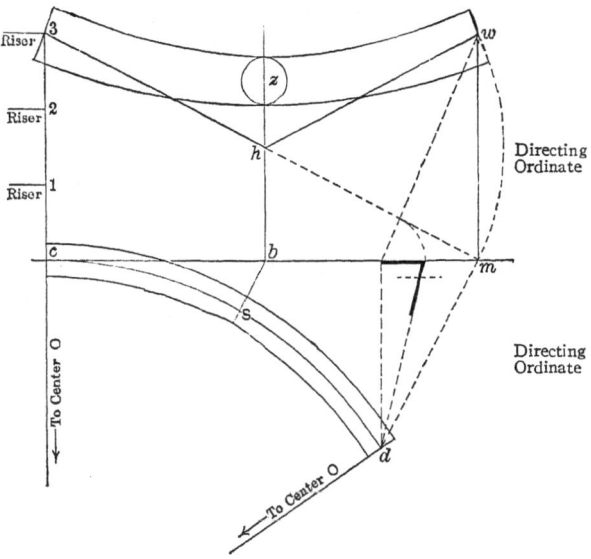

Fig. 309.—Plan and Development of Curved Band of Soffit Following the Wall Stringer.

connect *w* with *h*, thus obtaining the tangent angle of the band at *h*; the tangents are *3 h* and *h w* respectively. The manner of finding the bevel to twist the band is illustrated in the diagram.

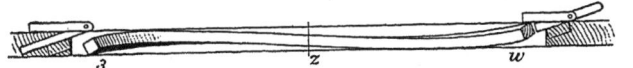

Fig. 310.—Appearance of the Band Twisted, After Application of Bevels

The points *3* and *w* are already determined in the curve of the band, and to find the point *z* draw a line from *d* in the plan to *m*, and another from *m* to *w*. These two lines are known as directing ordinates. From *b* draw a line to *S*, parallel to the directing ordinate *d m*, and from *h* draw a line to *z*, parallel to directing ordinate *m w*; make *h z* equal to *b s* of the plan.

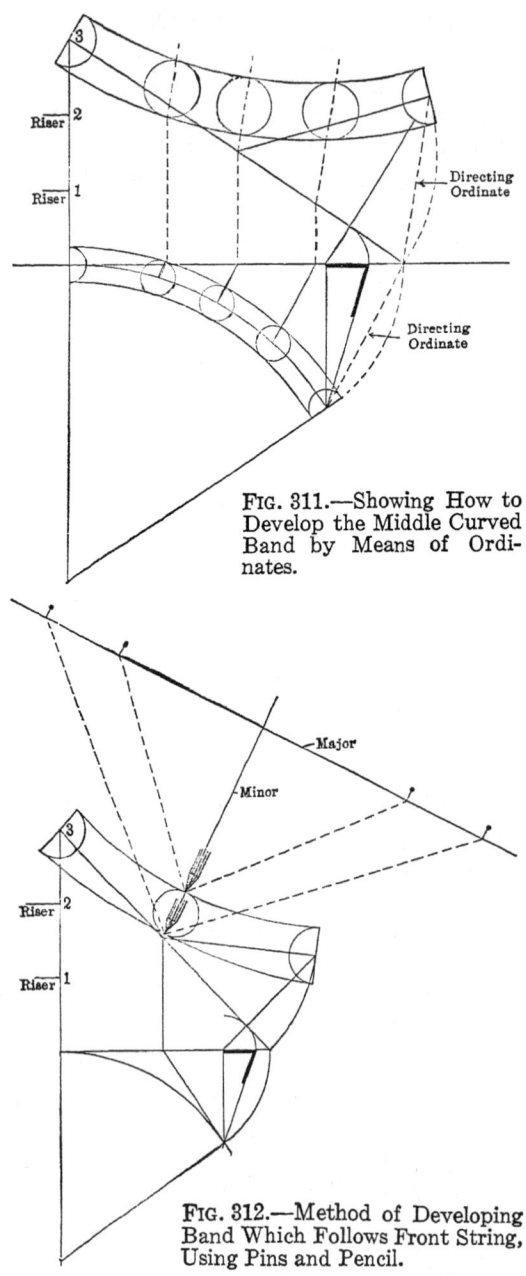

FIG. 311.—Showing How to Develop the Middle Curved Band by Means of Ordinates.

FIG. 312.—Method of Developing Band Which Follows Front String, Using Pins and Pencil.

Make the width of the band at *z* equal the plan width, and at the ends *3* and *w* about *3-16* of an inch wider.   Bend a lath to touch the points thus found to complete the curve.   Fig. 310 is the band twisted by applying the bevel reversely at the ends.

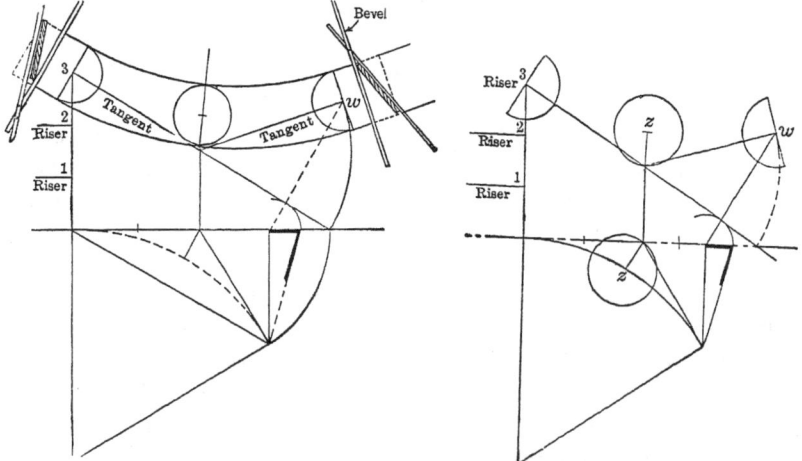

FIG. 313.—Plan and Development of Panel   FIG. 314.—Plan and Development of
No. 1 in Fig. 308.   Panel No. 2 in Fig. 5.

The development of the middle band is produced in Fig. 311 by means of the four ordinates; the process is the same as Fig. 309, except in the number of ordinates used.

The method of developing the front band by means of string, pins and pencil, which may be applied to all the other bands if preferred, is illustrated in Fig. 312 of the diagram.

To lay out the two panels between the bands, Fig. 308, commence with panel No. 1, draw a line through its center, and from

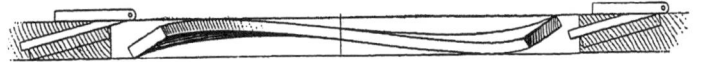

FIG. 315.—The Bevels Applied and the Appearance of Panel No. 2 After it
is Twisted.

each end of this line draw the tangents square to the radial bands.   Transfer these lines to the plan, Fig. 313, and develop each line by the process employed in Figs. 6, 8, or 9, for front, middle and wall bands.   The width of the developed panel is taken from the plan, Fig. 308, and its ends at *3* and *w* are made square to the tangents. The same process is employed in developing panel No. 2 in Fig. 314. Fig. 315 shows the bevels applied to form the twist in panel No. 2, and the cross-section indicates the thickness of material required. The developments for all the members, including the panels and bands, are very much alike and similar to the developments of hand rails.

All the remaining portions of the soffit with one exception are duplicates of the one developed, each one covering a space equal to the expansion of three steps; therefore, the molds developed for the one portion will apply to all the others except the top one.

To develop the molds for this portion, proceed as for the others; the only difference is in the length of the panels and curved bands; these are shorter, to correspond with the space they cover. The radial bands are precisely the same as the others, the exact width of the plan soffit in Fig. 304.

When a soffit like the one lilustrated contains a number of similar members, saving in time and material, is effected by using one of each member (after it is twisted) as a drum to bend the remaining members.

A few thin strips cut out to the width and length of the respective members may in this manner be bent by the use of glue and hand screws, and the work when finished appears as good as if the members had each been worked out of solid material.

CHAPTER XXVIII

HOW TO LAY OUT A RAIL OVER A 24″ QUARTER TURN AT THE BOTTOM OF A STAIRWAY

Fig. 316 illustrates a plan of a stairway having a 24-inch quadrant for a stretchout curve at the starting.

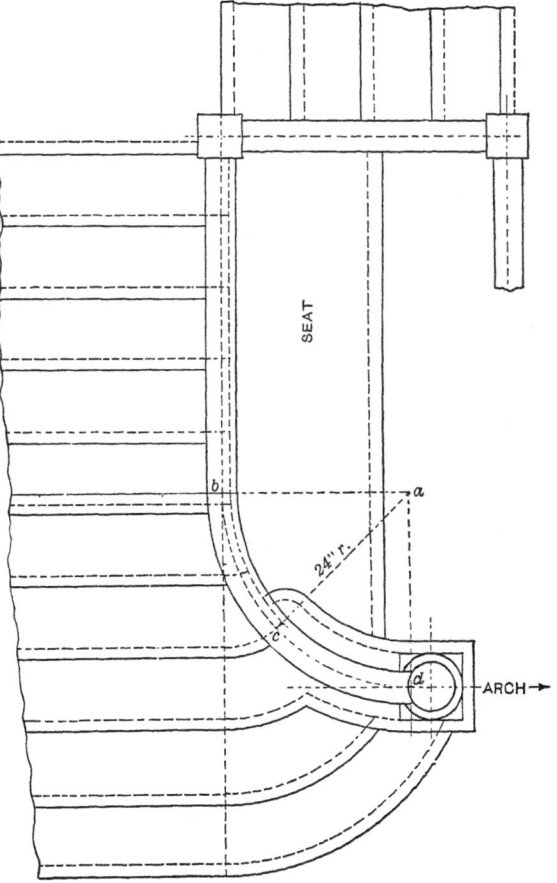

FIG. 316.—Reproduction of Correspondent's Sketch.

Fig. 317 shows the elevation and development of the tangents. This diagram should be drawn full size preparatory to

215

the laying-out of the face mold; and as the steps within the curve are uniform with those of the straight flight, they may be laid out with the pitch board in the ordinary way, on a straight piece of board for a common straight flight. It shows that the curve contains six risers, and that the springing

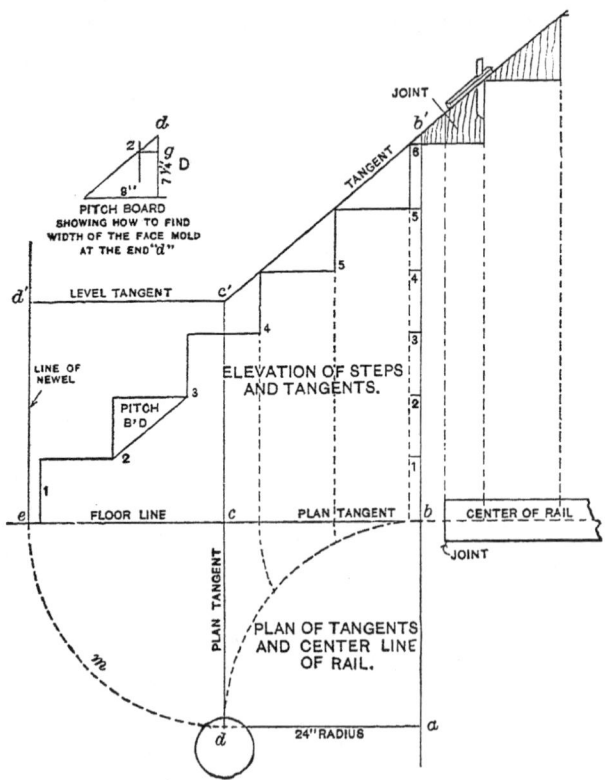

FIG. 317.—Diagrams Showing Plan of Tangents with Center Line of Wreath; Also Elevation of Tangents and Steps.

plan line a b of the curve, continued to b' in the elevation, cuts the pitch line in b'. The two steps shaded above b' are those of the straight flight, and are drawn merely to obtain the pitch of the flight, which, if continued downward through b' to intersect the plan tangent d c prolonged to c', determines the pitch and length of the elevation of the plan tangent b c.

To find the length of the elevation of the plan tangent $d\ c$, place one leg of the dividers in c, and extend the other to d, turn over as shown by the arc $d\ m\ e$ to the ground line. Upon e raise the perpendicular line $e\ d'$ and from d' draw a level line to c'; this is the elevation of the level plan tangent $d\ c$.

The line $e\ d'$ represents the inside face of the newel, and the distance from e on the floor line to d', where the level tangent cuts the line $e\ d'$, indicates the height from the floor of the center line of the wreath upon the newel, which is equal to the height of $3\frac{1}{2}$ risers., $7\frac{1}{4}$ in. each, a total of $21\frac{3}{4}$ in., the same height as the pedestal upon which the newel rests.

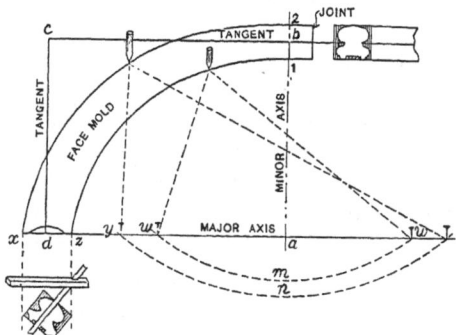

FIG. 318.—Method of Laying Out Face Mold by Means of String and Pins.

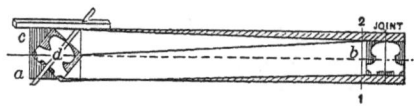

FIG. 319.—Appearance of Wreath After it is Squared and Showing Application of Bevel to the End d.

By adding to this dimension the length, 26 in., of the short baluster the exact height of the center of the rail from the floor is found to be $47\frac{3}{4}$ in.

To lay out the face mold proceed as indicated in Fig. 318 of the diagrams. Draw the square $a\ b\ c\ a$. Make the sides $a\ b$ and $c\ d$ equal in length to that of the level tangent $c'\ d'$, and make the sides $a\ d$ and $d\ c$ equal in length to that of the raking tangent $c'\ b'$ of Fig. 317.

The line c d in the square, Fig. 318, is the bottom level tangent, and the line c b the upper raking tangent of the wreath. The angle between the two at c is the angle between the tangents required on the face mold to give the correct direction to the tangents to square the joints of the wreath. The joint at d is made square to the level tangent line d c, and the joint at b to the line c b.

The line d a of Fig. 318 is the major axis, and the line a b the minor axis, of the elliptical curves that constitute the form of the face mold.

To draw the curves of the mold, place at each side of b on the minor axis a distance equal to half the width of the straight rail, at b 1 and b 2 respectively. This determines the width of the face mold at the end b.

To determine the width at the end d, place on each side of d, at d x and d z, a distance equal to d z of the Diagram D, Fig. 317 which is the bevel to square the wreath. The line z g in Diagram D is made equal to half the width of the straight rail.

To find the points (the foci of the ellipses) on the major axis to place the pins in order to describe the curves, take the distance on the major axis from a to z on the dividers, the point 1 on the minor axis for a center, and describe the arc m to cut the major axis in the points w and w. Again place on the dividers the distance from a to x on the minor axis, and taking the point 2 on the minor axis for a center describe the arc n, cutting the major axis in the points y and y.

To draw the inside curve of the face mold, place pins at the points w and w on the major axis, and a pin at 1 on the minor axis. Tie a piece of string around the three pins, and fasten it tight to the pins at w and w. Take off the pin at 1, and in its place fix a pencil, and describe the curve from 1 to z.

The curve for the outside of the mold is described by the same process, but the pins are fixed at y and y on the major axis and at 2 on the minor axis.

A short piece of straight rail called the shank, measuring 3 in. from b to the joint, is shown at the end b of the mold; at the end d the bevel is applied toward the inside to square the wreath.

Fig. 319 is a view of the wreath after it has been squared, also the application of the bevel to the end d, and a vertical section of the rail at the end b, showing that a bevel is not required at that point because it is on the minor axis.

The shaded portions of Fig. 319 indicate the slabs to be taken off in squaring the wreath, and the lines $a\ c$ and $1\ 2$, the thickness of the plank required. Inscribe the finished section of the rail within a circle; the diameter of the circle in all cases defines the thickness of the plank.

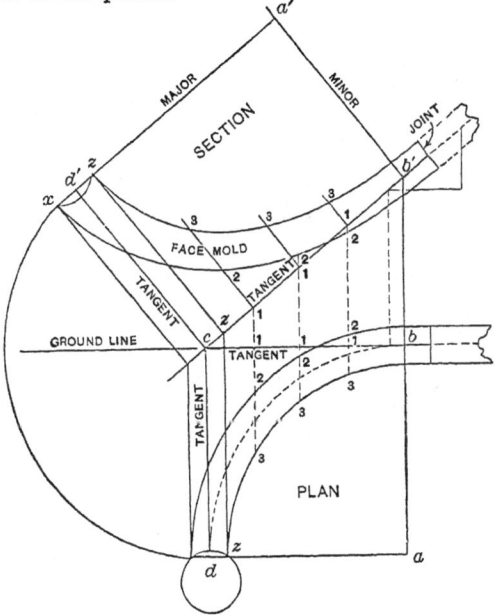

FIG. 320.—Diagram Showing Simple Method of Laying Out the Face Mold with Level Lines or "Ordinates."

The bevel shown at d in Fig. 319 is shown in Fig. 317 to be the upper angle of the pitch board.

A simple method of laying out the face mold with level lines or "ordinates" is shown in Fig. 320. First draw the line a, b, c, d, representing the square plan; then the plan of the curved portion of the rail from d to b. Place the pitch board at c, and draw the pitch from c to b' and beyond to the joint. From c draw $c\ d'$ square to the pitch line $c\ b'$. The line $c\ d$ of the plan is a level line, and the line *c d'* of the section is also a level line; these lines are called "directing ordinates".

Draw lines across the curved plan of the rail parallel to the plan level line *d c*, up to the pitch line *c b'*. From the contact points of these lines with the pitch line *c b'*, draw lines parallel with the level tangent line *c d'* of the section, and make all equal in length to their correlative lines in the plan. For example, make *1 2 3* extend across the face mold, equal to *1 2 3*, from the ground line across the plan curved rail; proceed in this manner with all the lines across the plan rail and across the face mold.

Trace the inside curve of the face mold through the points *3, 3, 3, z*, and the outside curve through the points *2, 2, 2, x*. Make the joint at *b'* square to the raking tangent line *c b*, and at *d'* to the level tangent line *c d'*. The same bevel and the same thickness of plank used for the wreath shown in Figs. 318 and 319 will suffice for the wreath laid out in this figure.

CHAPTER XXIX

HOW TO LAY OUT A RAIL AROUND A CYLINDER CONTAINING 4 RISERS AT THE JUNCTION OF A FLIGHT AND TOP LANDING

The plan of a stairway having a cylinder containing four risers at the junction of a flight with a level landing is shown in Fig. 321 of the engravings. A platform and two straight steps take the place of the winders around the cylinder. The first two risers in the cylinder are slightly curved, and the first one outside the cylinder is placed about two inches from the springing. The arrangement of the risers in and adjoining the cylinder greatly facilitates the manipulation of the wreaths.

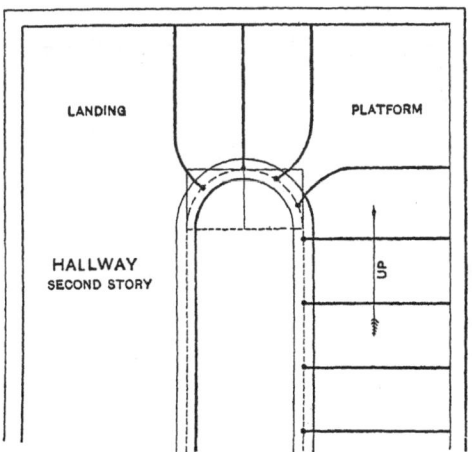

FIG. 321.—Plan of Stairs.

The elevation of the steps, where the pitch over the three lower tangents forms an inclined straight line, the inclination slightly in excess of the pitch over the flight, is presented in Fig. 322; the upper tangent at *1 2* is a level tangent, aligning with the central line of the landing rail. To draw this figure, unfold the side of the plan tangents *a b* and *c d*; and on the points *h, b, n, d* and g on the line $X\,Y$ erect perpendicular lines as h, l, b, 2, n, 3, etc. From h on $X\,Y$ to w on $h\,l$ measure the height of four risers, and from w to 1 measure the height of one-half a riser. Through w draw a line to represent the landing floor, and

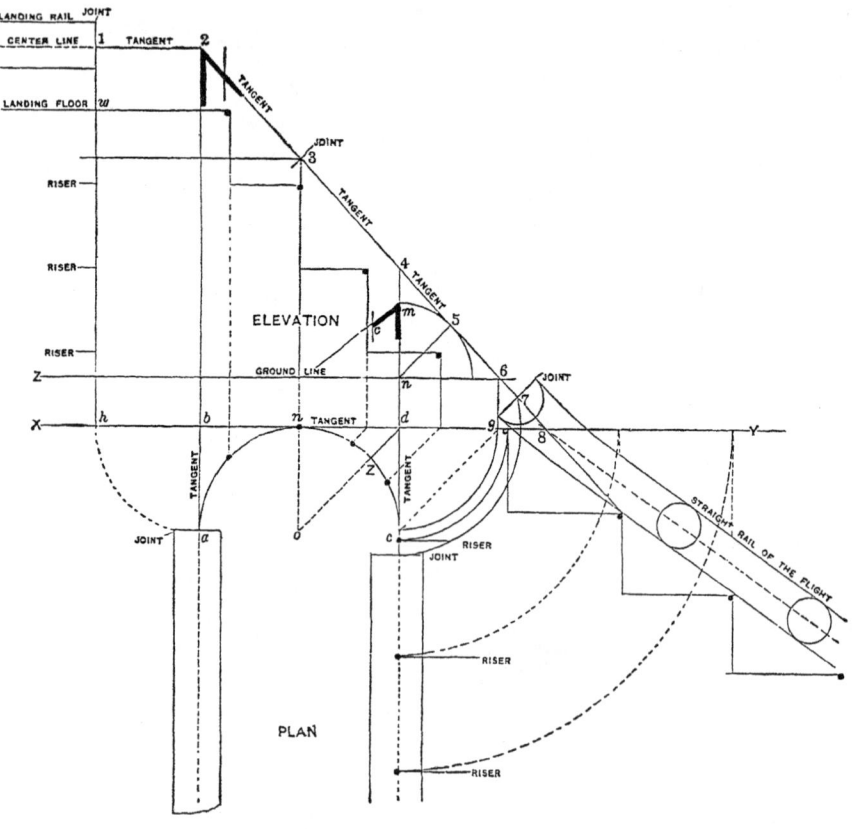

Fig. 322.—Unfolding of Tangents and Elevation of Steps.

through 1 a line to represent the center line of the landing rail. Continue the center line of the rail through 1 to 2; and from 2 draw the pitch line of the tangents 2, 3, 4, 6, 7, to intersect the center line of the flight at 8. Upon g erect $g\,6$, and draw the ground line $6\,Z$, which is raised to the height $g\,6$, to meet the necessity (arising out of the difference in pitch between the pitch line of tangents and the pitch line of the flight rail) of ramping the upper part of the flight rail to align with the pitch of the tangents.

The two wreaths in this figure are composed of three equally inclined and one level tangent. The conditions of the upper wreath, which extends from *1* to *3*, makes it necessary for tangent *1 2* to be level, so as to align with the level landing rail, and the tangents *2 3* to be inclined, to align with the inclination of the tangents *3 4* and *4 6* of the lower wreath.

The level tangent *1 2* stands above the plan tangent *a b*, and the tangent *2 3* above the tangent *b n*.

These tangents are presented in perspective in Fig. 323; the level tangent *1 2* is shown over and above *a b*, *2 3* over and above *b n*; and the center line of the wreath is also shown above the plan center of the rail.

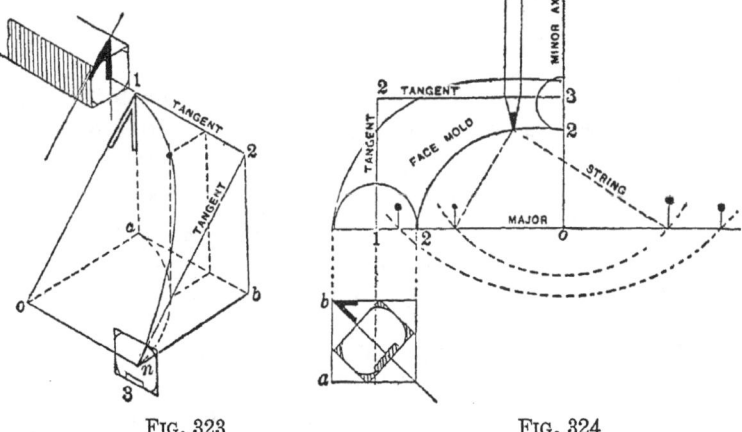

FIG. 323 FIG. 324

The geometrical problem encountered in the construction of the face mold in this case is merely the one to find the form of the section, cut obliquely to one side of a square prism; and the solution consists in forming a parallelogram having two sides equal the tangent *1 2* and the opposite two sides *2 3*. The outlines of the parrallelogram are shown in perspective in Fig. 323 at *1 2 3 0*, where *1 2* is the upper tangent and connects with the landing rail, and *2 3* is the lower tangent connecting at *3* as shown in Fig. 325 with the bottom wreath.

How to lay out the face mold for this wreath is shown in Fig. 324.

In Fig. 324 the points *1, 2, 3, 0* outlines the exact form of the parallelogram forming the section. The line *0-3* is the minor axis and the line *0, 1* is the major axis; the two remaining lines *1-2* and *2-3* represent the tangents. The width of the mold at *3* is the same as that of the straight rail, because it is on the minor axis and the width at the end *1* is taken from the

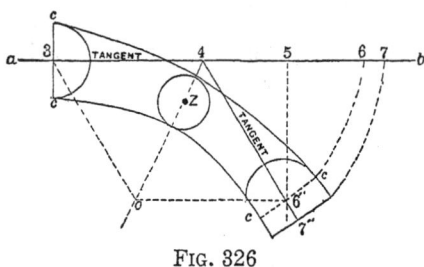

FIG. 326

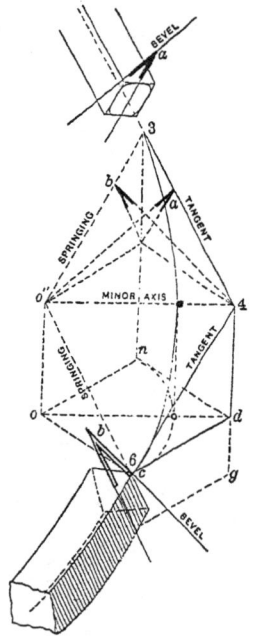

FIG. 325.—Square Prism Cut Oblique to Two of its Sides, and Showing Ramp in Rail.

bevel in Fig. 322. The outside and inside curves are described by means of the method known as the "pin and string method." The bevel to square the wreath is at *2* in Fig. 322, and is applied in Fig. 324, where the thickness of the plank required is shown at *a b*. The same bevel is applied in Fig. 323 to one end of the wreath; the other is squared without a bevel, as the section in the direction of the line *3 0* is level.

To draw the face mold for the bottom wreath, the tangents of which are shown from *3* to *6* in Fig. 322 to be equally inclined, the problem is to develop a section, cut through a square prism when cut obliquely to two of its sides. Such a prism is shown in Fig. 325. Its base, *o n d c*, is equal to *o n d c* in plan, Fig. 322, and its sides, *3 4* and *4 6*, represent the tangents, while the lines marked *0 3, 3 4, 4 6* and *6 0* indicate the outlines of the form of the section. The ramp in the rail of the flight to align with the inclination of the tangent *4 6* is also shown in Fig. 325. The distance shown from *g* to *d*, which corresponds with *g 6*

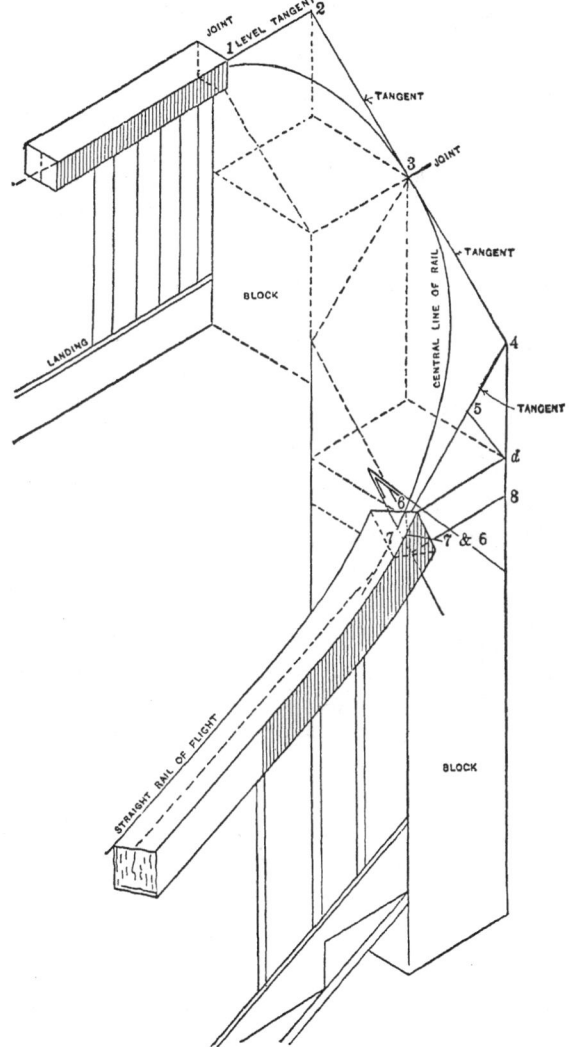

FIG. 327.—Combination of the Two Prisms in Figs. 3 and 5.

in Fig. 321, and indicates the height of the ground line, is raised to meet the necessity of ramping the rail.

To draw the face mold in Fig. 326, draw the line *a b*, and to it transfer the points *3, 4, 5, 6, 7* from the pitch line of the tangents in Fig. 322. From *5* drop the perpendicular line *5 6″*; place one leg of the compasses on *4*; extend the other to *6*, and turn over as shown to intersect the line previously drawn from *5* to *6″*; connect *6″* with *4*; this last line is the lower tangent required in the face mold; the other tangent is the line *3 4*.

Draw *3 0* parallel to *4 6″*, and *6″ 0* parallel to *3 4*; connect *4 0*; make *4 z* equal *d z* in Fig. 321, and draw the circle with a radius equal to the plan width of the rail. The circumference of this circle determines the width of the mold at this point, because the line *4 0* is the minor axis of the ellipses which constitute the curves.

The widths at the ends *3* and *6* are determined by the bevel *m*, shown in Fig. 322. The distance from *m* to *c* on this bevel placed on each side of *3* and *6″* in Fig. 326, at *3 c, 3 c* and *6″ c, 6″ c*, respectively, determines the width at each end.

Fig. 327 is an isometric figure showing more graphically the nature of the operations in the preceding figures.

It will be observed that the bottom section in this figure is similar to Fig. 325 and that the top section corresponds with Fig. 323.

The outside and inside curves of the mold may be described by bending a flexible lath to touch *c c* and the circumference of the circle for both inside and outside of the mold. The distance from *6* to *7* on the mold is taken from Fig. 322, and because it is below the ground line it is outside the cylinder, and therefore does not belong to the wreath proper, but is an auxiliary addition of a straight piece to extend the joint of the wreath beyond the springing of the cylinder, to secure a more graceful ramp at the junction of the wreath with the bottom straight rail.

The plane of the section has the same inclination in both directions to the sides of the prism, and only one bevel is required. This is applied reversely to both ends.

Fig. 327 presents a combination of the two prisms, to illustrate more graphically the utility of unfolding sections of prisms in geometrical handrailing. This figure also shows the development of the center line of the wreath, reaching from *6* to *3* along the plane of the section cut through one prism, and from *3* to *1* along the plane of the section cut through the other prism. The level tangent aligns with the level rail of the landing, and the bottom tangent with the ramp in the rail of the flight adjoining.

CHAPTER XXX

WOOD, STONE AND IRON STAIRS ERECTED IN RESI-DENCES, THEATRES AND PUBLIC BUILDINGS

This chapter contains a selection of artistic dining rooms, reception rooms and hallways designed by the leading archi-

FIG. 328—A Grand Staircase.

tects of the country. Many of them are from residences and other buildings in New York City and vicinity.

As a collection of modern stairway entrances, they present suggestions of such merit as will not fail to be of value in designing this most important branch of building construction. For of all the internal items in a building, the stairway and its immediate surroundings is most important, and therefore it calls

FIG. 329.—A Scroll and Balustrade Stairway.

for the best that can be conceived by the architect. The half-tone illustrations given in this chapter should consequently be of exceptional interest to the house owner, stair builder and architect.

The views from photographs of the finished stairways and

the name and location of the house owner, hotel, bank, public or office building in which they are located is given in each case. Further information may be obtained from the publishers, if desired. They should prove of exceptional value to the architect, stair builder or contractor in presenting suggestions to prospective customers or clients, and in this connection will

FIG. 330.—Entrance to World's Tower Building, West 40th Street, New York

doubtless save a lot of time and labor now lost in preliminary sketches or more elaborate drawings.

Practically all classes of work in wood, stone and iron are given, so that it is hoped that those who have occasion to refer to this chapter will always find suggestions that will be serviceable to them. Readers are invited to send photos of any stairways they may have constructed or designed which may be of interest in this connection.

The publishers are indebted to the Albee and Godfrey Company, the NcBride Mast Company, and the publishers of

Fig. 331.—A Colonial Stairway and Reception Hall.

Architecture and Building, Building Age and the National Builder for permission to use the illustrations shown.

FIG. 332.—Winding Stairway in the State Education Building
Albany, N. Y.

FIG. 333.—The Home of Dexter E. Wodworth, Quincy, Mass.

FIG. 334.—A New England Hallway about 1750.

FIG. 335.—Stairway in Entrance Hall of Centurian Building, New York.

FIG. 336.—This Southern Type may also be found in the north.

FIG. 337.—Interior of Living Room as Viewed from Stairway Above.

FIG. 338.—A Stairway in Lord and Taylor's Building, New York.

FIG. 339.—A Stairway Approach at the Second Floor in the New York
Post Office Building.

Fig. 340.—A Stairway in the Entrance Hall of the Montana Building, New York.

FIG. 341.—A Hallway Stairway with Iron Rail and Balustrades in Chas. Scribner's Sons, New York.

Fig. 342.—Lobby and Stairway to Second Floor, Hotel Bancroft, Worcester, Mass.

FIG. 343.—Reception Room Stairway with Scroll Handrail.

Fig. 344.—A Stairway in the Police Department Headquarters Building, New York.

FIG. 345.—A Hall and Dining Room of Homelitu Treatment.

Fig. 346.—Cylinder Stairway in Albany, N. Y. High School.

FIG. 347.—An Attractive Reception Hall and Stairway.

FIG. 348.—Hallway Stairway.

FIG. 349.—Entrance Hallway and Stairs.

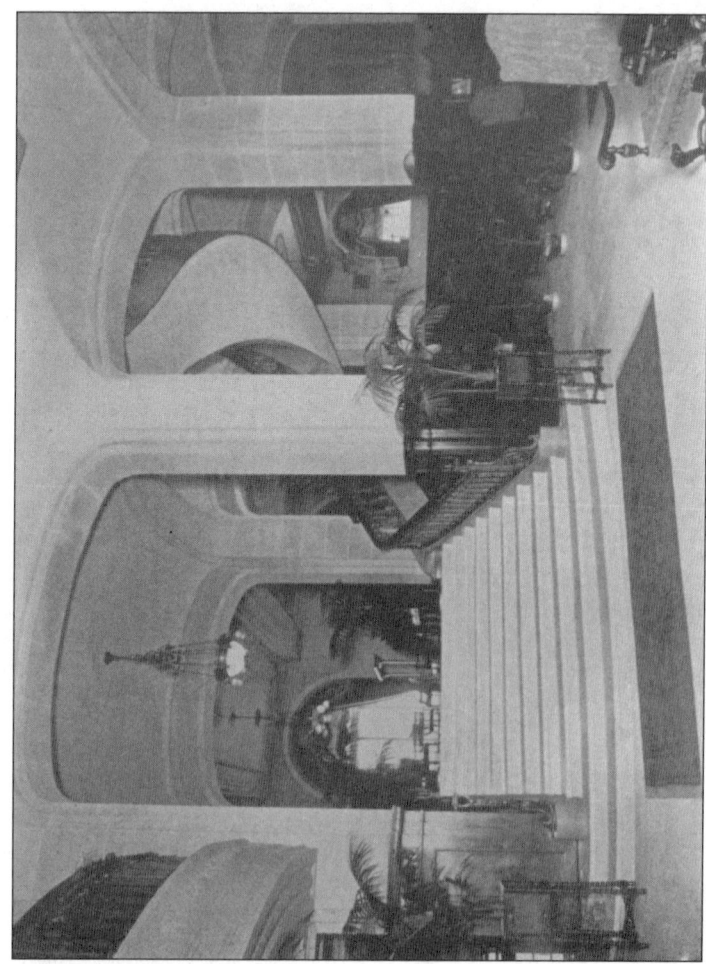

Fig. 350.—The Grand Stairway and Lounge in the Tutwiler Hotel.

Fig. 351.—A Colonial Stairway.

FIG. 352.—Main Stairway in Washington Irving High School, New York.

Fig. 358.—A Colonial Stairway with Scroll Rail.

Fig. 354.—A Stairway in the Foyer and Lobby of the Hotel Theresa, New York.

Fig. 365.—A Jacobean Staircase.

FIG. 356.—A Stairway in Aeolian Hall, New York.

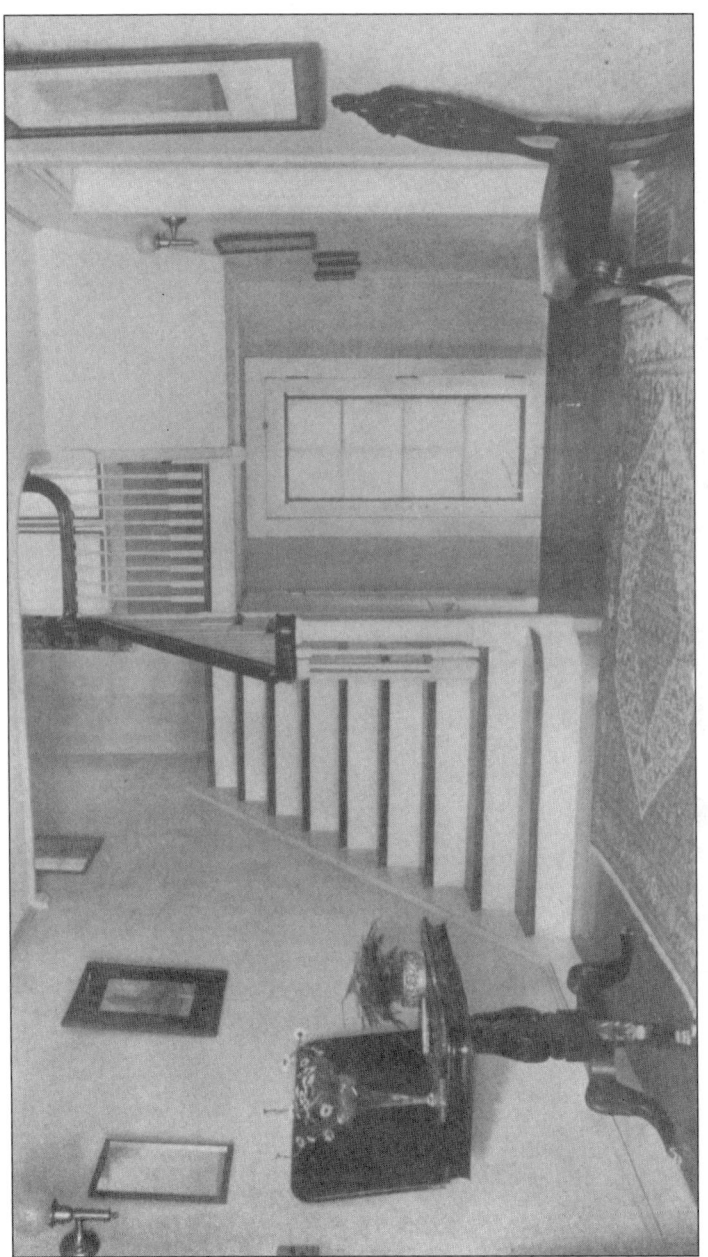

FIG. 357.—Reception Hall showing Stairway of Colonial Design.

FIG. 358.—Staircase leading to Second Floor in Irving National Bank.